School of American Research
Advanced Seminar Series

DOUGLAS W. SCHWARTZ, GENERAL EDITOR

SCHOOL OF AMERICAN RESEARCH
ADVANCED SEMINAR SERIES

The anthropology of war

THE ANTHROPOLOGY OF WAR

EDITED BY
JONATHAN HAAS

A SCHOOL OF AMERICAN RESEARCH BOOK

CAMBRIDGE
UNIVERSITY PRESS

Published by the Press Syndicate of the University of Cambridge
The Pitt Building, Trumpington Street, Cambridge CB2 1RP
40 West 20th Street, New York, NY 10011-4211, USA
10 Stamford Road, Oakleigh, Victoria 3166, Australia

First published 1990
Reprinted 1992

Printed in Great Britain by
Antony Rowe Ltd, Chippenham, Wiltshire

British Library cataloguing in publication data

The anthropology of war. – (School of American
   Research advanced seminar series.) (A school
   of American Research book.)
   1. Warfare. Anthropological perspectives
   I. Haas, Jonathan, *1949–*   II. Series
   III. Series
   303.6'6

Library of Congress cataloguing in publication data

The anthropology of war / edited by Jonathan Haas.
       p.   cm. – (School of American Research advanced seminar
series)
   "A School of American Research book."
   ISBN 0-521-38042-1
   1. Warfare, Primitive. I. Haas, Jonathan, 1949–. II. Series.
GN497.A58 1990
303.6'6–dc20   89-7286 CIP

ISBN 0 521 380421

wv

Contents

Contributors

McCAULEY, Clark Richard, Chair
Dept. of Psychology, Bryn Mawr
College

CARNEIRO, Robert L.
American Museum of Natural
History, New York

CHAGNON, Napoleon
Dept. of Anthropology, University
of California, Santa Barbara

FERGUSON, R. Brian
Dept. of Sociology, Anthropology
and Criminal Justice, Rutgers
University

GIBSON, Thomas P.
Dept. of Anthropology, University
of Rochester

GREGOR, Thomas A.
Dept. of Sociology and
Anthropology, Vanderbilt
University

HAAS, Jonathan
Field Museum of Natural History,
Chicago

ROBARCHEK, Clayton
Dept. of Anthropology, Wichita
State University

WHITEHEAD, Neil Lancelot
Oxford

Preface

This volume stems from an Advanced Seminar held at the School of American Research in March, 1986. It represents a cooperative endeavor between the School and the Harry Frank Guggenheim Foundation, which began with a series of conversations between Floyd Ratliff, president of the Foundation, Karen Colvard, its program officer, and me. The Foundation had been funding projects relating to the origins and role of warfare in prestate, "tribal" societies and was interested in integrating this recent research into a wider framework of the anthropology of warfare. The School's Advanced Seminar program seemed an optimum forum for attempting such an integration. Within this context, the goal of the seminar was to arrive at a better understanding of the causes of both war and peace in prestate societies and the impact of war on the evolution of those societies.

The participants were chosen to represent different theoretical positions, world areas, and perspectives on the phenomenon of prestate warfare. We recognized that in assembling such a diverse group of scholars, there was the potential for dispute, conflict, and lack of communication. However, there was also the possibility for cross-fertilization, synthesis, and resolution of at least some of the disagreements between opposing theoretical positions. In the introductory chapter of this volume, Clark McCauley summarizes the week's discussion and outlines the major arguments and eventual points of agreement. He also places the subject matter of the seminar in a wider context of human conflict.

The positions represented in the seminar can be discussed along several dimensions: different models of causation in explaining warfare; the origins versus the maintenance of systems of warfare; and the causes versus the effects of warfare in prestate polities.

The different models of causation in turn can be very roughly divided into three schools of thought: materialist/ecological; biocultural; and historical. Each of these "schools" had a common foundation of agreement, though there was considerable variation within each. The materialist/ecological school, holding that the causes of warfare in tribal societies are to be found largely in the material foundations of the cultural system, was represented at the seminar by Brian Ferguson, Robert Carneiro, and myself. The biocultural school, represented by Napoleon Chagnon and Rada Dyson-Hudson, generally maintained that the causes of warfare were ultimately to be found in a combination of ecological and biological elements. Finally, the historical school, in various dimensions represented by Clayton Robarchek, Thomas Gibson, Thomas Gregor, and Neil Whitehead, argues that the explanation of war is to be found in the specific historical context of the events in question and the personal motivations of the people involved in those events.

Looking at the origins versus the maintenance of warfare in prestate societies, we recognized early in the seminar that the causal factors important in initiating a sequence of armed conflicts may be very different from the reasons for the maintaining warfare once a pattern of conflict has begun. For example, a group suffering from a localized plague of locusts may initiate a cycle of war by raiding another group to acquire corn and squash. In the course of the raid, they kill someone in the prey village. If this village later stages a return raid revenge and retribution would have to be considered in addition to immediate economic variables. Furthermore, with the long-term perpetuation of a cycle of warfare, a complex social and ideological subsystem builds up around the pattern of warfare, and this subsystem to some (arguable) extent carries causal weight itself. Thus, we may have to look to one set of variables to explain the emergence of warfare in a particular area and a quite different set of variables to explain the development and maintenance of the pattern of warfare in that area.

Another dimension to the origins-versus-maintenance discussion is the question of why warfare does *not* emerge in some social systems. Not all tribal societies are in a constant state of war, and the reasons for "peace" provide an important perspective on explanations of the causes of war. Although there was some disagreement during the seminar about whether war or peace is the unusual condition needing explanation, we agreed that understanding why peace is maintained in some societies provides considerable insight into why other societies begin and maintain patterns of war. In this volume, Robarchek, Gibson, and Gregor all discuss the maintenance of peace in prestate societies; Haas discusses the transition from a pattern of peace to one of war; and Chagnon, Whitehead and Carneiro address the maintenance of a pattern of warfare. Ferguson crosses the field in offering a model of common causes for both the origins and maintenance of prestate war.

The final major dimension of variability in the seminar was that of causes versus effects of warfare in prestate societies. Although understanding why tribal groups come to fight one another is a critical issue in the anthropology of war, it is also important to know what happens to the social systems as a result of being in a state of war. Warfare has long been argued to play a central causal role in the general evolution of cultural systems, but this role – particularly in a prestate context – has seldom been rigorously examined empirically. In this book, Carneiro and I specifically address the evolutionary role of warfare, my paper in terms of the emergence of tribal systems in the southwestern U.S. and Carneiro's in terms of complex chiefdoms in Polynesia and Peru.

Assembling the protagonists in this seminar was one task; holding them together and channeling their energy into a constructive discussion was another altogether. Clark McCauley deserves abundant credit for his tact, patience, and authority in his capacity as chairman of the meeting. He guided the debates in productive directions and ensured that the myriad sidelines and tangents were brought back to the central themes of the seminar. I think it helped that he comes from a background in small group psychology. Karen Colvard is due great thanks not only for stimulating the seminar in the first place but also for contributing insightful comments and an alternate voice to the seminar throughout the week. Floyd Ratliff supported and encouraged the seminar from its inception and added a thoughtful outside perspective during the "off-hours" of the week. On behalf of all the participants, I would like to express our appreciation to the Harry Frank Gugenheim Foundation for making it all possible. To Douglas W. Schwartz and the board of managers of the School of American Research, I extend our collective gratitude for providing the supporting environment that made possible an exciting and successful seminar. Finally, we cannot begin to thank Jane Barbarrouse enough for being the most gracious and cooperative hostess, and Sarah Wimett, Jennifer McLaughlin, and Stephen Soule for making our week in the seminar house pleasant, nourishing and comfortable. It is so much easier to hold your attention to the subject at hand when your somatic needs are well cared for.

1
Conference overview

CLARK McCAULEY

In reviewing the conference discussion, I will compare this conference with the symposium on war at the 1967 American Anthropological Association Meetings. The symposium was held in the context of concerns about U.S. involvement in the Vietnam War, and attempted to bring together what anthropology could offer toward understanding and reducing war. Twenty years later, what has been learned? Or, more particularly, comparing the content of that symposium (as published in *War: The Anthropology of Armed Conflict and Aggression* [Fried, et al. 1968]) with the content of the present conference, how have the issues and the evidence advanced?

DEFINITION OF WAR

The foundation for meaningful comparison with 1967 is the definition of war, which, happily, has not changed. Carneiro was perhaps most explicit in the present conference in defining war as a subset of human aggression involving the use of organized force between politically independent groups. This is substantially the same as Livingstone's (1968) "intergroup aggression," Wallace's (1968) "sanctioned use of lethal weapons by members of one society against members of another

1

society," and Mead's (1968) "groups . . . in purposeful, organized and socially sanctioned combat involving killing." Carneiro goes beyond the older definitions in emphasizing political independence, but assessment of political autonomy can be difficult and can admit of differences of degree such as to make this portion of his definition problematic. Wallace and Mead go beyond Carneiro in emphasizing ingroup sanctions for killing, and Mead organized her whole paper around the origins and implications of the boundary between ingroup and outgroup. In thus emphasizing the perception of group boundaries and norms, Wallace and Mead appear to have been pointing the way to an analysis that could bridge cultural and individual explanations of war. In the present conference, the ethnographies provided by Gibson, Gregor, Robarchek, and Chagnon can be seen as moving toward and relevant to this kind of analysis.

BIOLOGICAL SELECTION AND WAR

The conference reflected a major change in biologically based explanations of war. Twenty years ago, Lorenz and Ardrey had popularized the idea of an aggressive or killer instinct for aggression in warrior societies, but which was present to some degree in all humankind. The implication of this view was that war might best be avoided by providing harmless outlets for aggression, and sports and the space race were both rated as above-average entertainments for this purpose. Anthropologists then and now find the hypothesis of a killer instinct not so much wrong as irrelevant to the kind of facts they want to explain. The Vikings of some hundreds of years ago are the notably peaceful Danes of today. The horse and gun made some people of the Shoshonean Basin – the Utes and Snakes – into warriors, and other people of the same Basin – the poor Diggers – into fearful refugees (Service, 1968). The gun and a market for slaves made both the Miskito kingdom and its Sumo victims "out of identical aboriginal material" (Service, 1968). Whitehead, at the conference, offered a similar history of transition from limited to unlimited war and slaving after the Carib came in contact with Europeans. In these examples, the rate of change in behavior – in culture – is too great to be a function of genetic differences (see Livingstone, 1968). Thus it hardly matters whether genetic selection for psychological characteristics may yet be going on in some human groups, since cultural change toward or away from war will remain to be

2

explained. This kind of argument was prominent in 1967, but appears to have been so successful as to need only briefest rehearsal in 1986.

Perhaps it is no accident that aggression as instinct has faded as an issue while sociobiology, another biologically based account of behavior, has risen to prominence. The possibility of explaining war in terms of behavior selected to maximize inclusive fitness was given considerable attention at the conference, at least as much as the killer instinct was given twenty years ago. A theory that promises to deal with cooperative as well as agonistic behavior is a priori attractive. And a theory able to comprehend altruism as self interest, as inclusive fitness can account for self-sacrifice if enough relatives with enough copies of the altruist's genes are thereby saved, generates real intellectual excitement. There was some feeling at the conference that a theory with this kind of excitement, one still under construction or at least in progress of explication, ought to be given the benefit of the doubt. More concretely, there were the vivid examples with which Chagnon illustrated his contention that the Yanomamö behave as if they sought reproductive opportunities. Still, the discussion did raise some doubts, one of which is already obvious: If war increases somatic and, ultimately, reproductive success of individuals who fight, why is war not continuous and ubiquitous like the incest taboo? That is, it is not clear how instincts leading to inclusive fitness can do better than instinct for aggression in accounting for the facts of cultural variation.

Another problem for the sociobiological approach was to specify how instincts leading to inclusive fitness could be represented in the motivations of the individual. It is clear that individual human beings are not motivated to maximize the number of offspring they and their kin contribute to the next generation. Infanticide is common in prestate societies, and abortion and contraception are common in modern societies. Likewise, celibacy is not nearly so rare as a biological motive for children ought to make it. The response was offered that individual human actors do not need to understand inclusive fitness, they need only be equipped with motives and behaviors which in the past have been associated with inclusive fitness. So, for instance, genetically based motives for dominance and for preferring similar others might be associated with success in getting genomes into the next generation. Even this example ran into some problems. The basis of similarity in humans appears to be susceptible to cultural interpretation that is independent of or even contrary to kinship relations. Chagnon reports

3

that Yanomamö brothers from nearby villages will attack one another, and some brothers did literally fight brothers in the American Civil War. Indeed the fissioning of Yanomamö villages means that nearby and feuding villages are likely to share more ancestors than more distant villages.

CULTURAL SELECTION AND WAR

At the conference, Chagnon and Dyson-Hudson argued for the importance of both biological and cultural selection in understanding warfare, while Carneiro and Ferguson remained largely unconvinced of the necessity of going beyond cultural selection. Although ideas about cultural selection were represented in the 1967 symposium, notably by Chagnon and Service, it seems fair to say that this perspective was considerably more elaborated in 1986 – perhaps by contrast with the advancing interest in biological selection. Most simply, cultural selection is group selection for norms and practices involving behaviors all humans are competent to perform (Skinner, 1981). That is, both cultural and biological selection explain behavior in terms of its consequences, but biological selection defines success in terms of relative contribution of genes to the next generation whereas cultural selection defines success in terms of relative contribution of norms and practices to the next generation.

The distinction between cultural and biological selection can be blurred by including mating opportunities as one kind of material resource, but the pure version of cultural selection espoused by Ferguson maintains that war, at least prestate war, is carried out for material resources such as land, water, food, and trade goods. Even war that appears to be for status can be understood as improving terms of trade for the group winning higher status. It is not necessary that individuals recognize the material goals that support their behavior; just as biological selection can operate via proximal motives associated with inclusive fitness, so can cultural selection operate on proximal goals of ritual, value, or religion that are associated with material success. Thus cultural selection can operate on variations in culture in the same way that biological selection can operate on variations in behavior anchored in genetic differences.

Cultural selection and biological selection can co-exist, but the pure version of cultural selection holds that biological selection of humans, if

4

it continues at all, is negligibly slow by comparison with cultural selection. Millennia ago, biological selection shaped human morphology, human motives, and human ability to satisfy these motives by analysis of means-end relationships. Now the morphology, basic motives, and intelligence of humans may be taken as essentially given, and the variation of culture understood in terms of cultural selection. Of course it need not be the case that all the motives biologically selected for in paleolithic times are as benign as the motives for food, water, and sex. It could be that motives for dominance and against difference that were selected for in the paleolithic are maladaptive today. If so, cultural variation must compete in satisfying these motives and the path of cultural selection is the more constrained.

An example of the opposition of cultural and biological selection cropped up in relation to identifying predictors of prestate war. Ferguson made a strong case for the importance of conflict over material resources such as land, food, and trade goods. Chagnon agreed to the importance of these but wanted to add mating opportunities and kin welfare as relevant to inclusive fitness and part of the material predictors of conflict. Ferguson resisted this idea as not necessary to explain examples of prestate war, but ended agreeing that resources related to inclusive fitness might well be important predictors of individual conflict even if not important as predictors of war. Chagnon agreed at least to the extent that it was fair to say that the Yanomamö fight over women but not fair to say that they go to war to obtain women.

One issue raised concerning cultural selection was the level at which it operates, whether only at the level of the group or at the individual level as well. That is, do individuals fare better or worse as a function of variation in belief, value, and behavior, or is individual variation within a culture negligible in the competition of group cultures? The beginning of data relevant to this question may be available in Gregor's description of a Xinguano man who denies the existence of witches and denounces killings for suspected witchcraft. If this individual lives and prospers, will others accept his beliefs? It is interesting to note that the question of level was raised as well for biological selection, but conferees agreed to consider biological selection only at the level of the individual. Biological selection at the level of genes, groups, or species remains controversial (see Barash, 1977), though perhaps not impossible (Gould, 1986).

The contest between biological and cultural interpretations of human

5

evolution continued throughout the conference. To borrow a metaphor from David Lykken, this is an issue of hardware versus software. Imagine the human brain evolving like the recent evolution of personal computers, that is toward both better hardware in terms of speed and memory and better software in terms of the programs and problems run on the machines. Biological selection is identified with evolution of hardware and cultural selection with evolution of software. Paleolithic selection can be thought of as selection of both hardware and software, with particular software to some degree limited to particular hardware. If biological selection is complete for humans, it can be thought of as having produced a very successful hardware that drove all other hardware from the marketplace so that further evolution is concentrated in the competition of software for the dominant hardware. The computer metaphor leads naturally to the question of whether the hardware is really so good that it places no limits on software development. There was general agreement at the conference that the greater speed of cultural selection recommends it for understanding cultural variation as studied by anthropologists, but the potential importance of understanding the products of biological selection was not denied.

SELECTION VERSUS HISTORY

At the conference, biological and cultural selection were seen as agreeing that material resources, including reproductive opportunities, are the currency in which different kinds of behavior are evaluated. That is, both kinds of selection explain group conflict in terms of competition for material resources, though both deny that human actors need be aware of the relations between their behaviors and these resources. Proponents of both biological and cultural selection (Chagnon, Dyson-Hudson, Carneiro, Ferguson, and Haas) found themselves in contention with more historically minded conferees (notably Gibson, Robarchek and Whitehead) for whom selectionist explanations were inadequate. The inadequacy cited was the blind and materialist quality of such explanations, and, in particular, the failure to connect distal contingencies in terms of material resources to the more proximal causes of conflict in the norms, thoughts, and goals of individual human beings. (At this point, I must confess that motives for dominance and against difference, offered above as possible proximal predictors of conflict, are more my own heuristics than hypotheses advanced in

6

discussion. Chagnon and Dyson-Hudson were especially consistent in limiting themselves to supposing indefinite proximal motives such that actors behave "as if" to maximize inclusive fitness.)

Discussion at the conference made clear that some participants were more concerned than others with connecting distal to proximal predictors of conflict, though there was eventual agreement that there was at least some value in identifying distal predictors. Still, the cultural historians were confident that the speed and direction of cultural change in relation to changed ecology could only be understood in terms of changes consciously directed by the perceptions of human actors. That is, cultural selection via random variation in culture seemed like biological selection via random variation of genes in that both are too slow to explain the speed of cultural adaptation.

The alternative offered was a view of culture as preadaptation, which was understood to refer to variation that may or may not have been affected by selection. In principle, this alternative can complement rather than oppose biological and cultural selection, but, in discussion, arguments on the basis of selection of either kind tended to be opposed to arguments on the basis of preadaptation. The idea of preadaptation is essentially historical; it is that ecological change or stress leads to cultural adaptation mediated by human choices based on pre-existing culture. The importance of this idea is that it emphasizes that ecological and especially material factors cannot be more than crude predictors of cultural change, since the same objective conditions can be interpreted very differently by different groups, depending on the culture through which they understand these conditions. With regard to war, preadaptation means that social or material challenge or stress may or may not lead to war, depending on the history of the group. Preadaptation especially means that war or peace, and particular directions of warlike or peaceful reactions, will be made more or less likely by the infrastructure of culture that is the product of group history.

For instance, Gibson was confident that the peacefulness of the Buid could not be explained by reference to physical or social ecology, since there were six other tribes he could point to with similar physical and social ecology, none of which is peaceful. His view was that the Buid culture could only be understood as a unique interaction of previous culture and present ecology, that is, that some important difference in previous history or culture led the Buid to react differently to their present ecology than did the other six tribes. He acknowledged that he

7

did not know and might never know what the important preadaptation had been, though historical investigation should clarify preadaptations for at least some kinds of cultural change. In a similar vein, Whitehead held that war and slaving by the Carib were reactions to contact with Europeans that could not be understood without reference to pre-European Carib culture. He suggested that the Carib kinship system was one important preadaptation for successful slaving. To a lesser degree, Robarchek and Gregor also resonated to the idea of preadaptation, and Robarchek's description of Semai reactions to the beginning of a cash market for durian fruit can be considered an extended example of the operation of preadaptation.

Relevant to the idea of preadaptation was considerable agreement at the conference that the origins of conflict must be distinguished from the factors maintaining conflict once begun. This distinction proceeds from both logical and experiential considerations. Logically, the effect of an adaptation cannot be its cause. Both biological and cultural selection can explain how a pattern of behavior can succeed and become more common because of its effects, but neither can explain how the pattern of behavior came to be there for selection to work on. In other words, selection works on the variation already available, and the origins of the variations need additional explanation. The kinship system of the Carib, for instance, existed prior to contact with Europeans and need not have originated in association with conflict, even though it was advantageous for slaving after Europeans made slaving profitable.

Gould (1986) makes a similar point by quoting Darwin with regard to the unfused skull bones essential to parturition of large-brained mammals. These cannot be explained as adaptations selected for their role in parturition, since similar sutures are found in birds and reptiles that need only break out of a shell. Indeed, Gould (1986: 54) summarizes the concerns of the historically minded at the conference:

Cardboard Darwinism . . . is a theory of pure functionalism that denies history and views organic structure as neutral before a molding environment. It is a reductionist, one-way theory about the grafting of information from environment upon organism through natural selection of good designs. We need a richer theory, a structural biology, that views evolution as an interaction of outside and inside, of environment and the structural rules for genetic and developmental architecture – rules set by the contingencies of history and physicochemical laws of the stuff itself.

Gould (1986) also makes a point about the asymmetry of selection

8

that is worth noting in the search for explanations of war. That is, structures that are harmful are likely to be eliminated by selection, but helpful structures can arise in many ways and need not be built by selection. Similarly in terms of behavior, motives and patterns of behavior that are harmful in either biological or cultural terms are likely to be eliminated, but helpful cultural practices can arise in many ways, not least from the accidents of unique group history.

In addition to these logical considerations, there are experiential considerations supporting a distinction between the origins and the maintenance of warfare. The conference discussed three kinds of force for continuation of conflict, once begun. The first is revenge: the injury or death of members of one's group, especially kin, is likely to lead to motivation and emotion for revenge. Feuding is likely to go on long after the original difference between two groups has become lost in myth or at least submerged in more recent injury.

The second force for continuation of conflict is related to the first but more rational: the strategy of physical conflict is dominant over more peaceful strategies in the sense that groups unable to respond to force with force are likely to be eliminated. That is, when choosing between cooperative and competitive behavior in a prolonged series of interactions with another, the strategy of responding to cooperation with cooperation and responding to competition with competition appears to be a very successful strategy (Axelrod, 1984). To the extent that individuals and groups appreciate the value of the tit-for-tat strategy, conflict once begun is likely to lead to additional conflict. The two forces for conflict continuation just described apply as well to individuals as to groups.

The third force applies to groups rather than to individuals and so may be said to be a force for continuation of war specifically, rather than for continuation of individual conflict. This third force is the class or common interest of those members of a group whose special business it is to fight or prepare to fight a war. This force, which may be identified with the interests of the military-industrial complex in modern states, exists as well in lower stages of political centralization. That is, a warrior class in chiefdom or village is likely to press for continuing conflict to the extent that their material interests and self definition depend on war and the threat of war.

Since these three forces for continuation and even escalation of conflict only come into play after conflict has begun, they act in

9

addition to whatever forces bring about the initiation of conflict. Thus predicting or explaining the initiation of conflict may be a different piece of theoretical business than predicting or explaining the continuation of conflict once begun. For instance, it is one thing to explain how the values and rituals of the Yanomamö, or the structure of their rewards and costs, operate to maintain and encourage conflict both within and between villages. It is quite another to explain how the system, the whole culture came into existence. The latter is an historical question, in which some previous culture presumably interacted with a change in ecology to shape the culture now observed. As an historical question, it is difficult to analyze scientifically since historical explanation is necessarily a highly contingent account of the interaction of unique circumstances.

The conference produced some lively discussion concerning the possibility and desirability of pursuing historical questions about why culture changes, as opposed to concentrating on predictors of war that can be useful across different cultures with the cultures considered as given. By the end of the conference, both kinds of approach seemed useful to most of the participants and examples of both kinds of understanding were cited in particulars of ethnographies presented by participants.

WAR AND THE DEVELOPING STATE

The end of the conference saw the beginnings of a promising model of the relation of warfare to the development of the state. This model will doubtless be further developed in the future by those involved with it at the conference (notably Carneiro, Chagnon, Ferguson, and Haas), but some of its directions can be briefly indicated here.

The foundation of this model was Carneiro's account of the development of the state via circumscription and resource competition. The states, from the least to the most hierarchical social organization, are the band, the autonomous village, the tribe or confederacy, the chiefdom, and the state. The stages are not meant to imply inexorable progress, since higher states can regress to lower ones (Carneiro suggested "pulsile tribalization" in reaction to external threat), but the stages are assumed to represent a necessary sequence such that, for instance, a tribe cannot become a state without passing through the stage of chiefdom. Parallel to these stages are several dimensions of hypothesized differences with

10

regard to war and conflict, and these differences are the main theoretical work of the model.

The first hypothesis is that conflict and war are the mechanism of increased social hierarchy and the impetus to progression from stage to stage. The band, whether family or supra-family, is seen as very egalitarian, and the state as very centralized. Progression from egalitarian to hierarchical society depends on conflict and war because, as often cited at the conference, "no one ever willingly gives up sovereignty" and because waging war successfully depends on hierarchical command and control and on specialized skills. Some question about this hypothesis was raised, however, in the context of Haas's work on Longhouse Valley. Here the data seem to show cooperation correlated with drought before the outbreak of hostilities, and there is as yet no evidence, such as a larger "chief's" village, of hierarchy or centralization after the beginning of hostilities. Thus war may not be the first or only response to scarce resources and may not always lead to hierarchical organization. Still, there was general agreement that war was typically associated with development of the state.

A second hypothesis concerned the role of material resources, including mating opportunities, in the origin of conflict and war. It was suggested that material resources are more likely to be at issue in war between bands, villages, and tribes than in war between chiefdoms or states. Chagnon, who sees conflict over resources occurring as the number of persons approaches the carrying capacity of an ecology, suggested that the concept of carrying capacity blurred at the level of the state, where organization and technology can effectively remove any limits on resources.

Closely related to the role of material resources is the third hypothesis, which concerns the interests of leaders and followers. In an egalitarian band, there is little distinction between leader and followers and the interests and outcomes of all participating in conflict are about the same. An autonomous village is likely to have a war leader different from the political leader, and there is some individual interest available for the war leader in the extra status and power during conflict. The same is true for confederacy or tribe, except that at this stage leaders begin to profit by information differences among group members that are not found in bands or villages. In contrast with lower states, the war leaders and political leaders of chiefdoms are usually the same persons, and the material resources available for chiefs are far greater than for

11

their followers. Indeed by the chiefdom stage, and to a still greater degree in the state, the interests of the leaders differ greatly from the interests of the followers, and the interests of the leaders are more likely to have to do with status and power than with access to material resources. A curious conclusion of this argument is that war of chiefdoms and states is like war of egalitarian bands in being mostly a matter of individual perception of personal interest, with the difference that in chiefdom and state it is the personal interest of only a very few that counts.

Along with differences in the interests of leaders and followers, a dimension of differences in power is hypothesized. Thus, in egalitarian groups, war occurs when a mob chooses to fight. In more hierarchical stages, war occurs by group decision, but, once decided, there is group pressure to stay and fight. Or war is declared by a leader, but war is waged only with consensus. Finally, at the stage of chiefdom or state, war is determined by leaders who have the power to compel participation by draft and taxation. Though it is clear that the power differences between leaders and followers do, in general, increase from band to state, there was some discussion concerning the difficulty of distinguishing the relative importance of consensus and compulsion in any particular case. In this regard, Chagnon noted that Yanomamö leaders prime their followers by repeatedly floating the idea of doing something, then waiting for consensus to build before saying *when* to do it – so that they may be seen to be deciding.

Lastly, the model hypothesizes differences across stages in the dynamics for conflict continuation. The three forces identified above – revenge, tit-for-tat, and military specialization – apply much more to the hierarchical than to the egalitarian stages. A band is less likely to have continuing contact with particular other bands than a village is with adjoining villages, a tribe is with neighboring tribes, and so forth. The dynamics of tit-for-tat and revenge are thereby reduced since both require a continuing relationship between the individuals and groups in conflict. Similarly, the increased specialization associated with more hierarchical organization enlarges the special interest of a warrior class or, at the level of the state, the special interest of a military-industrial complex. Thus in general, it appears that the intensity and duration of war should be greater in more hierarchical stages because the forces for continuation and escalation are greater once conflict is begun.

Without presuming to evaluate the model just outlined, it is possible to be impressed at least by its range and complexity. In relating the nature of war to stages in the development of the state, the model brings together physical ecology, individual motivation, and social structure and power relationships. The seeds of this kind of model are to be found in the symposium of twenty years ago (see especially Halloway [1968], Lesser [1968], and Wallace [1968] about the importance of personal involvement in prestate war by comparison with the impersonality of state war), but the model as advanced at the conference represents a flourishing development and integration of previous thinking. Perhaps the most notable aspect of the model is that it has something to say about the old question of what prestate war has to do with modern war; hypotheses about both similarities and differences are made explicit in the stages of the model.

ANTHROPOLOGY OF PEACE

Probably the most unusual aspect of the conference on war was its considerable discussion concerning three peaceful societies. In the symposium of twenty years ago, there was barest mention of the conditions of peace as relevant to understanding the condition of war (Leeds, 1968: 101). Ten years later, Scott (1976: 81) pointed out the limitations of studying war as if it were a disease to be eliminated by eliminating the bug that causes it, but he went on to recommend a U.S. Department of Peace rather than study of peaceful societies. Peaceful societies are rare, studies of peaceful societies likewise rare (Wiberg, 1981), and comparison of different peaceful societies is rarer still (Fabbro, 1978). But if war is the phenomenon of interest, conditions of peace and war must be contrasted. Thus the conference was indeed fortunate in having Gibson, Robarchek, and Gregor to present ethnologies of three peaceful societies, respectively the Buid, Semai, and Xinguano.

As with the model of stages of state development, the commonalities among the peaceful groups discussed at the conference will doubtless be explicated and extended in later work by the conferees. Here it is again appropriate to provide only a brief overview of some of the directions this work may take. To begin, it is important to recognize that the three groups are not equally peaceful. Among the Buid and the Semai,

13

violence among group members is almost unknown, and reaction to predatory raids by outsiders is always fear and flight. Among the Xinguanos, however, accused witches live in fear of members of their own group, and "execution" of a witch does occur every few years. Also, Xinguano reaction to hostile outsiders can include retaliatory raids which, in a recent case, were successful enough to leave a nearby tribe desperate for peace. Thus the Xinguanos are less consistently peaceful than the Semai or Buid, though the special achievement of the Xinguanos is association of four different language groups in a common culture of peacefulness.

Perhaps the most notable commonality of the three peaceful groups is what Gregor calls an "antiviolent" value system. Peace is supported by stigmatizing quarreling, boasting, stinginess, anger, and violence, and by according prestige for generosity, gentleness, and conflict avoidance. This value system is supported by supernatural beliefs in which helpful friendly spirits are opposed by malevolent and violent spirits who prey upon men. Further, the antiviolent value system is embodied in a contrast between the peacefulness of the ingroup and the violence of outsiders, a contrast that forms an important part of the everyday maintenance of the system. Outsiders are bloody, violent, dangerous, ugly, evil, animal-like and, in a real sense, less than human. Children are warned against outsiders and, especially, about behaving like outsiders. It is possible to imagine a value system in which peace is the great value and flight the only answer to attack, but without the extravagant ethnocentrism that characterizes the perception of ingroup and outgroup in these three peaceful societies. But the fact appears to be that hating violence requires violent people to hate.

Another commonality is the egalitarian nature of all three societies, and an associated impairment of personal relationships. The Buid believe explicitly that violence is the end result of uncontrolled individual emotions and wants and especially of attempts to dominate others; their society emphasizes adult autonomy and equality and avoids material or even emotional dependency. Individuals are encouraged to depend only on the group, and not on particular other individuals. The rapid turn-over of spouses among the Buid is one indication of the weakness of dyadic relationships in their society.

The peaceful Semai also see danger in individual emotions and wants. They experience any strong emotion as fear and believe the whole group is endangered by the unsatisfied wants of any individual. Voicing a want converts an individual need into a social responsibility, so an individual is reluctant to make any request that might be refused and, on the other hand, must be always alert to the wants of others. The result is that members of a Semai band see one another as responsibilities and relations between individuals are relatively formal and non-intimate. It might be said that the Semai are incorporated to share all gains and losses, whereas the Buid have shares in a limited liability partnership.

Unlike the other two societies, the Xinguanos do have some competition for status and position, and do have chiefs. But the power of the chiefs and indeed of any position or status is limited by fear of witchcraft and murder from anyone left unsatisfied and resentful, or equally, by fear of accusations of witchcraft if an enemy should fall ill. In addition to inhibiting power differences and stratification, the preoccupation with witchcraft inhibits spontaneity in personal relations. Aside from joking and practical joking that can become real hazing, relations between individuals are carried on with a careful courtesy that rests on fear. Both the joking and the careful courtesy keep people at a distance.

Thus, all three peaceful societies have very low degrees of social stratification, obtained by controlling expression of individual wants and emotions in various ways. (It is interesting to note that the Xinguanos are both a little less egalitarian and a little less peaceful.) The Semai internalize constraint by actually experiencing all strong emotion or need as dangerous, the Buid value self-control and autonomy in a more garden-variety form of internalization, and the Xinguanos depend on external constraint associated with threat of witchcraft. The cost for all three is some impairment in the quality of social and emotional experience within the group and a pervasive fear of outsiders – if witches can be thought of as outsiders disguised as insiders.

Other commonalities of the peaceful societies were discussed at the conference and can be mentioned briefly here. These include slash-and-burn agriculture, patchiness of resources, small villages, relatively open-ended groups with blurred cleavage planes, endogamy preferences, sources of disputes (sexual jealousy, gossip, stinginess), and absence of aggressive models.

The possibility of distinguishing between pacified and peaceful groups was raised, the former adopting peace as a strategy of weakness after losses to disease or war and the latter peaceful as personality types. Although this distinction was raised in connection with the greater internalized constraint against violence in the Semai than in the Xinguanos, there seems to be no evidence that the Xinguanos are remnants of earlier disasters. Thus there is no reason to see the Xinguanos as pacified rather than peaceful, though the possibility was raised that the Buid might have lost half their numbers to smallpox around 1948 and so might better deserve to be called pacified. Consistent with distinguishing between the causes of war and the functions of war once begun, there was sympathy at the conference for distinguishing between the historical origins of peacefulness and its current functions.

As was the case for the model of war in relation to the developing state, the commonalities of peaceful cultures that began to emerge at the conference were welcomed as a promising direction for future research. Further, the comparison of warlike and peaceful groups in rich ethnological detail was agreed by all to be an unusual and important impetus to creative thinking at the conference. It seemed clear that direct comparison of warlike and peaceful societies, particularly within a common ecology such as that shared by the Buid and their warlike neighbors, was a promising strategy for future research. What was not clear was whether the peaceful societies offered any real clues for avoiding war between modern states. It was undeniable that all three peaceful societies represented at the conference were peaceful at the expense of living lives obsessed with violence.

In retrospect, the conference was actually two conferences. The first took place from Monday through Wednesday, and was mostly occupied with conferees' defending their own papers and points of view and learning and criticizing the views of others. The second conference, which would not have been possible without the first, took place on Thursday and Friday as conferees sought and found common perspectives and the beginnings of integrated interpretations of their own and others' data. Many conferences can be efficiently apprehended by perusal of the papers submitted, but the five days of this meeting produced more than just the papers, even in revision. In concentrating on the discussions, here represented in terms of issues rather than in exact chronological order, this overview has attempted to convey some of both conferences but especially the second, and was written without seeing the revised versions of the conferees' papers.

THE SOCIAL PSYCHOLOGY OF WAR: SOME CONCLUDING OBSERVATIONS

This section offers a few personal observations of the writer, now exceeding his role as chairperson and reporter. As intimated earlier, these observations concern the importance of status competition and ethnocentrism in both war and peace.

The relative importance of status competition can be suggested by considering the nature and importance of individual aggression in warfare. Human aggression is behavior intended to hurt or kill another human. It is useful to distinguish two kinds of aggression, impulsive aggression and instrumental aggression (Buss, 1961: 10). Impulsive aggression is behavior in which the aggressor seeks satisfaction in the suffering of the victim. Instrumental aggression is behavior in which the aggressor seeks some other satisfaction for which the suffering of the victim is only a means. Killing for hire is instrumental aggression, and so is spanking a child, at least up to a point.

The two best known theories of aggression have to do with impulsive aggression. The model of instinctive aggression advanced by Lorenz and Ardrey holds that pressure for aggression is generated within the organism until released by an appropriate cue, and the greater the pressure the less required of the cue. Neither this hydraulic model nor its close relative, Freud's theory of aggression, is today taken very seriously by either anthropologists (see above) or psychologists (Krebs and Miller, 1985: 38–39).

The hypothesis that frustration is necessary and sufficient to produce aggression (Dollard et al., 1939) was another instinct-based model of impulsive aggression, but it, too, is a theory in disrepair today. Frustration does not always lead to anger, anger does not always lead to aggression, insult and pain are more likely than frustration to produce anger, and not all aggression is preceded by anger or frustration (Krebs and Miller, 1985: 39–40). Even Berkowitz, longtime exponent of frustration–aggression theory in manifold revisions, has come to see aversive events as the best predictor of impulsive aggression, with frustration reduced to one kind of aversive event (Berkowitz, 1982).

Perhaps the greatest dent in frustration–aggression theory has been the realization of the extent to which aggression is instrumental, rather than impulsive (Buss, 1961). That is, aggression in many examples, and certainly this is true of many examples of aggression cited by anthropologists, seems to serve some goal or purpose other than the pure satisfaction of inflicting pain or death on others. For instance, Chagnon describes a conflict between two Yanomamö villages in which the losers are trapped in a pit, but the winners leave them instead of finishing them off. And the losers are not later attacked any further. This is not behavior consistent with motivation to hurt and kill. Gibson's understanding of headhunting in southeast Asia is similar in that the goal is ceremonial life force or status improvement rather than the death of particular others. Indeed "any head will do."

Even if instrumental aggression is more common, impulsive aggression might yet be an important part of warfare. Impulsive aggression appears to be at issue in the model of war and the developing state outlined above. This is particularly true since hatred of the enemy is certainly the kind of personal interest hypothesized to be stronger in egalitarian than in hierarchical societies. There is evidence to support the weak role of impulsive aggression in state-level warfare. Research reported in *The American Soldier* (Stouffer et al., 1949) is clear in showing that pay, medals, ideals, and hatred of the enemy were only seldom mentioned as reasons for fighting. The greatest reason was not wanting to let down the other members of the squad, or to lose their esteem and support. Similarly, Marshall's *Men Against Fire* (1947) reports that only about a quarter of American combat troops would use their weapons against the enemy, even when hard pressed.

These data suggest that impulsive aggression is a minor factor in state-level warfare – though it would be interesting to have parallel data for Russian troops who believed themselves fighting for "Mother Russia" in World War II, or for Vietnamese fighting Americans in the Vietnam conflict. Notice, however, that it is incorrect to say that modern combatants are without personal motivation for fighting; there is nothing impersonal about a man's place in a group of other men. Indeed there is nothing impersonal about motivation to avoid punishment for cowardice or desertion. Thus it appears that the hypothesis about the weakness of personal interest in combat in more hierarchical societies should be understood to mean weakness of rewards. Compared to combatants from bands and villages, modern soldiers are not suffering any weakness of interest in avoiding punishment.

Although it seems that impulsive aggression is a minor factor in modern war, there is another possibility to consider. Perhaps the twenty-five per cent of soldiers who will fire their weapons are the minority who do hate the enemy, so that impulsive aggression is after all necessary for modern war. A superficial response to this possibility is to point out that the great majority of casualties in modern war come from weapons used at impersonal distance: artillery is the major source of infantry casualties. A less superficial response requires recognizing that wars are not fought only with artillery. Men must still face men with weapons in their hands, and it appears that we do not yet know the importance of impulsive aggression in this behavior.

But let us assume for a moment that impulsive aggression is relatively unimportant in modern war, as Givens and Nettleship do in their preface to *Discussions on War and Human Aggression* (1976: xi). What is the evidence that impulsive aggression is any more important in prestate war? Impulsive aggression should have brought the Yanomamö to wipe out their enemy, the more so to the extent that a beaten enemy is no longer dangerous. Impulsive aggression is not necessarily involved in taking a head, especially not to the extent that one head is as good as another.

These and other examples of aggression cited at the conference either do not demand or do not support interpretation in terms of impulsive aggression. Plains Indians counted coup above killing. Fighting for material resources, including mating opportunities, need not include impulsive aggression. Cannibalism may begin as impulsive aggression, but may come to be more a matter of taste or status. Perhaps the clearest examples of personal motivation to hurt and kill the enemy come from cases of revenge for previous attack, but even here it is difficult to distinguish the satisfaction of hurting back from self-protection or tit-for-tat.

There is even some indication that impulsive aggression needs to be incited or cultivated as a strategy of instrumental aggression. Propaganda to stir hate is not necessary if the audience already hates. The Yanomamö are quintessentially fierce people, but Chagnon describes young warriors practicing putting on rage as a tactic, describes warriors using drugs to put themselves in a fighting mood, and describes tempers rising only after exchange of blows or in the midst of a skirmish with spears. These examples suggest that impulsive aggression is weak unless actively cultivated or incited by pain. The point of these examples is not that impulsive aggression is irrelevant to prestate war, but only that the evidence of the importance of such aggression is no clearer for prestate war than for modern war. It is at least possible to argue that impulsive aggression is equally unimportant for both prestate and modern war.

If impulsive aggression is relatively unimportant in war and instrumental aggression relatively important, what can be said about the goals for which aggression is a means? As intimated earlier, male competition for status and dominance appears to have a central role in descriptions of both warlike and peaceful societies. Consider again some of the details of warfare cited above, and the greater sense to be made of these in terms of competition for status than in terms of motivation to hurt and kill. Competition for resources, including mating opportunities, is more proximately competition for status in a male dominance order. Counting coup is a blow for status. Revenge is status regained. Fierceness is status assertion that may be cheaper than fighting. Status is established by beating the enemy, but does not require finishing them off. Status can require getting a head to get ahead. From a biological perspective, competition for status in a dominance hierarchy is easily linked to similar behaviors in many infrahuman species, and aggression in the service of establishing dominance is commonplace animal behavior. Indeed it is hard not to imagine some biological foundation for a behavior pattern powerful enough to put survival in doubt. This is the case for the Yanomamö, whose village size is a constant compromise between the military value of larger numbers for inter-village warfare and the value of fewer status challenges in smaller villages. Chagnon says that the Yanomamö are "delighted" to live in smaller villages and fight less.

Of course, all of these examples have other possible interpretations. In particular, the material benefits of status are sufficiently reliable that it is in practice extremely difficult to disentangle status competition from material interest as predictor and explanation of war. Ferguson (1984a: 41) recognizes this problem and suggests two kinds of evidence that may serve. One is to look at a regional pattern of war to see if who attacks whom and changing intensity of war can be understood in terms of material interest. It is not clear how this will cut through the tangle. The second is more promising: to determine if individuals behave in ways that conform to expectations of material benefit. In the examples above, the details of individual behavior in warfare are more consistent with a competition for status than with materialist self interest. The contrast comes strongest when competition for status endangers material self interest, as it appears to for the Yanomamö when villages fission, for the Plains Indians counting coup, and for modern soldiers who stay at their posts in order to maintain their status as men in a small group of men.

Do the details of individual behavior in peaceful societies offer another means of separating status competition from competition for material resources? It appears that they do not. First of all, even if competition for material resources is necessary for war, it does not necessarily follow that the absence of competition for material resources is sufficient for peace. Second, the Buid, the Semai, and the Xinguanos all show low levels of both resource and status competition, the Buid by ascribed equality of independence and prescribed sharing of resources, the Semai by ascribed equality of dependence on the group and prescribed sharing of resources, and the Xinguanos, less radically, by threat of witchcraft against anyone rising in status or resources. Thus peacefulness in these three societies does not distinguish the two kinds of competition. It is interesting to note that the Buid do compete with poetry for the favor of women, even as Yanomamö compete with fierceness. Evidently, status competition can serve peaceful values as well as warlike ones, though the paradox of competition to serve equality may have something to do with the emotional and social costs experienced by these societies. And there is some hint here that status competition is more basic than competition for physical resources, since status competition remains after competition for resources is reduced to a very low level.

There are more modern examples of status competition in service of peaceful values. Cult members competing in recruiting and fund raising are one example, and canonization of saints the indication of another. Old-order Amish compete in simplicity, work and peacefulness, but have to warn one another about getting puffed up. Musical, athletic, and scientific competitions are more prosaic examples. In some of these examples – cult and scientific competitions, for instance – the connection with material resources, including mating opportunities, is sufficiently strained as to suggest that resource competition has been separated from status competition and status competition yet appears. Examples of the other kind, resource competition appearing in circumstances where status competition is a strained interpretation, are not so easy to find.

The view of male status competition advanced here can be contrasted with Tiger's view of *Men in Groups* (1969). Tiger sees males attached to other males in a process of self-validation that is associated with instinctive ingroup cohesion and instinctive outgroup aggression. Status competition is similar in implying both attachment to the reference group and contest within it, as explicated by Festinger's (1954) social comparison theory and the research that came from it (Suls and Miller, 1977). But status competition does not imply any necessary or instinctual connection between attraction to the ingroup and aggression toward the outgroup (e.g. in religious groups), and status competition actively denies any instinctual ingroup cohesion. The Yanomamö and their fissioning villages should alone suffice to sink the contention concerning instinctive ingroup cohesion. Additional evidence is available from U.S. crime statistics showing that almost three quarters of all murders involve a murderer and victim who are friends or family members (suggesting that murder, by comparison with war, is much more a matter of impulsive violence).

It appears, then, that status competition, particularly among males, is an important mechanism of the translation of values into behavior. Values are anchored in groups, and status competition is the connection between the group and the behavior of individual group members. But status competition, found in both peaceful and warlike groups, cannot explain the difference between peace and war.

Neither can ethnocentrism. Ethnocentrism, or ingroup preference, is often cited as an important ingredient of group conflict and hostility, notably by Mead (1968) in her contribution to the 1967 symposium. Chagnon (1968a), in his contribution to the 1967 symposium, illustrated the importance of ethnocentrism in the *waiteri* complex by noting that the Yanomamö not only see themselves superior to all other peoples but even stigmatize tiny differences between groups of their own people – differences of pronunciation, for instance. However, ethnocentrism cannot alone explain the difference between war and peace any more than status competition can. Like status competition, ethnocentrism is found in both warlike and peaceful groups described at the conference. Ethnocentrism may be an ingredient in making war, but what other ingredients are necessary? Brown (1985: Ch. 15) has recently offered an analysis that puts ethnocentrism together with group stereotyping and perceived inequity in resources to explain group conflict.

Brown's analysis is pessimistic in that he sees both ethnocentrism and stereotyping as primitive and universal aspects of individual psychology. He understands stereotyping as perception of group differences in a process of category formation that is no more to be got rid of than categorization of non-human objects of perception. And he reviews evidence that the most arbitrary division of individuals into groups, including random assignment by coin-flip, is enough to elicit significant ingroup preference over outgroup in the individuals thus divided. This ingroup preference effect is linked to the individual's desire for a positive self image, a tendency as basic as the tendency to categorize. Finally, Brown sees perception of inequity as the factor that moves a group from ethnocentrism to aggression and hostility. Here it is not the fact of inequality of resources (either material or status resources) that is crucial, but the perception of unfair or illegitimate inequality that leads to anger and aggression. Brown holds that any aversive event tends to elicit anger and aggression, but sees perception of inequity as an aversive event particularly important in explaining group conflict.

Another way of thinking about the inevitability of stereotyping and ethnocentrism is to consider the role these phenomena may play in the evolution of culture. Whether by biological or cultural selection, cultures are likely to be favored that hold their own values as objectively true and competing values as objectively false. The reason is that morality is cheaper and more reliable than coercion (Schweder and Miller, 1985). To the extent that cooperation in group goals requires the individual to put group outcomes ahead of individual outcomes, the individual must be either coerced or persuaded. But persuasion that goes no deeper than personal preference is not likely to have much power over the individual. To get beyond mere preference to an obligation, a "should" that has power even when the individual is unobserved by others, requires the concept of an objective moral order from which at least some values and behaviors can be defended as objectively correct. It is not surprising that cultures including this moral quality have succeeded in competition with those, if ever there have been any, that did not. But an objective moral order implies that some behaviors and some groups of people are not merely different but wrong.

From several perspectives, then, it appears that stereotyping and ethnocentrism are characteristic of all human groups. The details of ethnographic descriptions at the conference are in accord with this generalization: as noted above, both warlike and peaceful societies show ethnocentrism and unflattering stereotypes about outgroups. But what about the perception of inequity? Here may be a more promising prospect for peace than Brown makes it. Brown sees inequality of resources as essentially inevitable, but distinguishes the fact of inequality from the perception of inequity. The latter is an interpretation, an interpretation peculiarly susceptible to group definition. Brown discusses the psychological work to be done in creating this definition, work which amounts to a conflict within the group between those who would go to war to gain equality and those who would not. Although invasion or attack makes a strong case for inequity and thus for war, there appears to be considerable potential for peace in understanding the dynamics by which inequality is translated into inequity.

Here it must be acknowledged that Brown's analysis is aimed at understanding ethnic group conflict between minorities and majorities, as for example between black Americans and the majority Anglo culture. Thus it might be argued that Brown's analysis is not relevant to war, at least not to modern war. What, for instance, does perceived inequity have to do with U.S. involvement in twentieth century wars? But Brown's analysis of inequity can be extended to any difference between groups in which moral values are at issue – extended, in other words, from perceived inequity to perceived iniquity. Perception of inequity is perceived violation of values of fairness and legitimacy in relation to distribution of resources. These are values understood to have the status of objective moral standards, so we may understand Brown to be saying that it is perceived moral violation that moves a group from ethnocentrism to hostility and conflict. By extension, we may hypothesize that violation of any value having the status of objective morality can incite hostility and conflict. Thus U.S. involvement in twentieth century wars may better be understood as reaction to perceived iniquity than to perceived inequity.

Of course, war is not an automatic reaction to either inequity or iniquity. These may explain the transition from ethnocentrism to hostility toward outgroup, but neither contributes much to our understanding of the transition from hostility to conflict and war. It appears then that either perception of iniquity or the impact of that perception is moderated by the potential costs of conflict. Still, Brown's analysis is interesting in pointing to the potential importance of socially constructed definitions of moral violation in the origins of conflict and war. Perceived moral violation can provide the foundation for ingroup sanction of violence against outgroups. The Buid, the Semai, and the Amish are encouraging indications that there are viable nonviolent reactions to even the clearest moral violations, though it must also be

24

said that response to perceived iniquity is likely to include violence so long as groups believe that there are values more important than life and peace.

2
Explaining war

R. BRIAN FERGUSON

This paper proposes a materialist synthesis of theory, towards a comprehensive explanation of war in stateless societies. War by states is
discussed, but only as the end point of the range being examined.

War itself is difficult to define. Elsewhere (Ferguson 1984a: 5) I
describe the broader phenomena underlying war as "organized,
purposeful group action, directed against another group . . . involving
the actual or potential application of lethal force." War is not merely
action, however. It is a condition of and between societies, with
innumerable correlates in virtually every dimension of culture.

Because it is so pervasive, the genesis, processes, and consequences of
war can be studied from diverse perspectives, which can lead to radically
different kinds of conclusions. Before any analysis even begins, crucial
decisions have already been made. What will be the form of the analysis
– attribution of causes, demonstration of functional linkages, achievement of subjective understanding? What aspect(s) of war and society will
be the focus of the investigation? What level of analysis and what time
frame will be used?

Depending on these decisions, different analysts could look at one
case of war and conclude that it is a conflict over political status,
women, natural resources, or trade goods; an expression of witchcraft

26

beliefs, cognitive orientations, pent-up frustration, rules of conflict, or belligerent personalities; a quest for prestige, revenge, security, power, trophies, or wealth; a consequence of residence patterns, level of political evolution, men's organizations, sovereignty, or inadequate conflict resolution mechanisms; and that it is generated by individual decisions, the functioning of societal subsystems, or cultural selection. Possibly, all of these conclusions could be correct. Each could accurately identify one aspect of the multiple interactions involved in that particular case of war.

This complexity must be recognized and dealt with. Not having done so up to the present is one reason that anthropological analyses of war tend to the particularistic and eclectic. When theoretical controversies do develop, they tend to be non-comparable, and the points are argued only among specialists in one region. Arguments about Great Plains Indians' warfare, for instance, do not overlap with arguments about the Northeast Woodlands (compare Biolsi 1984; Trigger 1976), and neither is cited in the currently hot debates over war in Highland New Guinea and Amazonia (see Ferguson 1984a: 30–31). Such provincialism is expectable given the limited development of general theory. Several more general hypotheses have appeared over the years, most of which will be mentioned in the text. But these have rarely been connected to each other or to other research findings.

Cumulative growth in understanding war requires that order be imposed on this explanatory chaos. We need theoretical templates to test against the burgeoning descriptive material (see Ferguson 1988a), lest it remain merely raw data. We need syntheses of findings, to show where approaches may agree, and to clarify where they do not.

This paper is an attempt to construct such a synthetic theory or model, one that is capable of coping with the sociocultural complexity involved in war. It does not center on any specific hypothesis, although the theory is capable of generating many testable predictions. The present effort is more deductive than inductive. The criterion of fit with empirical data is secondary to criteria of the explanatory power and parsimony of a few initial premises, and the logical integrity of the hypotheses they generate.

The theory outlined here is generally consistent with the research strategy of cultural materialism (Harris 1979a: part I; Price 1982), even though it differs significantly from some earlier analyses of war associated with that strategy. Inadequacies in earlier theoretical conceptions led to reformulations which are incorporated here, including a de-emphasis of functional models and the concept of adaptation, a greater emphasis on conscious strategizing, level of political evolution, histori-cal processes, and explicit recognition of the possibility of multiple levels of analysis (see Ferguson 1984a: 28–37). In addition, there is one major point where this theory diverges from the existing cultural materialistic research strategy.

Three mutually reinforcing premises make this a materialist approach. The first is the endorsement of the causal primacy of the infrastructure. Basically, this is the proposition that variables relating to demography, technology, the organization of work, and interaction with the natural environment shape structural patterns of kinship, economics, and politics, and that the latter in turn combine with infrastructural variables to shape ideological or superstructural patterns (Harris 1979a: 56). The causal primacy is expressed both in the existing organization of society, and in its patterned responses to new circumstances.

I disagree with Harris's formulation, however, that structural and superstructural factors should be invoked as explanations of other cultural patterns only after the possibilities of infrastructural explana-tions have been exhausted. In my view, these are not explanatory variables of only second or last resort. Rather, they expectably will operate in specific ways, determining specific kinds of patterns. This is a programmatic difference, and one which provides the basis of the synthesis to follow.

The perspective employed here is of a nested hierarchy of constrain-ing factors, progressively limiting possibilities. More powerful and general constrains leave latitude for secondary but more specific determinants. Many well-substantiated findings about the incidence and conduct of war have been made without reference to the infrastruc-ture, which are nevertheless perfectly compatible with a materialist approach framed in this way. These findings can be anchored in a network of deductive linkages based on materialist premises, thus expanding the scope of materialist explanation and making the incorporated findings something more than a formless assemblage of mutually irrelevant facts (see Price 1982: 712).

The idea of hierarchy of constraints is not the only materialistic premise in this model. The second is that there may be competition between and selection among groups, and that behaviors affecting

28

military ability can be made uniform in a region as groups with less effective military patterns are eliminated. Group selection models have been largely discredited in biology (Williams 1966; 1971). Whatever the general relevance of those criticisms to cultural processes (Harris 1984a: 130–133; Irons 1979: 10–13), they clearly are not relevant in the present case. First, the selection here is for "traits" concerning military capacity, rather than reproduction rates, which is what the biologists argue about. Second, the mechanism producing group extinctions – another thorny issue in biology – is war itself (see Naroll 1966; Otterbein 1977). Warfare can result in the elimination of local groups by death, dispersion, or absorption. If their elimination is due to some cultural pattern related to the practice of war, it is likely that other local groups will take appropriate steps to avoid a similar fate, even if that requires that individual interests and tendencies be overruled (see Alexander and Borgia 1978: 470–471). This view is applied elsewhere to explain the universality of redistributive exchange such as potlatching among Northwest Coast societies (Ferguson 1983; and see Harris 1975: 272; Webster 1977: 347).

The third and final materialist premise concerns motivation. All explanations of war are premised on some assumptions about human psychology, although these are usually not made explicit. I discuss "the question of motivation" elsewhere (1984a: 37–42), where I propose that three basic material goals are the maintenance or improvement of (1) available resources, (2) work situations, and (3) security against threats (cf. Chagnon, this volume). These three are, of course, always accompanied by a host of other concerns. Under some conditions, other non-material goals can outweigh material incentives in decisions to fight. But in the view advocated here, those cases will be exceptional. Non-material goals will not regularly lead to war unless they accompany material objectives. That is because war itself typically involves major costs. This must be emphasized: war costs lives, health, resources, and effort. So, if the motivational premise is correct, we should expect peace if the probable costs of war are not outweighed by potential benefits. This perspective is also applicable to understanding transitions from one phase of war to another. It is compatible with a perspective which stresses the role of purposeful decisions made by thinking cultural beings (see Robarchek, this volume), but contradicts the view that war is in some sense normal, and it is peace which requires explanation (see Gregor, this volume).

29

The motivational premise can be expressed in one general proposition: wars occur when those who make the decision to fight estimate that it is in their material interests to do so. (This is a more precise and correct formulation than statements made previously [Ferguson 1984a: 32] that wars are conflicts over scarce resources.) The material interests of decision-makers can take the form of six strategic objectives of war: (1) to increase access to fixed resources; (2) to capture movable valuables; (3) to impose an exploitative relationship on another independent group; (4) to conquer and incorporate another group; (5) to use external conflict as a means of enhancing the decision-makers' position within their own society; and (6) to forestall attacks by others. Objective (6) suggests an important clarification. A "material interests" perspective does not imply that war is always deliberately chosen and planned. It may be so, or it may be an unplanned and unwanted last resort, the outcome of a "prisoner's dilemma" brought about as the result of previous self-interested strategic decisions. Even in such a situation, however, decision makers will continue to act in accord with their perceived material interests.

The three complementary materialist premises form a base for a structure of explanation extending through various areas of social life. The model can be summarized as follows.

Infrastructural factors explain why war occurs. In the absence of a pressing scarcity of some essential material resource(s), or when an existing scarcity can be addressed by alternatives less costly than war, the model indicates a low likelihood of war. The infrastructure also accounts for basic parameters of how warfare is actually practised, and that in turn affects all other dimensions of war.

Within these constraints, structural factors explain the social patterning of war, even as they themselves are responsive to war and to requirements of production and reproduction. Kinship affects how people are grouped to fight. Economics translates resource scarcity into hostile relations between groups. Politics is the means through which antagonistic interests become purposeful, violent, group action. Structural factors can make the difference between war and peace in situations where scarcities are generating tensions; and economic and political organization have a limited (at this evolutionary level) ability to create significant additional incentives for war. But generally, structural factors do not generate war in themselves. They do largely determine such matters as why a particular war starts just where and when it does.

Superstructural patterns shape the way individuals perceive and act on conditions related to war. Calculation of material loss and gain necessarily must consider relevant properties of the existing social universe, and that includes the values and rules by which individuals are expected to live. Those which affect war are strongly conditioned by war, but they also respond to everything else in the social system. War-related quirks of the superstructure, or even of its manifestation in one individual, may tip the scales in a situation already at the edge of war. But independent of infrastructural and structural patterns conducive to war, superstructural elements have a very limited effect. (That does not mean that we cannot use ideas to lessen the risk of war in the contemporary world. Changing ideas can have an important effect over the long run, if, and only if, the actual significance of ideas is understood [Ferguson 1988b; 1989a].)

The following sections describe posited relationships within and between these areas, which are consistent with the initial premises, with other relationships, and at least arguably, with known facts. But any thorough comparison against existing data would be an enormous undertaking, and that is not the task here. Citations of relevant cases are more for illustration than evidence.

All relationships posited here must be seen as probabilities. "Probabilistic causality" has always been an explicit part of the cultural materialist strategy (Harris 1971: 594–596; 1985: 528–529), but the idea has been invoked regarding the study (and practice) of war by many scholars (Andreski 1968: 5; Boulding 1963: 4; Von Clausewitz 1968: 108–109).

Complicating the presentation of the model is the fact that all of these areas experience major changes as a result of general sociocultural evolution and of contact with Westerners. The initial discussion of the above areas will factor-out those changes, concentrating on war in relatively egalitarian societies – bands and tribes – and on relationships not dependent on contact. Following that, separate discussions will address the significance of general evolution and contact.

INFRASTRUCTURAL FACTORS

A usable description of the infrastructure is a population with given characteristics, using a given technology, working to obtain necessities via interaction with its natural environment. Factors related to those

31

areas have typically been implicated in "ecological" analyses – for a quarter century the dominant theoretical approach to war (Bennett Ross 1971; Harris 1974: 61–80; Hickerson 1965; Netting 1973; Rappaport 1967; Siskind 1973; Suttles 1961; Sweet 1970; Vayda 1969a; 1969b; 1976). Ecologists have most often invoked infrastructural factors to explain cross-cultural variations in war – why society X has the general war pattern that it does – rather than particular variations in the practices of war within one society (cf. Vayda 1979).

Despite extensive changes in ecological theory, the basic idea has remained that war can be a reaction to population pressing on resources, and that it can lead to a relaxation of that pressure. So, war can be "adaptive." (Although Vayda [1976: 3–7] and others reject population pressure as the general cause of war – adopting a broader view of war as a means of coping with any type of environmental hazard – population pressure remains the principal hazard demonstrated in this work.) It is certainly not inevitable that human populations expand until they are stopped by scarcity of some crucial resource. When they do not, one major cause for competition and conflict is eliminated. But populations commonly do grow, leading to resource scarcities, and prompting some remedial action.

This action need not be war. A consistent theme in ecological analyses for the past decade has been the possibility of functional alternatives to war (Balee 1985: 488ff.; Morren 1984: 169–170; Netting 1974a; Price 1984: 220–222; Vayda 1976: 4–5; Webster 1977: 345–348). Intensification of production efforts is one possibility, if infrastructural conditions allow it. Trade is another, but costs of transport may eliminate trade as a solution to basic subsistence problems. Movement is often a real alternative, provided a group is not strongly fixed in one place (below). Movement apart commonly resolves intergroup conflicts before they reach the point of open warfare. This may be especially true in situations where villages or bands fission due to increasing scarcities, and that is one reason why an explanation of conditions leading to local group fissioning is usually insufficient by itself as an explanation of war between fissioned segments (Ferguson 1989b). But when these and other functional alternatives are not viable in themselves, or entail unacceptable costs, or are rendered impossible by the presence of a competitor relying on force, war may be the only option left.

Conflict between competitors for scarce environmental resources has frequently been identified as the underlying generator of war. Vayda's

(1969a) early and influential study of expanding swidden cultivators invoked competition over desirable secondary growth forest land. Materialist participants in the debates over war in Highland New Guinea and interriverine Amazonia have argued for land and game shortages, respectively (see Ferguson 1984a: 30–31; 1989b). I assert competition for prime subsistence areas, notably estuaries, on the Northwest Coast (Ferguson 1984b). The list of such studies is easily expanded (e.g. Balee 1984; Boehm 1983; Graham 1974; Larson 1972). Also, ecological scarcities have been identified as the immediate cause of conflict in analyses which stress that the scarcities are primarily determined by cultural patterns (Biolsi 1984; Kelly 1985). Ecological crises, obviously, can intensify conflict over resources (Bonner 1981: 78; Haas, this volume; Netting 1974b: 152; Tornay 1979).

One point derived from these studies is especially relevant for discussions to come. Conflict situations generated by environmental resource scarcity vary in the specificity of the oppositions they create. Competition may be generalized, so that somebody has got to go, but who exactly does not matter. Or there may be more specific conflicts, so that a group of one type will regularly go after a group of another type. The less specific is the basic conflict, the more room there is for the influence of structural factors described below.

Although ecological theory has been most concerned with how resource scarcity may generate war, infrastructural factors exert a profound influence on war in many other ways. General subsistence orientations will have multiple consequences regarding the causes and practice of warfare. For most hunters and gatherers, and for horti-culturalists whose numbers are limited by unevenly distributed game rather than by land availability, defense or conquest of territory expect-ably will not be a goal in fighting (Dyson-Hudson and Smith 1978; Ferguson 1989b; Winterhalder and Smith 1981). When tribal people rely on domesticated pigs for nutrients, pigs can figure prominently in war patterns: theft of pigs or garden damage caused by pigs is a source of hostility, pig acquisition is an incentive to fight, pig herd size sets constraints on the possibility of waging war, etc. (Meggitt 1977; Rappa-port 1968).

Pastoralists may be prone to war for several reasons: they typically need to obtain some necessities from agriculturalists; they are often subject to environmental perturbations which force them to capture new livestock or expand pasturage; and their mobility over large areas

33

makes them candidates for trade controllers or mercenaries (Fukui and Turton 1979; Golden 1986; Peires 1981a).

Both hunters and gatherers and pastoralists have subsistence technology and skills which can be carried over into combat (Cohen 1984: 339; Ekval 1961; Turney-High 1971). The technology of war itself is an infrastructural factor with direct bearing on military planning and action (Engels 1939: 185–192; Mason 1966; McNeil 1982: 9–20; Turney-High 1971 and see Pitt-Rivers 1906) – a fact which should be obvious to all who live in the nuclear age.

Whatever the general subsistence orientation, many factors affect the ability to make war on targets at varying distances, including distance between local groups, topography and ground cover, the technology of movement and communication, the existence of unoccupied territory allowing free passage, and the feasibility of a column literally living off the land (Fadiman 1982: 30–31, 36, 105; Vayda 1960: 12–13, 67–80; Whitehead, this volume). The size of local settlements and their demographic profiles obviously will affect the size and composition of combat groups, and that will affect tactics. (Many of the inadequacies of "primitive" fighters identified by Turney-High can be attributed to their small scale of operations.) The fixity of settlements on the landscape, their circumscription, may determine the choice between fight or flight situations (Carneiro 1961: 61; 1970; Chagnon 1973: 136). The fixity of target groups affects the costs of attacking or conquering them (Gibson, this volume; Goldberg and Findlow 1984). Conversely, highly mobile groups often have the capacity to expand by force over large territories (Cohen 1984: 341; Kelly 1985; Malinowski 1966: 27). The discussion could be extended, but the point should be clear that infrastructural conditions are largely responsible for many aspects of the characteristic practice of war in any culture.

What about the infrastructural consequences of war? If, as argued above, scarcity leads to conflict, does the conflict somehow diminish the experienced scarcity? Here, too, long-standing ecological assertions seem unshaken. By forcing relocations, war can result in reapportionment of resource territories to the size (and so military strength) of groups; and to weaker groups being forced to leave an area entirely (Ferguson 1984b, 1989b; Meggitt 1972; 1977; Vayda 1969a; and see Robbins 1982). Hostilities can create buffer zones where natural resources may be replenished, free from human exploitation (Bennett Ross 1984: 97–99; Hickerson 1965; Netting 1974b: 155; Trigger 1976:

103, 623). Various direct and indirect demographic consequences of war can slow or even reverse a population growth trend (Cook 1973; Divale and Harris 1976; Ferguson 1989b; Vayda 1968: 470; Werner 1983). On the other hand, war captives may be taken to replenish a dwindling population (Oberg 1973: 191–192; Trigger 1976: 72), or to add to a geographically expanding one (Evans-Pritchard 1940: 221; Wagner 1940: 228).

Does this mean that war is 'adaptive'? Adaptation is a concept as problematic to employ technically as it is indispensable for general usage (see Ferguson 1989b). It might be better restricted to general use, referring – with deliberate imprecision – to the ability of an individual, local group, or culture to survive and prosper within its natural environment. In that general sense, war may be adaptive. It can lead to a reduction of the pressure of population on resources which led to the fighting. In doing so, war might protect the integrity of the environment by preventing over-use and long-term degradation of the resource base. But, this assessment of adaptive value needs major qualification. War usually entails major costs in resources, effort, and lives, for both winners and losers, and it is not self-evident that these are outweighed by observed or hypothetical benefits of war. Moreover, because war is a blind process, triggered by localized scarcities, it will expectably keep regional populations far lower than the maximum possible. And local scarcities will often be aggravated by war, since efficient use of available resources commonly is hampered by forced population nucleation for defensive purposes (see Haas, this volume). So there should be no mistaking that war somehow creates the optimum balance of people to resources for a region.

Another qualification is that war may be caused by factors other than scarce environmental resources. In these situations, the demographic consequences of war described above may still result, often in intensified form. That may lead to a reduction in population numbers, even to the point of local extinctions. Such war could only be described as maladaptive.

STRUCTURAL FACTORS

For convenience, these can be discussed under the headings of kinship, economics, and politics. Discussion of each will follow a similar pattern: beginning with comments on its general significance regarding war, then describing links of warfare variables to specific structural arrangements, and followed by discussion of the patterning of within-group and between-group relations.

Kinship

Relations of descent, affinity and co-residence provide the basic organizing principle of daily life in the societies under consideration. The immediate family and larger circle of kin are context not just for biological and social reproduction, they also are the main bases for organizing any cooperative effort. War parties are organized according to existing kin structures. Reciprocally, the demands and hazards of warfare affect kinship patterns.

A consistent and well-substantiated body of research has demonstrated correspondence between aspects of kinship systems, particularly post-marital residence, and war patterns (Ember and Ember 1971; Divale 1985; Divale et al. 1976; Murphy 1957; Otterbein 1968; 1977; Thoden Van Velzen and Van Wetering 1960). Patrilocal post-marital residence and other correlated patterns produce "fraternal interest groups" of co-resident agnates. Men in these groups share basic interests, and are relatively unencumbered by conflicting loyalties. Such groups regularly resort to violence to protect their interests, and are strongly associated with localized warfare. Matrilocal post-marital residence weakens or eliminates fraternal interest groups, and creates cross-cutting ties between men in different local groups. This encourages the peaceful resolution of conflict among neighbors, and is commonly associated with localized peace. The cross-cutting ties of matrilocality, however, facilitate more extensive cooperation among men, which makes it possible to mobilize larger military forces. That makes longer distance warfare more feasible, and matrilocality frequently is linked to "external warfare." While it has been argued that fraternal interest groups by themselves cause war, these correlations can be interpreted as consistent with the materialist perspective presented here because (1) the pattern of conflicts over resources may play a large role in shaping residence patterns (Ember and Ember 1971), and (2) both conflict and residence patterns are mutually conditioned by basic production arrangements (Ferguson 1988c).

Other major structural features display similar linkages. The development of corporate unilineal descent groups is related to competition

36

over scarce critical resources (Ember, Ember and Pasternak 1974; Harner 1970). Their presence can add definition to groups involved in war (Bell 1935: 253–259; Berndt 1962: 165–266); and one variety, the segmentary lineage, has been identified as "an organization of predatory expansion" facilitating military cooperation of local agnatic groups (Sahlins 1967; and see Brown 1964; Kelly 1985; cf. Peters 1967). But very intense and deadly warfare can work against unilineal descent as an exclusive basis of group membership, as high battle losses can make flexible recruitment a necessity (Langness 1964: 174; Lepervanche 1968). Other structures which affect the organization of military forces include men's houses (Maybury-Lewis 1974: 306), male age grades (Fadiman 1982; Fukui and Turton 1979), and non-kin sodalities (Lowie 1963: 105).

The nature of interpersonal relations within a group also affects the practice of war. In some situations, domestic authority patterns are carried over to military action (Kiefer 1968: 226). In some, the structure of male-female relations can foster the transformation of resource scarcity into violent conflict between men over women (Ferguson 1989b; Siskind 1973). Choosing sides in a conflict, individual decisions on who is "us" and who is "them" (when that is necessary) is influenced by strength of kin ties (Berndt 1962: 234; Chagnon 1979a; Mair 1977: 34–35). And when conflict does develop among related people, kinship provides an idiom for conceptualizing and acting on diverse and sometimes incommensurable issues (Netting 1974b: 157–161).

Between groups, military relations are partially determined by kin ties related to marriage (Berndt 1962: Ch. 12; Burch and Correll 1971; R. Rosaldo 1980: 65). Close kin ties are no guarantee of peaceful relations, however (Gregor, this volume; Hayano 1974; Kang 1979). Commonly, people both marry and make war on their close neighbors (Bell 1935: 255–256; Peters 1967). Yet the basic link between intermarriage and peace may still hold true even in those circumstances, as individuals try to maintain peaceful relations with their own affines among the enemy (Brown 1964: 335–336; Robbins 1982: 245). Other structural patterns may further complicate these between-group relations (Fadiman 1976: 12; Peters 1967: 272–277).

That related groups are capable of slaughtering each other does not invalidate the idea that kinship generally fosters cooperation. Close kin are usually bound by generalized reciprocity (Sahlins 1972), a sharing of material resources as part of the obligations of kinship. Increasing scarcity will lead to progressive strain in fulfilling these obligations, and eventual failure to do so, beginning with more distant kin. These failures constitute violations of the norms of proper kin behavior, at a time when their fulfilment may be most needed (as a source of material assistance). The hostility created by these breakdowns may be in direct relation to the previous closeness of the ties (Malinowski 1964: 251). The situation can tend towards polarization of factions (Coser 1956), to threats and accusations of witchcraft (Marwick 1970), and ultimately to division and war.

Economics

The preceding paragraph calls attention to the overlap of kinship and economics near the egalitarian end of the evolutionary spectrum. They cannot be understood apart. If kinship provides the structure of social relations, economics provides much of the substance. The organization of work, property relations, expectation of rights and duties in production, distribution, and consumption – all are expressed through kinship (Leacock 1982; Lee 1982; Siskind 1978). But as kinship is directly influenced by the necessities of biological and social reproduction, the economy is shaped by the exigencies of material production. And as with kinship, the distinctive structures of the economy influence the practice of war. That influence becomes more prominent with increasing elaboration of the economy, i.e. with evolution, but economic patterns are important variables even in relatively simple societies.

The possibility of intensification of production, as noted above, may offer an alternative to war. This possibility is strongly conditioned by infrastructural factors, but economies operating within infrastructural constraints can take on their own dynamics, which can influence the practicality and consequences of increased production (Price 1984). Some economies are limited by labor, instead of or in addition to land (Lepervanche 1968: 176; Price 1984; Reay 1973). Such economies may generate a demand for captive labor, or slaves. Slave-taking is often a major goal of raiding and of full-scale war (below), although it usually requires at least mid-level ranking as a political pre-requisite. Even among relatively egalitarian societies, however, raiding may be promoted by a structurally generated demand for captured domestic animals (Fadiman 1982: 42–47; Kelly 1985). Another structurally determined factor is the degree to which an individual can enhance his position within existing economic relations through success in war. That can occur directly, when booty or new territory is acquired by a warrior, or indirectly, when the main direct benefit is prestige, but prestige serves one's material well-being (below). However, continuous development of economic inequality will lead to other and more fundamental changes in war. These, and the results of elaboration of economic structures and processes, will be considered in the section on evolution.

The relation between kinship and economics comes to the fore again when one considers the definition of a group and the structure of intergroup relations. As already noted, "us," bound by dense kin ties, is also a community of interests linked by economic cooperation and/or common property. The kin ties that bind different communities are usually conduits for exchange. The latter merit particular attention.

Levi-Strauss (1944) observes that war and exchange can be understood as opposites, two sides of one relation. It may not be wise to go that far, but war and exchange certainly are related in many contexts (Gibson, this volume; Gregor, this volume; Mauss 1967; Sahlins 1965). Redistribution, at multiple levels, can be a means of building alliances beyond the limits of daily reciprocal sharing (Ferguson 1983; Gregor, this volume; Robbins 1982: Ch. 7). Simple barter may compensate for local ecological imbalances and so remove a basis of war, but such trade may run up against practical limits (Balee 1984: 258; Price 1984: 220; Trigger 1976: 62–63), and it is quite common for a mutual interest in trade to lead to a special relationship of peace between individual trade partners within an environment of war (Harner 1973: 125–132; Numelin 1963: 102; Oliver 1967: 295–296).

As exchange affects war, so war shapes exchange. Demonstrated military superiority, especially if coupled with other advantages in trading position, can lead to unbalanced exchange (Ferguson 1984b: 286–288). Taken a step further, unfavorable trade verges into open tribute, which is a more common concept in anthropology (Krader 1968: 84–85; Pershits 1979; Rosenfeld 1965: 77–78; Sabloff and Lamberg-Karlovsky 1975). In areas with extensive inter-societal trade, military force is often an inseparable correlate of control of trade routes (Golden 1986; Peires 1981a; Rosenfeld 1965; and below).

Politics

At the most elementary level of political organization, politics is firmly embedded in the conditions already discussed. If kinship is the structure of social life, and economics a large part of the content, politics is an expression of the interests they generate. Through the medium of politics, conflicting interests become war, and the links between warfare and politics are extensive.

Political groups and alignments reflect the various divisions of social structure and the interests of their members. What are the significant kinds of political divisions? One possible division is between political leaders and followers. But in relatively egalitarian societies, leaders and followers may be hardly distinguishable. Political leaders are representatives primarily of kinsmen (plus any other followers they can attract). They are closely scrutinized, and given their lack of authority, a leader's actions are, to varying degrees, circumscribed by the wishes of his supporters (Lepervanche 1968: 176–178; Price 1981). Still, even these leaders are in a somewhat distinctive social position and generally have some latitude to influence group action. Also, their status is sometimes dependent on their military accomplishments (Berndt and Lawrence 1973; Chagnon, this volume). This creates the possibility that leaders may manipulate conflict situations to further their own particular interests. By the time one reaches the level of Melanesian big men, such manipulation is already a very significant factor in processes leading to war (Langness 1973; Lepervanche 1968: 177; Oliver 1967: 412–418; Sillitoe 1978; and see Chagnon, this volume; Trigger 1976: 68). More will be said about leaders shortly.

Kinship and economic distinctions based on gender, age, and sometimes generation are accompanied by political inequalities. While mindful that this inequality may be very limited in many egalitarian societies (Leacock 1978; Leacock and Lee 1982), decisions to go to war are typically made by senior males. Women and children have less if any direct say, and it may be that their interests in conflict situations are both distinctive and under- or misrepresented (Langness 1968; Meggitt 1977: 98–99). Internal conflicts related to gender, age, and generational differences may play a role in deliberations leading to war (Ferguson 1988c; Siskind 1973), but this possibility has received so little attention that no generalizations are possible.

Other and more obviously significant divisions are the various

40

cleavages which separate similar groupings of kin: clans, lineages, factions, etc. All can have their collective interests and the potential to act on them. These units may be completely independent, or joined in some larger coalition or structure, or merely latent divisions within a single group. Arrangements are often complicated and fluid, with political relations among units at one organizational level affecting relations between levels, and vice versa (Bennett Ross 1984: 102–104; Berndt 1962: 253–254; Langness 1973: 304–213; Maybury-Lewis 1974: 194, 212).

Such common situations put in question the claim that making war is an expectable attribute of sovereignty (Chagnon 1977: 163; Sahlins 1968: 4). Not only is this assertion tautological (sovereignty is diagnosed by the ability to wage war), but the very concept of sovereignty seems inadequate to deal with the manifest complexity and degrees of political independence regarding military policy (Berndt 1962: 309–310; and see Bennett Ross 1980; cf. Carneiro, this volume; Chagnon, this volume; Robbins 1982: 71–83).

The possibility of fighting within a group highlights the weakness of authority relations so characteristic of relatively egalitarian societies. Koch (1974a; 1974b; 1979) gives particular emphasis to the structural inability to decisively resolve conflicts, and claims (1974a: 173–174) that this explains warfare. But this explanation is just a modified version of the sovereignty theme – groups without any overarching authority can resort to force to resolve conflicts – and no more instructive.

Weak authority patterns mean that war, as an activity involving an entire group, requires group consensus. But weak authority also means that individual warriors cannot be prohibited from leading small-scale raids (although raiders can often be restrained by informal pressure [Ekvall 1964: 1123–1124; Trigger 1976: 68]). This can produce a pattern with two distinct levels of intergroup combat, although each will, of course, affect the other (Biolsi 1984: 143; Kiefer 1968: 241; Langness 1973: 306; Meggitt 1977: 74–76; and see Kelly 1985: 51).

However, the non-authoritarian pattern of decisions on whether to enter into war does not necessarily carry over into the actual practice of war. Misunderstanding on this point is the basis of Turney-High's (1971: 26; 1981: Ch. 2) unfortunate distinction of "primitive" and "civilized" war (see Ferguson 1984a: 26–27), since he claims that the sophisticated tactics diagnostic of the latter are dependent on authority relations found only in more hierarchical societies. There does exist a

41

general correlation of political centralization and military sophistication (see below), but the meaning of the correlation is clouded by the existence of substantial variation between the two.

When war breaks out and survival is the issue, there are often major changes in internal authority patterns. If peacetime leaders remain in charge, their decision power is broadened and strengthened, to relax again when peace is restored (Chagnon 1974: 162; Collins 1950). Often authority is handed over to men of known military skill, who are not peace leaders, and who may even be excluded from the actual decision to fight (Fadiman 1982: 97; Hoebel 1978: 43; see also Meggitt 1977: 68–69; Numelin 1963: 73–74; Trigger 1976: 55–56). Various types of social pressure are brought to bear to get men to fight and follow orders (below). The result is that even where general decisions are made by consensus, there can be a form of command in war, and the use of virtually every tactical principle specified by Turney-High (Lewis 1970: 183–188; Meggitt 1977: 67–68; Stewart 1947: 264–266). And perhaps more interesting, in some cases sophisticated tactics are employed even without field command (Fadiman 1982: Ch. 5; Robbins 1982: 186–189).

Political patterns within a war-making group are only one side of the coin. War is a relation between groups. It is strongly affected by other between-group relations, such as the specificity or generality of conflicts over resources, existing linkages of marriage or trade, and of course, previous military engagements. These relations create social fields which can be complicated, unstable, and obscure. Political leaders, constrained by the requirement of consensus among their own support-ers, must steer a course through these treacherous seas. This is a task requiring intelligence and great diplomatic skills. Anthropological theory has little to say about this type of diplomacy (cf. Numelin 1950; 1963). From case descriptions of war, however, it seems clear that the key issue is the negotiation and utilization of politico-military alliances. (The following two paragraphs are based on discussions in: Berndt 1962: Ch. 2, 309–310; Chagnon 1977: 97–99; Fadiman 1982: 31–39; Glasse 1959; Gregor, this volume; Hallpike 1977: 210–211; Hames 1983: 404; Kiefer 1968; 1972: 73–74; Langness 1973: 308, 312; Lepervanche 1968: 178–181; Meggitt 1977: 68–70; Trigger 1976.)

Possibilities of alliance are created by the existing web of between-group relations, but it is up to political leaders to transform possibilities into actual alliances, and often they have substantial freedom in doing

42

so. Leaders try to select the most desirable allies from the set of possibilities, take the steps to bring about a general alliance, and negotiate specific understandings for specific conflicts. Their actions crystallize political alignments, and in doing so have a major impact on the process of war. But the task is an endless one, as alliances may hold together for only one action. They, and the home-group consensus, may have to be reestablished at every step in a conflict.

Alliances are crucial for success in war. Allies can provide combat assistance, intelligence, material support, places of refuge, and secure flanks. In plotting campaigns against an enemy, no move may be contemplated without estimating its impact on existing alliances. Alliances also affect the balance of power between opposed groups – itself a factor of great importance in shaping military actions (Berndt 1962: 266–267; Boehm 1984: 166–170; Chagnon, this volume; Heider 1970: 126; Langness 1973: 309–311). The structure of alliance not only affects who wins, but also the initiation, spread, and cessation of hostilities.

Instability of alliances seems the rule at relatively egalitarian levels, although there are exceptions (Bell 1935: 254–255; Heider 1970: 99; Kaberry 1973: 63–65; Langness 1973: 304–305). Certain evolutionary developments above that base line, into ranking, are themselves forms of relatively stable alliances linked to war. One is tribe formation, discussed extensively by Haas (this volume; and see below; cf. Fried 1975). The other is the development of confederacies, which at one time was seen as a distinct level of sociocultural evolution (Jack Bernhardt, personal communication; and see Boehm 1984: 184–185; Drucker 1951: 5; Ferguson 1984b: 280; Trigger 1976).

Recognition that alliances are significant factors in war, and that they are significantly affected by the actions of individual leader-diplomats, adds an element of individual variation to the structure of explanation being offered here. The personalities and skills of leaders do make a difference, which brings us to the next topic: the general significance of attitudes toward war.

SUPERSTRUCTURAL FACTORS

Probably the most frequent type of explanation of war, especially in ethnographies, has been to relate a war pattern to some aspect of culturally patterned beliefs and attitudes. These efforts take various forms. Benedict's (1974) approach is to explain war as an expression of a general cognitive pattern. The analytical drawbacks of her approach are well known (see Harris 1968). Unfortunately, similar problems remain in more recent efforts (Burch 1974; Hallpike 1977), rendering the constructed patterns questionable in themselves and useless as explanations of war. More substance is found in several overlapping approaches, which look at war in terms of modal personality types, particular values, and cultural norms of warfare.

People who make war often have belligerent personalities (Berndt 1962; Chagnon 1977; Koch 1974a). But the relationship between aggressive personalities and war is hardly a necessary one. People with normally pacific personalities can be quite brutal in war (Ellis 1951; Heider 1970: 127; Murphy 1957; Robarchek, this volume; Wallace 1972: 39–48). As the discussion of leadership indicated, oftentimes aggressive fighters are kept out of or are secondary in making a decision to fight. (The "hotheads" may be young men, bachelors, who have less to lose and more to gain from combat than older family men [Baxter 1979: 83–84].) Even very aggressive persons can find outlet for their feelings in non-violent actions (Codere 1950). Then there is the question of where these attitudes come from. Several studies in this volume (Chagnon, Gibson, Gregor, Robarchek, Whitehead) discuss orientations to violence. In my reading, all are consistent with the view that attitudes are products of (different) social circumstances. Generally, individual bellicosity would seem to be of secondary and derived significance. However, in specific cases of high politico-military tensions, unusually aggressive individuals, especially leaders, can take actions which precipitate new hostilities (Biocca 1971: 217–238; Li Puma 1985: 64; Trigger 1976: 69).

"Martial values" include a variety of culturally patterned goals. Three are regularly invoked by anthropologists. One is an emphasis on individual bravery, exemplified by the Great Plains coup-counters (Lowie 1963: 117–122; Mishkin 1940: 38–40), but also found in other parts of the world (Meggitt 1977: 68; and see Kiefer 1970: 590). (This contrasts with the far more typical pattern where warriors attack only when victory seems certain, and withdraw when resistance is met.) An emphasis on doing brave deeds certainly can stimulate raiding. But on the Plains, this emphasis seems derivative of the demands of the regional pattern of violence (see Biolsi 1984).

Another goal is to acquire specific war trophies: heads, scalps, sacrificial captives, etc. Often these trophies have direct material value, as when Jivaro could trade a shrunken head to Westerners for a rifle (Karsten referenced in Bennett Ross 1984: 90). Trophies which are taken and kept may serve as tangible proof of military accomplishment, which in turn has material rewards (Baxter 1979: 82–83; Zegwaard 1959: 1040). Or they may be used to signal a group's ferocity to potential enemies, as when Northwest Coast peoples staked heads on poles in front of their settlements (Ferguson 1984b: 308–309; and see Trigger 1976: 70).

A final value, and probably the most widely cited of all, is a desire to avenge past offenses. Again, this truly is an important motive in some conflicts, especially those with small and closely related decision groups (Bennett Ross 1984; Langness 1973: 308). It does not stand up as a useful explanation of war, however, first because the existence of tremendous variation in the situations calling for revenge itself requires explanation, second because revenge-seeking often cannot possibly operate in the automatic form suggested by ethnographers or every member of the society would be killed (see Peters 1967), and third because revenge requirements are frequently and obviously manipulated by decision-makers, with offenses "forgotten" or "remembered" at convenience (Berndt 1962: Ch. 12; Vayda 1960: 45; and see Balee 1984: 246–247; Ferguson 1984a: 39–40). Analyses of revenge are on firmer ground when the goal is examined not as an autonomous cultural value, but as an element in tactics calculated to ward-off future attacks and serve other interests (Mair 1977: 37–42; Vayda 1960: 118).

War, like any human activity, follows established conventions or rules: on proper behavior towards different types of people, how to start and end a conflict, when and how to move from one level of hostilities to another, etc. Rules of war pose interesting questions, and must be investigated. It may even be that these rules have an inherent tendency toward elaboration into ritual (Kennedy 1971; cf. Kiefer 1970: 591). But rules and normative standards should not be mistaken for practice, as was common in earlier studies of war (Fathauer 1954; Smith 1951; and see Vayda 1960: 3). An important point is made by Zegwaard (1959: 1037) regarding the tangle of rules surrounding Asmat headhunting. Despite the surface appearance of strict and unchanging custom, his fine-grained research revealed that individual decisions were producing changes in practices "all the time".

The suggestion that rules of war have a tendency to be elaborated into ritual brings up the next topic: the connection between war and magico-religious beliefs and practices. Source citations on this topic are superfluous, since it is hard to find cases where the connection is not evident (but for a compilation, see Turney-High 1971: 213–220). Ritual commonly precedes, accompanies, and follows an engagement. Military success and safe return are divined. The enemy is attacked and confused by supernatural means. Oaths and curses maintain discipline in combat. Supernatural rewards are added to other potential gains for warriors.

Despite the abundance of data on this connection, I could find no general theoretical study devoted to it. Perhaps that neglect stems from a prejudice that war and religion do not belong together – a bias revealed, for instance, when the militarist's claim that "god is on our side" is viewed as ironic. But the linkage of war with religion and magic is quite expectable. War involves, in an extreme form, virtually all of the circumstances which have been invoked to explain the genesis of religion and magic. It is a collective activity, closely linked to group solidarity and survival. It forces individuals to confront a hazardous unknown, beyond their rational-instrumental control. It places a premium on the efficacy of social control. It poses "the question of meaning" repeatedly, as it leads to tragedy, injustice, and immorality. For all these reasons, war is a virtual magico-religious magnet.

All these factors affect how war is practiced and thresholds of violence, but generally, they alone do not cause war (Koch 1979: 200). What they do is reinforce the resolve of warriors (Whitehead, this volume). The decision to fight might be made according to material interest, but those ultimate benefits may seem to pale as men march toward possible death. The rules, values, and attitudes described above give an added and more immediate incentive. They are hammered into boys from an early age, sometimes accompanied by severe punishment for failure to learn them. Individual military accomplishment may be a prerequisite for achieving adulthood; and is reinforced for adults by shame for cowards, and prestige for accomplished warriors (Fadiman 1982: Ch. 3, 4; Heider 1970: 129; Voget 1964). Shame and prestige do not stand alone, however. They often have very tangible correlates, in marriages, in resources, and in influence (Chagnon, this volume; Meggitt 1977: 60–66; Turney-High 1971: Part II; Zegwaard 1959: 1040–1041). All these within-group reinforcements will be backed up by the threat that war will "select out" groups which have not sufficiently motivated their fighters. (Consideration of all these means of reinforcing the resolve of warriors should eliminate any notion of war being the result of an "aggressive instinct.")

These layers of motivation complicate testing of the proposition that war happens when it is in decision-makers' material interest (see Ferguson 1984a: 37–42). Expectably, individuals will express the cultural values as their motives in war, so emic accounts will often be at variance from the material gain view. Evaluation of the material motivation proposition is still possible, however, by investigating whether it – in contrast to other motivational premises – can explain actual military behavior, viewed on a regional scale (Ferguson 1984b); or by evaluating whether current and prospective material conditions, individually assessed, carry the most weight in group deliberations about war (Ferguson, work in progress; and see Chagnon, this volume). This ends the survey of factors involved with war in relatively egalitarian societies, excluding the effects of Western contact.

EVOLUTION AND WAR

The concept of general sociocultural evolution has a long history, and also longstanding associated conceptual problems (Fried 1967; Haas 1982; Harris 1968: 634–653; Mann 1986; Service 1971; 1975). Fortunately, most of those can be avoided because the concern here is not with evolution per se, or with the role of warfare in promoting evolution (see Carneiro, Haas, this volume), but with the changes in war which go along with evolution. For this purpose, the concept of evolution can be left at centralization of political control, greater structural inequality, and more intense production efforts resulting in surpluses.

It has long been known, probably since before there were states, that evolution is associated with greater military sophistication in formations, tactics, weaponry, and defensive preparations, although there is also substantial variation in the relation between political and military levels (Broch and Galtung 1966; Otterbein 1985; Wright 1965). And it frequently has been suggested that more evolved polities make war more frequently, more intensively, or more deliberately as policy. Such changes were a major concern in anthropology at an earlier time (Fried 1961; Hobhouse et al. 1965; Malinowski 1964; Newcomb 1960; Sumner 1911; Wright 1965; and see Carneiro, this volume). All these

47

changes are most apparent when one arrives at the state level of organization, but they are changes of degree and can be studied throughout the evolutionary range.

General developments associated with evolution will affect the significance of infrastructural sources of conflict. The direct constraints of ecology are loosened as other elements of the infrastructure develop, and production moves away from simple lithic technology, limited storage capability, and relatively autonomous household production. Increasing productivity supports, and in turn depends upon, an increasingly elaborate pattern of circulation and controls, many of which are far removed from any direct encounter with an environmental check. The general subsistence requirements of a population become less determinative of demand for resources. They act only as a floor, and even that can be circumvented if the costs of reproducing the work force can be passed to outside the system, as with slave capture (below). The functional necessities of the economic system and the structurally determined pattern of consumption determine actual demand for resources.

The infrastructure continues to set the general boundaries of the economic system, and perturbations of infrastructural factors will cause adjustments in the economy, sometimes traumatic ones. But during normal times, structural patterns and dynamics are more salient, and they will have major implications for war. These implications are apparent in Price's (1984) comparison of ranked societies where production is limited by resources or by labor scarcities. The contrast is accompanied by differences in descent rules, exclusiveness of property claims, emphasis on redistribution, and so on – all of which affect orientations in war (see Gibson, this volume). (That discussion also develops the related point that evolution of political and economic structures increases the ability and incentive to wage wars of conquest [see Carneiro, this volume].) One particularly important manifestation of a demand for labor is the taking of slaves. Although patterns are often complicated and obscured by Western contact, a wealth of recent research indicates that slave capture is a major goal in many indigenous raiding and war patterns of chiefdoms and states (Ferguson 1984b; Gibson, this volume; Kopytoff 1982; Kopytoff and Miers 1977; Lovejoy 1983; Meillassoux 1971; Mitchell 1984; Warner 1982; Watson 1980; and see Engels 1939: 199–202).

An increasingly elaborate division of labor allows for the creation of military specialists. In states, the organization of production and transportation can be sufficient to support a specialized army. The costs of any particular military effort may be reduced, and so its likelihood increased, if a society is already diverting major resources to the routine maintenance of a military force. Andreski (1968: 232) coins the term "polemity" as "the ratio of energy devoted to warfare to the total energy available to society." The priority diversion of scarce resources is one of the major characteristics of contemporary industrial societies (Dibble 1967; Melman 1974; 1984). It is impossible to say how this compares with polemity in early states or pre-state societies, since virtually no work has been done on it (cf. Robbins 1982: 224–231). The topic merits investigation, especially in regard to the point where the military and their associates acquire enough structural distinctiveness to develop into a powerful interest group. Like any interest group, these compete with other power groupings over the distribution of society's resources (Claessen 1979; Fortes and Evans-Pritchard 1940: 11–14). Since they can hardly justify more support if there is no danger of war, they may have an interest in promoting military confrontations. On the other hand, some state armies must largely support themselves, and perform additional work besides (Beemer 1937: 179–183; Mair 1977: 129). A recent seminar on Zulu history concluded that it was the development of regimented labor which facilitated the rise of militarized states (Peires 1981b: 9–10).

In chiefdoms and states, one's material interest depends more on position within the structure of society than on the general relationship of population to natural resources. Costs and benefits of war likewise depend on structural position. People or organizations at different levels in a society may have even contradictory interests in war (Peires 1981a; Warren 1982; Webster 1977: 363–365). Gains for those who decide military policy may be accompanied by losses for those who follow their commands. Further, since the structure of inequality itself is the key to prosperity for the elite, they will be vitally concerned with strengthening their position within that structure.

The purposeful expansion of resources claimed by the military is one example of struggle over controlling positions, but there are others. Junior upstarts may challenge current rulers (Boone 1983; Epstein 1975: 215; Gluckman 1965; Ogot 1972), the military may pose a danger of overturning established rule (Andreski 1968: 104–107; Otterbein 1980: 354), centrifugal tendencies may weaken power structures (Cohen

1984: 345; Golden 1986; Kiefer 1972: 109), rival strong men may contest control of the central administration (Mair 1977: 62, Numelin 1963: 20; Wolf and Hanson 1972: 205–225), or popular discontent may threaten the entire political structure (Crummey 1986; Ferguson 1984b: 290; Peires 1981c: Wolf 1973). All represent dangers to a ruling elite which often can be neutralized by mobilizing forces against an external enemy. In some cases, the connection is more direct and constant, as the continued rule of an elite is dependent upon the ability to wage successful war more-or-less continuously (although here some non-elite groups clearly do benefit from the violence) (Beemer 1937: 176; Golden 1986; Peires 1981a).

Manipulation of external conflict for the benefit of a few suggests substantial control over military decisions. State political leaders are distinctive less in their ability to make war, than in the control they exercise over warmaking (Cohen 1984; Otterbein 1985). One side of this control is that subdivisions of a state are prohibited from resorting to force to advance their interests. Even if fighters still mobilize along kin lines, they will do so at the command of the central government (Mair 1977: 129–130). That is the other side of control, that central authorities can demand and compel acceptance of their decision on war (Fortes and Evans-Pritchard 1940: 14; Webb 1975: 157–162; Webster 1977: 364). This is not the case in chiefdoms (Spencer and Jennings 1965: 430–431; Vayda 1960: 15, 28; Wallace 1972: 39–48; cf. Carneiro, this volume), and it represents one of the key aspects in the long-noted shift from kin-based to territorial organization with the advent of the state (Maine 1861). Obviously, this represents a major diminution of the military significance of kinship.

The genesis and ultimate foundation of this control in states is controversial (Andreski 1968; Giddens 1985; Goody 1980; Haas 1982; Mann 1986). The critical point here is that it exists. (Although the claim that the state administration monopolizes the legitimate use of force [Weber 1964: 156; and see Mair 1977: 31–32; Vansina 1971: 143] is often contradicted by the existence of diverse sorts of partially independent local-elite-controlled armed forces [Drago 1970; Gibson, this volume; Kiefer 1970: 587; Willems 1975: Ch. 5; Wolf and Hanson 1972: 223–232].) Non-elite may materially benefit from war in particular cases – in terms of increased security, new resources acquired, external tribute mitigating the effects of internal stratification, etc. But whether they do or not is in itself secondary. The principal question is, will those who decide military policy benefit? Subjects can be compelled to accept a policy decision, and compelled to fight. The old maxim that a soldier must fear his officers more than the enemy was appreciated by rulers of proto-states in Africa, as epitomized by Shaka of the Zulu, who heaped rewards on brave warriors, but executed those who held back (Turney-High 1971: 83). That, along with changes in the organization of forces, transformed the Zulu from nomadic warriors to a disciplined army of infantrymen, capable of conquering an empire (Gluckman 1940; Otterbein 1980; Peires 1981a; Ritter 1957; and see Beemer 1937: 67–74; Mair 1977: 129–130). With the advent of the state, compulsion replaces consensus as the ultimate basis of mobilization. No change could be more fundamental.

Reliance on brute force alone, however, is an expensive and inefficient form of control. Ideological manipulation is a cheaper way of achieving compliance with decreed military policy. The degree to which this is possible will vary widely, according to the circumstances of a particular crisis and the overall organization of control. As a general rule, it can be assumed that those who seek to enhance their own position via war will take whatever measures are possible to make the war seem for the general good.

Evolution modifies the significance of infrastructural, structural, and superstructural factors in war. It is an error to apply generalizations based on war in relatively egalitarian societies to war in more evolved societies, without considering the implications of these changes. The error is magnified when such generalizations are carelessly extrapolated to current geopolitical crises.

WESTERN CONTACT AND WAR

A different kind of distortion occurs when analysts fail to consider the effects of Western contact on indigenous war patterns. Western contact is only a type of the more general process of acculturation involving societies of radically different evolutionary levels (Gibson, Robarchek, this volume). In an even broader sense, it is only one type of historical change. But of both more general categories, it is the type most immediately relevant for an accurate anthropological understanding of war. The significance of contact for war has been regularly slighted by anthropologists, perhaps due to a professional bias toward the study of (supposedly) "pristine" culture patterns (cf. Rodman and Cooper 1983).

One illustration of that bias is that study of the most dramatic military consequence of contact – wars of resistance to Western expansion – has been largely consigned to the domain of historians. But even if that division of academic labor is accepted, Western contact must be appreciated for the major changes it produces in "native" warfare.

The three aspects of contact which are most relevant here are the introduction of new epidemic diseases, development of new trade patterns, and actual subjugation of native peoples and their incorporation into Western state control. The first two can precede the third, or even any face-to-face contact, by great distances and long periods of time (McDonald 1979; Trigger 1976). All three affect the infrastructure and have direct and pervasive implications for war.

Disease and other consequences of contact regularly produce drastic reductions in native population numbers that can prompt raiding for captives to make up for losses (Oberg 1973: 191–192; Trigger 1976: 62). Depopulation can reduce pressure on and so conflict over scarce subsistence resources (Ferguson 1984b). However, other changes may counteract that effect. Contact can touch off mass migrations away from the Western frontier, which in turn create a chain reaction of dislocations and migrations. These intrusions can aggravate pressure on resources, especially since the established residents and newcomers will lack any established basis of peaceful cooperation (Balee 1988; Biolsi 1984: 154–155). Other changes may aggravate conflict over access to environmental resources. Geographic range for resource exploitation may be restricted (Biolsi 1984: 147). Disruption of ecological chains may result in unexpected losses of basic food resources (Ferguson 1984b: 296). Commodity production for trade to Westerners can create new resource demands and scarcities (Biolsi 1984: 158–159; Bishop 1970; Ferguson 1984b; Trigger 1976). In short, contact has different and contradictory consequences regarding competition over environmental resources.

Trade with Westerners brings changes in the technological base of society. It is often the case that a lithic technology is supplanted by metal tools, and in the process, a locally produced technology is replaced by one that must be obtained from outsiders. A technological transformation will affect the structural conditions discussed earlier, but will also have direct implications for war. People may raid to plunder steel tools or other manufactures, or to take items, including slaves, which can be traded for manufactures (Ferguson 1984b; work in progress; Golob

1982; Trigger 1976: 626; Vayda 1960: 106; Whitehead, this volume).
The new technology may include new and more deadly weapons (cf.
Townsend 1983). That can lead to major changes in tactics (Lewis 1970:
183–188; Trigger 1976: 417); and, since possession of these weapons
may be crucial for survival (see Naroll 1966: 20), it may trigger an arms
race which itself generates more raiding for tradeable plunder and slaves
(Bennett Ross 1984: 90–93; Chagnon 1983: 202–203; this volume;
Ferguson 1984b: 299–300; Gamst 1986). On the other hand, skillful
distribution of manufactures by an outside agent can be used to foster
peace among local indigenous groups (Gordon 1983: 206, 209).

Structural patterns related to war are restructured by contact
(although such three-way interaction has received relatively little study).
Kinship structures often go through major changes due to depopulation,
changing work patterns, and direct intervention by Westerners.
Residence patterns can change completely. Normative expectations
among kin can be undercut by increased value of movable property and
general monetarization of social relationships. Marriage rules may be
changed by fiat of new authorities, and by the new local realities of
power which are considered when arranging marriages (Podolefsky
1984). More elaborate structures of kinship may be eroded by a variety of
forces. To the degree that warfare is shaped by kin structures, change in
those structures will produce changes in warfare (Ferguson 1988c;
Murphy 1956; 1960; Murphy and Murphy 1974).

A major focus of economic interest shifts to relationships with
outsiders. If commodity production expands, this will affect relations
with the environment, work groups, etc. If this reaches the extreme of
full-time wage or forced labor, there may be a virtual collapse of native
cultural patterns. Long before that, however, war patterns can go
through sweeping reorientations related to changes in trade patterns.
The directly negative correlates of contact (epidemics, slave raiders,
etc.) may initially rupture established trade networks, which could
aggravate hostilities between neighboring groups (Golob 1982: 265–
266). A more common occurrence is for natives to seek closer integration into Western trade networks because of the benefits associated with
Western technology. Intensive warfare may be generated by efforts to
control this trade, as one group seeks to impose itself as a monopolist of
one form or another, and others try to break that control and achieve
more direct access to Westerners (Ferguson 1984b; work in progress;
Hunt 1940; Jablow 1950; Macdonald 1979; and see Ballard 1981; Webb

53

1975; Whitehead, this volume.)

Political patterns also change in various directions. Group identities and boundaries alter in the process of contact-induced "tribalization" (Fried 1975: cf. Haas, this volume). The position of leaders may be strengthened at first due to their position in newly important trade networks, and because of direct military advantages gained in their relationships with Westerners (who may want "their chief" to be stronger than any rivals) (Ferguson 1984b: 288; Lewis 1970: 178; Whitehead, this volume). A more authoritative leader may promote his own interests via warfare, or he may launch attacks at the bidding of Westerners, to obtain slaves, to pacify hostile natives or because Westerners want to keep natives divided and fighting (Forbes 1960: 121; Murphy 1960: 30–38; Whitehead, this volume). But as acculturation proceeds, the authority of traditional leaders is lessened or completely destroyed. This may happen by stages, as when indigenous states impacted by the West break up into predatory warlordships (Lovejoy 1983: Ch. 4). The actual incorporation of local indigenous populations brings them within the scope of the state's claimed monopoly on force, and local military autonomy is eliminated. Missions and schools in this context illustrate rather clearly the use of ideology to achieve effective control over formerly independent polities (Berndt 1962: 423; Rodman and Cooper 1979).

An expanding Western frontier produces direct and indirect changes in war as extensive as those associated with evolution. The initial net result of these changes is to produce an increase in warfare, and this may occur long before any Western observers arrive on the scene. A consequence of this, I believe, is a systematic exaggeration of images of warlike behavior in supposedly "first contact" accounts. Recognition of these extensive changes should not, however, lead to a different error, that of supposing that endemic war patterns are totally transformed or replaced (see Hunt 1940; Trigger 1976). Post-contact warfare should be investigated for both persisting and new patterns (Bennett Ross 1984; Ferguson 1984b; Gamst 1983; Vayda 1976: Ch. 4).

CONCLUDING REMARKS

The general theory developed here encompasses most anthropological interests in war. The "either–or" attitude demonstrated in some recent debates must be rejected if explanation is ever to reflect the complexity of the topic. Recognition of this fact opens the possibility that both sides in an argument sometimes could grant the validity of the opponent's view – if both opponents take care to precisely define the questions they are addressing.

Obviously, there will be objections to the causal priorities suggested here. Objections would be more productive if they were framed in terms of alternative hypotheses, rather than being purely negative, and even better if they were connected to other findings on war, in the manner attempted here. The existence of alternative general theories would establish that there is much common ground between them, and allow for true comparison of their merits where they do differ.

Motivations and material causes: on the explanation of conflict and war

CLAYTON ROBARCHEK

> There is always an easy solution to every human problem –
> neat, plausible, and wrong.
>
> H. L. MENCKEN

The explicit *raison d'être* of the Advanced Seminar on the anthropology of war was our concern as anthropologists with the surpassingly important tangle of human problems of conflict, violence, and war. The subtitle of the seminar, "The Sources of War," succinctly expressed the nature of our objective: gaining some understanding of the causes of organized conflict in order to move toward an explanation of war. This paper, therefore, has two objectives: (1) to make some contribution, however minimal, to an understanding of the sources of conflict, violence, and war; and (2) to examine some current approaches to the explanation of these phenomena. My point of departure is an ethnographic case study, an example of a specific conflict among a specific group of people, and the course it took.

Understanding this event will, I believe, give us some insight into the nature of conflict, not only as it occurs in this one society, but as it occurs among human beings everywhere. I thereby want to highlight some considerations that must necessarily be addressed by adequate explanations of human conflict. The perspective demonstrated here, and the ethnographic material through which it will be exemplified, are the outgrowth of more than ten years of involvement by my wife and myself with a people whose anthropological claim to fame is their antipathy to violence, a small band of Semai Senoi living in the mountains of central West Malaysia.

There are about 15,000 Semai, mostly living in small hamlets of fewer than 100 people scattered along the steep river valleys that dissect the mountains of the central Malay Peninsula. Although the degree of acculturation to and integration into Malaysian society varies widely from area to area, the traditional Semai pattern is one of independent and politically autonomous settlements. Each occupies a specific territory, usually a small river valley, and subsists by swidden cultivation of manioc and hill rice supplemented by hunting, fishing, trapping, and gathering. Under the encroachment of the modern world, this traditional way of life is rapidly giving way. Yet the traditional pattern still persists in the less accessible highland and deep forest areas and, to a substantial degree, in the settlement where we conducted our research.

The Semai are best known in the anthropological literature for their nonaggressiveness and avoidance of physical conflict and violence. Robert Dentan (1968) characterized them as "a nonviolent people of Malaysia," and others have used them as an example to counter arguments for people's innate aggressiveness (e.g. Alland 1972). In the communities where my wife and I lived, we also found Semai social life to be virtually free of interpersonal violence (see Robarchek 1977a,b; 1979a,b; Robarchek and Dentan 1987). This is not to say, however, that the community was free of conflict. Pettiness, jealousy, theft, gossip, disputes over property and marital infidelities, and so on, were as common as they probably are in any small group of people. What was remarkable was that, unlike in most societies, these conflicts never resulted in violence.

The roots of the dispute that I will be examining lay in changes stemming from the band's increasing involvement in the larger Malaysian socioeconomic system. Under pressure from the government, the band was being encouraged to settle permanently near a road. The band was divided on this issue, with about two-thirds of the group having relocated near the road, partially in response to their own desire for manufactured goods and for access to the wage labor that would provide money for their acquisition. The remaining third still lived in a secondary hamlet several miles further up the valley.

Recent years had seen a great increase in the volume of trade with the lowlands, especially in the export of durian fruit to the lowland Malays and Chinese. The sale of durian (a large, thorny, aromatic fruit highly prized throughout the region) was the primary source of cash for most Semai. It was the source of the money they used to buy sarongs, machetes, axes, radios, flashlights, tobacco, sugar, and all the other luxuries that were rapidly becoming necessities. As this trade had developed (primarily since the Second World War), the rules of land use and of access to places where durian and petai (another forest tree product) could be planted had been evolving, based primarily on the notion of territories which individual kindreds had traditionally occupied (C. J. Robarchek 1981). As the durian trade has become more important, however, there are increasingly frequent disputes over access to territories in the lower end of the valley, from which fruit can be more easily transported. (It is carried in large backbaskets along the narrow and precipitous trails that snake through these valleys.)

It has been recently discovered that members of one kindred, and especially its acknowledged leader, Nyam, a bright and articulate young man (son of the previous headman and himself the probable next headman of the band) had planted large numbers of durian trees in places claimed by other individuals and other kindreds. They complained to the headman (whose territory had also been infringed), and he informed an elder of the offending group that a *becharaa'*, a formal debate and discussion by the involved kindreds, would be convened in several days, and that all members of his kindred should attend.

Several young men whose territories had been usurped were threatening that if something wasn't done they would pull out the trees or chop them down. This would have escalated the conflict, since Nyam now had a legitimate claim to the young trees on the basis of understandings (predating, I am sure, the idea of exclusive territories) which confer ownership of fruit trees on whoever planted and/or tended them. Talk in the villages in the intervening days stressed that "We must get this settled or there will be fighting, people will start cutting down each other's trees and shooting each other with poisoned darts."

THE *BECHARAA'*

What follows is a lightly annotated and condensed description from my field notes of the resulting *becharaa'*, one that is thoroughly typical of many that I have attended (cf. Robarchek 1979b).

Principal Characters:

> Tidn: The present headman (*Penghulu*) of the band.
>
> Nyam: A son of the former headman, and probable next headman, and the one who precipitated the conflict.
>
> Entoy: The headman of a neighboring, related band.

As night falls, people begin to assemble in the headman's house. The headman of a related band from a nearby valley has been called to oversee the discussion, since the headman of our band is himself a party to the dispute. The headman's wife has prepared rice and fish for any who are hungry. The dispute is not mentioned. [No one should ever come to another and confront him with a complaint or dispute without first observing the necessary amenities: sit for a while, talk, smoke, accept an offer of food or tea; only then can the issue of contention be raised. To do otherwise would be a severe breach of sociality, implying that the dispute took precedence over the relationship.]

Nyam finally arrives; makes an elaborate production of greeting Carole and me. He spends at least an hour telling us how much he has missed us and talking about the death of his wife. [My wife and I had only recently returned to the valley after a 6-year absence.] During this time and a few feet away, the preliminary speeches begin, stressing the need to settle this matter so our minds can be at ease, how we are all siblings here, how we must care for each other, and so on. Several times Nyam is called to come and take part, but he says, "Later, I'm talking to my old friends." Tidn states his case, and Nyam is listening with one ear all the time. Finally, Nyam joins the circle, makes an expansive entrance, jokes with everyone. Others state their complaints that people have been planting in their territories.

Nyam tries to justify, on a variety of grounds, his right to trees in several of the disputed areas; in some cases he denies planting, saying that the new trees just sprouted as "children" of trees he already owned there and, since he cleared the ground and tended them, they are legitimately his. At one point he calls on a young kinsman to come and support his argument. The young man refuses, saying "I don't know anything about it." At times, both Tidn and Nyam are speaking simultaneously; not arguing directly, but talking past one another, each stating his own case.

[After several hours of this] Entoy starts to speak, says that (at the simplest) each couple has claim to a place; if there are 10 couples, 10 places; 20 couples, 20 places [the implication being that these are inviolate]. Tidn agrees, so does his wife. Entoy says that once when a Malay was stealing his durian, he set a spear trap to wound him in the leg and the Malay spent two weeks in the hospital. (It was impossible to tell if this is true or not, though I seriously doubt it, Entoy being a notorious liar; in any case, his point in telling the story here is that this sort of thing could happen among ourselves.) He says, "When Nyam's father [the previous headman] was alive, he taught him the correct ways," [implying that Nyam knows better than this].

Nyam is arguing with Tidn's wife, saying he will give her an example of something. He calls Yagng, another kinsman of Nyam, to come over, but he refuses. Entoy asks Nyam why his kindred didn't come tonight. Nyam launches into a long explanation to try to account for it: because of the rain today, because they were fishing, because somebody passed worms. Entoy isn't having any; "You only have four people here," he says. "When people are called to talk, they should come. There is a tiger eating our goats, but I left my shotgun and came here. The law is when you are called to talk, you come, whether you shit worms or not." Entoy goes into a long discourse on how a *Penghulu* (headman) takes responsibility for his people: "Before the Malays came, before the pale people, this was our way. A *Penghulu* has to watch out for his children, he can't quarrel and wrangle."

This is all directed at Nyam, who will probably be the next headman. "Who is the *Penghulu* here?" Entoy asks.

This is the *Penghulu*; the old one is dead; if you follow the one under the ground, go under the ground; if you follow the one in the house, then come into the house . . . If we don't hear it all [the dispute] now, tomorrow there will still be bad talk [dissatisfaction and disagreement] about the *Penghulu* and the assistant [Nyam]. I want our minds at ease. If you don't listen to the *Penghulu*, how will things work? Tomorrow there will still be trouble.

"True!" several people respond. Entoy continues, expounding on how disaster will overtake us if we don't follow the *Penghulu* and our customs. "We'll have to run to the hills because of the fighting."

Entoy has the group in the palm of his hand; everyone is listening, laughing at his jokes. He tells of giving five dollars to a stranger who needed help [highly unlikely]. "I'll be friends with anyone who is good; the evil ones, I abandon . . . We want to get along with each other; I want to leave this group at ease, not fighting." He addresses some remarks to me, telling how he came here tonight to smooth things out for these people, so that they will heed the *Penghulu*. "We aborigines are poor, but you don't see us begging in the towns; we take care of our own, of each other." [Of course, all of this is directed to the group and is, among other things, an attempt to justify, affirm, and extend the clearly limited authority of headmen, including himself.]

The talk goes on like this for several more hours with numerous old claims and disputes being brought up and discussed. Occasionally Entoy tells people to share the produce of some disputed tree and not to quarrel over it any more or they will be fined. Finally, he asks if everyone's mind is at ease. When all agree that they have had their say, he lectures the group, admonishing them not to interfere with each other's rights, not to quarrel. Nyam is given all the trees he planted in others' territories, but told not to plant any more. In a long summing up, Entoy emphasizes the sharing of food and how we are all siblings, how we must all stand together: "We can't make a house with one support post; even six isn't enough; we need nine."

Discussing the affair the following day with Tidn and others, I asked why it was that Nyam, who nearly everyone agreed was in the wrong, had been allowed to get away with it. One man, in whose territory Nyam had planted, said "It's as if he had forgotten the law; he is forgiven this one time, but he mustn't do it again." Tidn says "If we treat Nyam too harshly (interestingly, the word he used was "kill"), we lose a man, so we let him plant; we take pity on him." Several times the assertion was made that "these quarrels don't matter for us, because we will all die soon; but they are important because they will result in dissension among our children and grandchildren" [because of the conflicting claims to inherited land and trees that they will cause].

Compared with the dramatic accounts of human conflict presented by some of the other participants in this seminar (see Carneiro, Chagnon, this volume), this little dispute seems anti-climactic. Nonetheless, this too was a conflict among individuals and groups involving access to scarce but important material resources. Coming to understand how and why it occurred the way it did will raise some important issues and considerations concerning both the dynamics of human conflicts and the nature of explanations of them.

THE EXPLANATION OF CONFLICT

Currently the most commonly advanced anthropological explanations of conflict in these sorts of preindustrial societies are one or another species of materialistic and deterministic "final cause" argument that sees human behavior as ultimately caused by and explainable in terms of the material ends that it serves. The most fashionable current versions of this orientation are ecological functionalism (especially the "cultural materialism" of Marvin Harris and his followers) and sociobiology. Although the proponents of these two approaches are frequently at each other's throats, this should not obscure the many fundamental assumptions that they share. Foremost among these is the assumption that the ultimate causes of human behavior (warfare, in this case) are in the material realm – food, mates, land or other scarce resources, or even in human genes – rather than in the realm of ideas and ideals, beliefs and values, purposes and intentions, that many anthropologists call "culture." Methodologically, this assumption is reflected in the attempt to identify the material concomitants and consequences of conflict and warfare (e.g. looting or sexual conquest) as their causes (Divale 1971; Harris 1972, 1974, 1977, 1979a; Divale and Harris 1976; Gross 1975; Ross 1978, 1980a; Bennett Ross 1980; Ferguson 1984b, this volume; Haas, this volume).

This focus on material causes leaves little room for consideration of human decision-making, and such concerns are often explicitly disavowed (Harris 1964, 1974; Ross 1980a; Price 1982). Such disclaimers notwithstanding, any theory of human behavior must necessarily presuppose a theory of motivation. It must at least incorporate some assumptions about why people behave at all. In most materialistic approaches the motivational theory, while implicit, is nevertheless straightforward: human motivation is material maximization. More is better, and more of everything is always sought, whether land, meat, women, or offspring. If this striving results in conflict with others, the material ends are its cause (Durham 1976; Chagnon and Bugos 1979; Biolsi 1984; Price 1984; Ferguson 1984b; cf. also Barnett 1983).[1]

Given our explicit concern here with the sources of warfare, it is, I think, appropriate to examine the utility of an approach which has such wide currency. What can it contribute to our understanding of specific conflicts, such as the one just described? This example is especially appropriate in view of the fact that it bears some striking similarities to

62

the paradigmatic model of conflict that the materialist–determinist model asserts. It was a conflict among individuals and groups, and one involving access to important and scarce material resources. Moreover, and relevant to sociobiological theory, it involved people who were kin and non-kin, and who were very much concerned with their own and their descendants' well-being. Understanding the course this conflict took will, I believe, demonstrate some serious inadequacies in these materialistic approaches. These inadequacies are specifically manifested in their inability to explain conflict in terms that provide any understanding of the causal dynamics of particular conflicts.[2]

One thing I trust is apparent even from the brief ethnographic excerpt presented thus far: this was a dispute among specific human beings who were deciding whether or not to plant trees, whether or not to cut down others' trees, whether or not to support their kinsman, and whether or not to shoot their opponents with poisoned darts, as some feared would happen. Their decisions and the actions that flowed from them were not incidental epiphenomena; rather, they ultimately *constituted* the outcome of this conflict. While material factors – especially land scarcity – were clearly involved in precipitating this conflict, no accounting of the material correlates of these people's actions can truly explain them unless it addresses these decisions and the intentions and goals of those who made them. It is also necessary to take into account how those material factors were translated into human concerns, into components of human motivational equations (cf. Kobben 1973). Understanding the trajectory of this dispute thus requires putting the brute "material facts" into cultural and social contexts, attempting first of all to comprehend how the situation was conceptualized and defined by the people involved.

This discussion focuses on the subjective and social meanings of people's actions and on the various and multilayered contexts in which they occurred. My concern is explicitly with motivation, but conceptualized not as some unitary force (like a need to maximize protein intake or inclusive fitness, or even a "need for achievement") within passive individuals, that mechanically impels them to action, "pushing out" certain forms of behavior. Rather, people are conceived of as active participants in their own destinies, goal-directed decision makers in pursuit of particular goals and objectives. They pick their ways through fields of options and constraints, many of which are indeed biologically and environmentally conditioned. Motivation, as this paper conceives

63

of it, involves all the forces, factors, options, and constraints, both intrinsic and extrinsic, that influence the choices people make. It affects these choices both in terms of the goals they strive for and the purposes they intend, and the means they employ in their achievement.

THE CONTEXT OF SEMAI NONVIOLENCE

In order to begin sketching a picture of the motivational context within which life in a Semai community is played out, as well as to exemplify the differences between the approach that I am advocating and the materialistic determinisms outlined above, I want to begin by examining several Semai concepts for the image of reality that they help to define. The discussion begins, as with the materialist approaches, from a consideration of human needs and their satisfaction. A crucial difference, however, is that in the perspective presented here, "needs" must become "wants." That is they must be cognized by the actors themselves before they can become relevant to people's actions. An unrecognized need, such as a vitamin deficiency or protection from exposure to cosmic radiation, cannot give direction to the behavior of a human being or a society. Once cognized, a material want is still not a determinant of behavior, but is merely one factor (perhaps a very salient one, perhaps not) in a complex motivational equation.

The image of human wants

The Semai concept of *pehunan* refers to a state of being unsatisfied in regard to some specific and strongly-felt want. This is most commonly the result of a hunger for some particular food, but it may also result from other unfulfilled desires. While incurring this state may be purely accidental – the result of losing one's tobacco pouch while hunting, for example – it is most likely to be the result of action (or, even more likely, inaction) on the part of others in the settlement (cf. Dentan 1968; Robarchek 1977a, 1977b). The danger of *pehunan* is, moreover, greatly increased if an explicit request has been made and not granted. Voicing a want converts an individual need into a social fact, magnifying the potential danger in its frustration.

Other concepts similarly define the dangers inherent in the frustration of wants or goals involving sex and cooperation. Together with *pehunan*, they encompass the most likely and most important potential

64

sources of frustrations arising from personal interactions in a society such as this.

The reciprocal of this image is a conception of the community as the source of that nurturance. One aspect of that conception – also entailed in the concept of *pehunan* – is the obligation of individuals, as members of the community, to give support and assistance when it is needed. This can also be seen in another Semai concept, *tinghaa'*, a punishment inflicted by a vaguely-conceived guardian 'spirit' for failure to provide nurturance. *Tinghaa'* is persistent bad luck in the quest for food: the swiddens fail or are ravaged by animals, the hunter's blowpipe does not shoot true, dart poison loses its potency, animals evade the snares and spear traps, the fruit trees do not bear, etc. *Tinghaa'* is seldom mentioned until a death occurs, but when that happens, everyone, down to the smallest child, helps with the burial – clearing the ground, digging the grave, cutting poles and weaving thatch for the grave house, and so on. All are anxious to take this last opportunity to aid the deceased, and to show that they have not been remiss in fulfilling their obligations (Robarchek 1977b, 1986).

Implicit in all this is a conception of the dependent position of the individual vis-à-vis the group. We can see clearly the cultural recognition that to be given nurturance by the community is to be given life; to have it withheld is to be left helpless in the face of danger and death that menaces in the world outside the group. The implication is clear: without the nurturance of the band an individual cannot survive.

There are three points that I would like to emphasize from the foregoing. (1) For Semai, the non-satisfaction of a band member's wants is explicitly a social as well as an individual fact. (2) The response to situations of frustration, a response entailed by the cultural definition of the state of non-satisfaction, is not the anger and aggression expected in our own cultural context. Rather, fear and actions directed at alleviating the threat are the normal responses (cf. Robarchek 1977b). (3) *Pehunan* and related conceptualizations emphasize that there are no independent individuals and that without the support of the band, individual survival is impossible.

The image of the band

Implicit (and often explicit) in the foregoing, in addition to the images of the helpless individual and the nurturant band, is another culturally-crucial dichotomous image: that of the band versus the danger outside. One of the clearest cultural statements of this image is in the division of the human world into two components: *hii'* and *mai*. *"Hii'"* are kinsmen and co-villagers – those whom one can depend upon and trust. The rest of the human world, even Semai from other bands, are *"mai,"* outsiders and strangers whose intentions can never be known with certainty.

Hii' are those who will feed us if we are unable to work, call the spirits to treat us when we are sick, and stand beside us in disputes with outsiders or non-kin. This image of benevolent *hii'* is endlessly reiterated. Any formal public meeting will (as we saw in the *becharaa'*) begin and end with reaffirmations that "We are all siblings here; we take care of one another. When I couldn't hunt, you took care of me; when you were sick, I fed you . . ." and so on, all stressing the interdependence of the group and the responsibility of each to care for the others (see also Robarchek 1979a, 1979b). What I want to emphasize is that Semai social reality is extremely tightly circumscribed. The only source of nurturance and support, the only place where a person can feel secure, is in the band, that tightly knit little group of perhaps a hundred others with whom life is bound up from birth to death (see also Robarchek 1985).

The image of the world

The forest world surrounding these encapsulated communities is a world of unremitting hostility and danger. It is a world filled with malevolent beings and forces, nearly all of which are aggressively hostile to human beings. Even the most mundane activities – gardening, hunting, fishing, eating, even children's playing – are enveloped in taboos and circumscribed by ritual in a vain attempt to avoid precipitating the dangers which menace from all sides.

This view of reality can be seen clearly in a recapitulation in the "spirit" world of the contrasts between kinsmen and strangers, between nurturance and danger, that we saw as fundamental to the Semai conception of the human world. In the nonmaterial world, the contrast is between *mara'* and *gunik*. *Mara'* are, in the words of one informant, "they that eat us," beings that may or may not have material form at any given time and who prey upon human beings.

Gunik, on the other hand, are allies with human beings against these dangers. They are personified forces who can be called upon to assist individuals or the community, especially in treating illness. *Gunik* were once *mara'*, but they have come to humans in dreams, asked to become kin, and given songs to their human kin. The *mara'*, now a *gunik*, is called "son" or "daughter" by its human "father" or "mother", and becomes "sibling" to their children. By singing the dream song, they can call it into the settlement from the forest to aid its human kin, especially to ferret out and eliminate the sources of their illnesses and to ward off other attacking *mara'*. As inmarrying *mai* become *hii'* by joining the band, contributing to its well-being, and becoming incorporated into the network of kin relations, so do *mara'* become *gunik*. As *mara'* is the malevolence of *mai* given cultural form, *gunik* is a reified ideal image of *hii'*: powerful, protective, and benevolent (if outnumbered) kinsmen. What is described once again is a tightly circumscribed world where the only security is in *hii'*, in the band and its spirit kin. All else is danger and death.

The image of the person

If the foregoing is reality as Semai culture defines it, who are the people attempting to make their way in it? How do Semai see themselves and their purposes, opportunities, and means in a world so constituted?

Sentence-completion test responses provided some insight into Semai self-concepts. The pattern is quite clear: when stressed, one does not fall back on one's own resources. Rather, one seeks (and finds) relief in the security and nurturance of others. Semai culture stresses not individualism, self-reliance and independence, but rather dependence, affiliation, and mutual aid.

Major determinants of Semai (or any one else's) self-concepts are the assessments that others make of them and that they make of themselves, in terms of some set of culturally-defined values. Guided by the fundamental values and assumptions of the society, the responses of kin and community constitute a mirror in which children and adults alike see themselves reflected. People come to evaluate themselves largely in terms of these cultural values which thus become incorporated as components of individual self-images, developed and maintained by the continuing feedback of daily interaction.

Sentence-completion responses also provided some clues to this value set and, thereby, to the individual self-images that it helps to develop and sustain. Nineteen informants made 102 value-related statements in response to items relating to "goodness" and "badness," and only three of those responses were not clearly related to the two core values of nurturance and affiliation. Analysis also revealed that "goodness" and "badness" were not simple negations of one another. They were defined instead on different dimensions, with "goodness" defined primarily positively in terms of nurturance (helping, giving, and so on) and "badness" defined primarily negatively in terms of behaviors inimicable to affiliation (especially aggressiveness – fighting, getting angry, quarrelling, and so on). These are the standards against which people are judged by their neighbors and by themselves. Ideals of generosity, friendliness and nonaggressiveness, largely realized in the behavior of most people, constitute central components of individuals' self-images as well (see also Robarchek 1981).[3]

How does all this relate to action, to people behaving in the real world, the world of occasional pettiness, frequent gossip, inevitably conflicts of interests, evaded obligations, jealousy, anger, deceit, duplicity, in short, to a greater or lesser degree, the world we all live in? These images of self, the band, and the world are incorporated into the personalities of individuals as fundamental assumptions about the nature of reality. They are thereby components of motivational complexes (the action strategies they use to operate in such a world) and channel individual behavior choices into nonviolent directions. The collective behavior of individuals thus directed in turn constitutes the learning environment of the next generation. It is an environment where children have little opportunity to learn how to utilize violence. In a reality so defined, violence simply does not come to be seen as a means for settling disputes or resolving difficulties (cf. Robarchek 1977a; Dentan 1978).

MATERIALIST EXPLANATION OF CONFLICT

It is, I hope, clear by now that no understanding of (or, for that matter, predictions of) the course that these events took is possible without knowledge of the motivational context of these people's behavior, or their culturally-constituted reality and of the assumptions, values, purposes and intentions of the people whose actions constituted the social drama that we witnessed. Without these data, no collation or correlation of the "objective," "material" "facts" of the matter would provide any insight into what happened, into the psychosocial dynamics of the process.

Yet, as we have seen, it is precisely this intentionality and the decision-making capacity that underlies it that is either implicitly or explicitly denied by much current theorizing on the subjects of conflict and war. There is, in most ecological and sociobiological formulations, no concern with the translation of putative material "causes" of behavior into human concerns. In short, precisely what is lacking is any conception of human motivation beyond simple maximization. Behavior seemingly happens spontaneously as a result of the exposure of human beings to material conditions which thus constitute the "causes" of warfare. Needless to say, I see such approaches as open to criticism in a number of areas, beginning with the fundamental orienting assumption of the primacy of "material" factors as "causes" of human behavior.

Material causation

Both terms of the "material cause" equation are open to serious question. Are material causes, in fact, "material"? And are they "causal"? That is, even if people specifically reason together and decide to go to war to acquire more wives, or more buffalo horses, or a better salmon stream, does the ultimate cause of the behavior lie in the "material" end to be served? Or is it to be found in the cultural values that put a premium on salmon over other foods, or on buffalo horses as sources of status, or on multiple wives as symbols of virility or success?[4] If we put aside the assumption of an innate drive to maximize material good, is greed a material cause? Put another way, if I own a Volkswagen and I steal a Mercedes, is the cause of my behavior "material"?

Also questionable is the denial of the causal relevance of beliefs and values, of goals and intentions, and the assertion, thereby, of the causal primacy of the material world. In much anthropological speculation – ethnological, historical and, especially archeological – concerning the causes of human social behavior, including war, the technical and methodological constraints that favor the collection of material data are transformed into the theoretical proposition that only material factors are relevant to the explanation of behavior. From there, the ontological assumption is made that only material causes are "real," thereby banishing human intentionality from the realm of science. Marvin

Harris, the leading theorist of materialist anthropology, for example, argues for an approach ". . .linking together separate portions of the behavior stream without invoking the actor's subjective understanding of what his 'purpose' or 'goal' is supposed to be." He then holds that ". . .the assumptions [that the human actor knows the purpose or meaning of his behavior]. . .are totally alien to the spirit of science" (1964:91).

It might be worth noting that materialist psychology – behaviorism – rested on precisely this same transformation; the behaviorists reasoned that since only observable behavior was measurable and objectively verifiable, all else was irrelevant or imaginary, leading academic psychology to spend half a century digging itself into a hole from which it has only recently begun to emerge.[5] It is no coincidence that it was Harris who tried to introduce behaviorist methodology into ethnography with the "actone" approach to ethnographic description (Harris 1964). This approach, however, has never been widely accepted or applied.

It is, of course, often difficult or impossible, especially in historical or archeological research, to recover data concerning the sorts of psychological and cultural factors that we observed at work in the Semai case. Saying that data bearing on certain factors is difficult or impossible to obtain in the investigation of some particular chain of events does *not*, however, imply that those factors were necessarily irrelevant in the process being investigated (cf. Haas, this volume).

The statuses of the material conditions proposed as causes of human behavior are of two sorts – initial conditions and final conditions – and there are serious problems in the conceptualization and treatment of each.

Final states as causes

In these sorts of formulations, the causal explanation of some cultural phenomenon is sought and found in its effects. The processes alluded to (but never specified) are frankly teleological, with the end result (e.g. increased inclusive fitness or ecological efficiency) existing entirely outside the consciousness of the actors (e.g. Harris 1974; Ross 1980a; Bennett Ross 1980, Price 1982). From the Semai case study it is clear that understanding behavior is, as a purely practical matter, impossible in the absence of motivational information. It is also clear, however, that final cause explanations are unacceptable *in principle* in the absence of human intentionality (cf. Kobben 1973:90). As Spiro

(1967:66) cogently argues:

If. . .the function of the phenomenon to be explained is an unintended consequence, it is a logical fallacy to explain the phenomenon by reference to its function. Indeed, the contrary is the case: the function is explained by reference to the phenomenon by which it is achieved.

In some functional formulations, considerable lip-service is paid to "decision-making" and "information processing." Close examination, however, almost invariably shows these usages to be metaphorical (if not metaphysical). The "decisions" appear to be made without the participation of human minds and seem inevitably to be restricted to the teleological process of "choosing" courses of action that maximize ecological efficiency or inclusive fitness. (Analytically these are determined on the basis of a cost/benefit analysis that has nothing whatsoever in common with the conscious factors – insults, sorcery, perceptions of relative strength and weakness, etc. – on the basis of which human actors are actually seen to make choices [cf. Chagnon, this volume].) The final causes once again turn out to be functional "goals" existing entirely outside the consciousness of the actors who putatively make the decisions (e.g. Alexander 1979; Ferguson 1984a, 1984b, this volume).

Initial conditions as causes

Perhaps as a consequence of the difficulties inherent in teleological functionalism, some materialist approaches, while still seeing the ultimate explanation (cause) of warfare in the final state toward which it progresses (acquisition of territory, control of trade, etc.), stress initial material conditions. Climatic change, new trade opportunities, and so on, are seen as the material determinants of warfare (e.g. Divale and Harris 1976; Ferguson 1984a; Harris 1984a). There are a number of problems with this approach, the most important of which is the mechanistic and deterministic assumption which underlies it. This assumption is that having identified even a necessary condition for human behavior is to have explained the behavior by virtue of some (never specified) mechanical linkage through which the material condition automatically generates the behavior.

Both initial and final cause arguments are usually based on the demonstrated (or assumed) co-occurrence or correlation of material events or conditions with warfare: climatic change, population growth, annexation of territory, numbers of offspring, etc. (e.g. Divale and Harris 1976; Bennett Ross 1980; Ember 1982; Harris 1984a; Ferguson 1984b; Betzig 1986). A correlation is, of course, only an empirical generalization about the co-occurrence of events which, in itself, tells us nothing about causation. Causal statements require the postulation of processes connecting the correlated variables. Noting the correlation between swidden gardening and malaria, for example, tells us nothing, in the absence of intervening processes, about the efficient causes of the disease. The generalization will, in fact, make such understanding impossible if we assume, as do most materialist analyses (on the presumption of the primacy of material causes) that the correlation already describes the causal process: climatic change causes warfare; protein shortage causes warfare; resource competition causes warfare, and so on.

The solution most common in ecological and sociobiological approaches to the problem of linking material "cause" with behavioral "effect" has been to relegate the intentionality to Culture, reifying and ascribing purposes to it, to "make society and culture think for the people" (Nadel 1953:276; cf. Kobben 1973:91).[6] Somehow, the "correct" (in terms of inclusive fitness or ecological efficiency) decisions were institutionalized as part of the culture, as cow worship or female infanticide or polygyny or warfare. Individuals thereafter do not have to make decisions, they simply obey the dictates of their cultures (e.g. Harris 1974, 1979a; Gross 1975; Divale and Harris 1976; Bennett Ross 1980; Ferguson 1984a). Once made explicit, however, this sort of "solution" to the problem of motivation is obviously also unsatisfactory on several grounds. Not the least of these is that it simply pushes the decisions back into the past where the analyst does not have to deal with the processes involved. More seriously, it entails a degree of cultural reification and a level of cultural determinism not taken seriously in a generation.

All the foregoing notwithstanding, shared sets of values, beliefs, meanings, and assumptions – culture – must, as I hope the Semai case demonstrated, be an indispensable part of any explanation of any human behavior, including warfare. Cultural traditions certainly do define certain options as more desirable than others, and certain methods as legitimate and others as illegitimate means to those ends. Thus, for example, like the Yanomamö, most Semai men would probably like to have sex with more women than they do. Yet no Semai man ever gets up one morning, turns to his brother-in-law and says, "Let's get a bunch of the guys together and go raid the next valley and see if we can kill some people and steal some women." For Semai, murder and rape are simply not legitimate means to any ends, no matter how "objectively" desirable.

However, while culture provides us with at least a partial answer to our question about the basis for choices among options, considered as a determinant it, too, is unacceptable. The existence of a culturally institutionalized pattern of behavior (such as Yanomamö warfare) is at most a necessary, and not a sufficient, condition for its performance. (It is not, in fact, even a necessary condition; if it were, culture change would be impossible.) Ever since the Kinsey report, for example, it would be difficult to argue that marital infidelity is not an important component of the American cultural–behavioral inventory. That does not mean, however, that we are all constantly occupied every day in cheating on our spouses. Nor do the Yanomamö, even with their culture of war, fight, rape and kill every day, or every week, or every month, or even every year. That is to say that the individuals and groups must consciously decide whether or not to put their culturally-legitimized behavioral potentiality into action. Once again, we are faced with the problem of discovering why, on any given day, a man or a group of men decide to attack a neighboring band, and why they choose to attack one band rather than another. Was it because of an insult? because they were raided by that group recently? because their group recently split and they are weak while others are strong? (All of these, according to Chagnon, are cited by raiders themselves as reasons for going to war.) These daily decisions are not trivial or irrelevant or epiphenomenal. In the aggregate they and the actions they motivate, in fact, *constitute* the behavior of the group. When the subject is human behavior, materialist explanation must at least acknowledge (even if it does not address) the question of how the posited "material causes" become parts of actors' motivational schemata.

CONCLUSION

I trust I have made it clear above that my objections are not to the assertion of the significance of the material world in relation to human conflict. Denying the relevance of the material world to human decision-making would be as counter-productive (and counter-intuitive) as the reverse denial has been. My objection is rather with the assumption, explicit or implicit in many of the most influential of the avowedly materialist approaches to warfare, that identifying the material concomitants of war essentially exhausts the explanatory process and provides us with an understanding of the causal processes and the dynamics of organized human conflict.

What we saw in the Semai case (and, for that matter, in all of the other examples of conflict presented during the seminar) were people choosing courses of action based on what they believed and what they wanted. These choices were certainly not unrelated to their material circumstances – in the Semai case, to the opening of a road and to the increasing penetration of the market economy; or to technological changes – improved transportation, radios that brought the outside world to them, access to improved medical care, and other factors. Against this background, one man saw an opportunity to materially improve his position, and he took it, regardless of the fact that it violated the accepted cultural rules. Others, his own kinsmen, decided not to support him, even though it might have been in their material best interests to do so. Most importantly, everyone in the community saw the potential for violence inherent in the dispute, and consciously rejected it as an option.

Even though the matters at issue were extremely important for everyone involved, we did not see the spontaneous eruption of human violence in response to conflict over scarce material resources. Rather, people defined the situation in terms of the cultural values and ideals that they brought to it. Dissention, selfishness and quarreling were continually equated with violence, feud and murder. Lack of harmony within the band was seen in terms of its potential (*never* realized) of producing the war of each against all. Constantly reaffirmed were the necessary unity, mutual aid and support of the band, and the responsibility of each person for the others. We also saw people making decisions on the basis of these personal and cultural values. We saw individual self-interests downplayed in the service of restoring relations. "We take pity on him," they said, "these quarrels don't really matter for us, we'll be dead soon, but they will cause quarrelling among our children and grandchildren." While it is abundantly clear that no one really believes that all this is unimportant here and now, it is also clear that a prime consideration, beyond the issue of material gain, is the dissention that could be caused in succeeding generations. Moreover, the ideal image evoked in that assertion, of a cohesive, cooperating group persisting through time, is used as a way of justifying and accounting for (as well as describing and explaining) the existence of dissention and deviation from the ideal here and now. Finally, conspicuously absent was the kin group support that Nyam had a right to expect, if only he had been aware of kin selection theory and reciprocal altriusm. Rather, his kindred, recognizing that he was violating the rules as they were consensually understood, provoking conflict with other kindreds, and theatening the unity of the band, chose to abandon their own spokesman. They thereby chose to ignore the opportunity to increase their own inclusive fitness by advancing the well-being of their kinsman.

The point of all this is simply that in all conflicts, as in this dispute, there are always multiple levels of causality and conditionality, multiple levels of contexts within which conflict occurs, indeed within which all human behavior occurs. There is, moreover, no reason to suppose that Semai are different in terms of fundamental psychological and social processes from the Yanomamö, the Tlingit or the Anasazi. For them no less than for the Semai, There is only one condition that is both necessary and sufficient for organized conflict – warfare – to occur: the decision on the part of individuals and groups – always within the contexts of particular environmental circumstances and particular sociocultural institutions – to engage in it.

The motivations of individuals, the proximate causes of their behavior, are not the self-evident stimulus-response reactions of a universal human psychobiology to an objective external reality. Rather, they are generated in the appraisals and interpretations of situations, largely in terms of culturally given meanings. Warfare or nonviolence, like other behaviors, occur when they are perceived and selected from among a field of possible alternatives as viable means of achieving specific, largely culturally defined, goals. Biology and the environment are most assuredly relevant, imposing constraints upon and providing opportunities for the generation and realization of goals in human societies. But the process does not end there. Psychological and cultural information structures mediate between biological and environmental constraints and individual and collective behavior. They are the constructions of reality within which purposive human action takes place, and any framework of explanation must be at least potentially (even if not actually) capable of encompassing these if it is to be both intellectually satisfying and truly explanatory.

75

Notes

1. As opposed to the overwhelming primacy of material conditions of motivation in Marxist–materialist theories, one might wonder whether a different view of motivation – as satisficing (settling for some acceptable minimum), for example – would have the same implications. Of course, such a view would require taking actors seriously in terms of *their* intentions and purposes, not relegating people to the status of passive pawns, manipulated by the inexorable logic of material transactions in energy and substance, but seeing them instead as active seekers of meaning and coherence.

2. I want to make it clear that it is not my intention to resurrect the old materialist/idealist and ideographic/nomothetic dichotomies. Rather, I hope to show the pitfalls of thinking in terms of these sorts of antinomies which has led, in much of the theoretical literature on primitive warfare, to the *a priori* rejection *on principle* of just the sorts of factors that prove to be critical for an understanding of specific cases.

3. There were six of these items which were intended to elicit both positive and negative values by seeking their expression in both approved and disapproved behaviors:

   "They praise him/her because (s)he . . ."
   "If (s)he is a true friend, (s)he . . ."
   "(S)he is a good person, (s)he always . . ."
   "(S)he is angry at her/his friend/relative because . . ."
   "(S)he is a bad/evil person, (s)he always . . ."
   "His/her friends/kin reject him/her because (s)he . . ."

   The first three were intended to elicit positive values, the last three, negative values. All, in Semai, can be completed statements either about what people do or what they do not do. For a more detailed discussion and analysis of this technique see Phillips (1965), and of these data, see Robarchek (1981).

4. Sahlins deals at great length with this issue in *Culture and Practical Reason* (1976).

5. In anthropology, this same assumption can be seen in the title of a recent collection of essays entitled *Beyond the Myths of Culture: Essays in Cultural Materialism* (Ross 1980b).

6. Harris, for example, approvingly cites Durkheim, Malthus and Marx as holding that ". . . actor's 'purpose' is frequently subsumed by a social 'purpose' of which he is totally unaware" (1964:91).

4
Reproductive and somatic conflicts of interest in the genesis of violence and warfare among tribesmen

NAPOLEON A. CHAGNON

This paper is a preliminary step in the development of a more comprehensive treatment of warfare among band and village societies, a study that will be based heavily on my own field research among the Yanomamö Indians of the Venezuela/Brazil border region. My ultimate goal for the longer study will be a synthesis of the most useful concepts of the cultural ecological (culture materialist) approach in anthropology (White 1949; Steward 1955; Vayda 1976; Rappaport 1968; Netting 1977; Harris 1979a; Chagnon 1968a; Johnson and Earle 1987) with a number of new concepts and theoretical developments from evolutionary biology (Hamilton 1964; Trivers 1971; Williams 1966; Wilson 1975; Alexander 1979, 1987; Alexander and Borgia 1978; Chagnon and Irons 1979; van den Berghe 1979; Dawkins 1976; Symons 1979; Daly & Wilson 1983, 1988; Flinn and Alexander 1982).

As in any attempted synthesis, one must first demonstrate how or why particular well-defined approaches such as materialism fail to provide satisfactory explanations in the face of new evidence and theory, and how or why new theory can provide better or more satisfactory explanations. Space does not permit an exhaustive justification of that order of magnitude in this paper. I will, however, lay out a few of the issues that appear to be most central to the success of my projected future attempts to synthesize these two bodies of theory, and I will provide a few examples to illustrate how some of the issues of conflict and violence in a particular tribal society can be interpreted when both bodies of theory are taken into consideration.

I am convinced that the developments in theoretical biology since approximately 1960, and the stunning field research on many different species that these developments have provoked, can not be ignored by social scientists. They must be considered in our formulations about and explanations of the social behavior we customarily deal with in our studies of humans. Historically, anthropologists have borrowed many ideas from biology and most of us use them without much reflection on their provenience – notions such as "adaptive," "evolved," "selected," etc. At the same time, few of us keep abreast of the changes in the biological meanings of these concepts, changes that have occurred in theoretical biology *after* social sciences had appropriated the original concepts.

Darwin's view of the evolution of life forms by natural selection is now a standard dimension in social and cultural anthropology, modified, of course, to apply to "cultures" or "societies." It is the modification, however, which is today a major issue, since the changes necessary to extend his original arguments by themselves distorted and changed his arguments. Specifically, problems with the "group" versus the "individual" controversy are now beginning to appear in anthropological discussions of the evolved functions of human behavior. This has long been resolved in favour of the individual or lower levels of organization in the field of biology (Williams 1966, 1971).

Another deficiency in our use of evolutionary theory has to do with our almost exclusive focus on "survival," when, in fact, evolutionary theory is about both survival and reproduction. On the one hand, this is probably related to the difficulty of imagining cultures or societies "reproducing" like organisms. On the other, there is a general bias in materialist/evolutionary anthropology to play down or ignore the issue of the individual's role in shaping societies and cultures. Furthermore, when we deal with survival, our concerns appear to be more about the survival of systems (cultures, groups, populations, etc.) than of individuals. This makes it difficult for us to evaluate and discuss the relationship between societal rules and what individuals actually do. We thereby preclude the possibility of understanding the evolved biological correlates of conventions and institutions.

My proposed approach will treat warfare as only one of a class of conflicts which, in band and village societies, must be examined carefully to determine the extent to which they can be traced back to conflicts of interest among individuals (Chagnon 1988a). This will provide the historical and developmental matrix of particular conflicts that ultimately reach the level of inter-group warfare. In addition, the focus will be primarily on individuals, who will be viewed as expending two basic kinds of efforts during their lifetimes: somatic effort (in the interests of survival) and reproductive effort (in the interest of fitness) (Alexander 1985; Chagnon, 1988a). Both of these entail costs and benefits. While I will provide no empirical date on costs and benefits in this paper, I will eventually use differential survival rates and rates of reproductive success among the several projected measures of costs and benefits.

Let me now turn to a few of the issues that are central to an attempt to synthesize materialist, or ecological, anthropology and theoretical biology.

WARFARE AS A KIND OF CONFLICT

Warfare in band and tribal societies must be put into a more general context, one that treats it as a species within a larger genus. That larger category can be called *conflict* and, within it, we can identify and list a number of specific kinds of conflicts that actually do or potentially can occur between individuals and groups of individuals. I see this as an essential step that will obviate many definitional and theoretical issues.

An analogy might illustrate why this is an important step. In looking, for example, at the comparative study of political leadership in order to develop a theory of political power, it would be imprudent to begin our study by defining political leadership as something that presidents and kings do. This would force us to try to put !Kung, Eskimo, Cheyenne, Ona, etc. leaders into either the "president" or "king" category. We either have to make their leaders presidents and kings, or conclude that they do not have political leadership (Fried 1967). I think we have a similar problem with warfare. Conflicts between individuals and groups of individuals break out within many band and tribal societies, but the groups contesting are not always (at the time) politically independent. Indeed, a common consequence of such conflicts is the fissioning of the groups along conflict lines, and an escalation/continuation of the conflict. It is at this point that groups become visibly "independent" of each other and more conveniently fit into categories that enable us to define the *extended* conflicts as "warfare." However, we could not do so initially when the contestants were members of a common group. By insisting that our approach to warfare focus only on conflicts between politically independent groups, we run the risk of losing sight of the genesis of the conflict. We are also tempted to restrict our search for causes to just that inventory of things that "groups" (politically independent societies) might contest ever, such as a hunting territory or water hole – resources that may be intimately identified with members of specific local groups.

This is a crucial issue. First, conflicts of interest in band and village societies often occur between individuals within the same group and are provoked by a wide variety of reasons. Second, individuals in kinship-organized societies tend to take sides with close kin and/or those whose reproductive interests overlap significantly with their own (e.g., wife's brothers). "Groups" are therefore often formed on the basis of kinship, marriage, or both, and by definition their members have overlapping reproductive interests. They usually have economic and other interests that overlap as well, but it is theoretically important to keep in mind that, from the perspective of evolution, the ultimate interests of individuals are reproductive in overall scope.

Owing to the fact that no two individuals are genetically identical (save, of course, for identical twins), conflicts of interest between individuals are bound to arise since the nature of some life's resources are such that they cannot be secured by one individual without depriving other individuals. Such conflicts frequently lead to competition between individuals (or groups of related individuals) for significant resources. However, the competition need not take violent forms and conflicts can be resolved by means other than violence, such as cooperative agreements to share a scarce resource. The point here is that while conflicts of interest over resources may be inevitable, violent (competitive) resolutions of the conflicts are not. Axelrod's game theory analyses of social strategies such as "tit-for-tat" in competitive milieus (Axelrod and Hamilton 1981; Axelrod 1984) persuasively argue that cooperative solutions work extremely well where interactants must repeatedly confront each other and where each has approximately the same degree of ability to conflict harm on the other (Chagnon 1988a).

LIFE EFFORT

A basic assumption in my model is that the lifetime efforts of individuals can be partitioned into two conceptually distinct categories that incorporate all or nearly all of the activities that an individual (an organism in any species) engages in if it is to be biologically successful. These categories are *somatic effort* and *reproductive effort* (Alexander 1985). The former has principally to do with those activities, risks, costs, etc. that ensure the survival of the organism in a purely somatic sense – seeking shelter from the elements, protection from predators and conspecifics, obtaining nutrients, maintaining hygiene and health, etc. This would include most items we traditionally focus on in studies of technology, economics, settlement patterns, cultural ecology, grooming, ethnopharmacology, curing, etc.

The second category is one that is not normally considered in traditional cultural ecological/materialist approaches to intergroup conflicts, warfare, and cultural adaptation. While the category's overall content is "reproductive," it includes a number of specific variables not normally considered in traditional anthropological studies of reproduction as such (see Figure 4.1). Herein lies the value and power of theoretical developments in evolutionary biology that can shed new light on conflicts of interest between individuals and, ultimately, intergroup conflicts between politically independent groups such as bands and horticultural tribes.

A review of the literature pertaining to warfare and conflict in such societies reveals that much of the conflict emanates over such factors as rape, abduction of females, failure to deliver a promised bride, niggardliness in paying bride price or executing bride service, and seduction (Daly and Wilson 1988; Chagnon 1988a). Whereas warfare and conflict in industrialized societies and many "ranked" or "stratified" societies (Fried 1967) can be convincingly shown to be associated with relative scarcity or protection of material resources, the proverbial "means of production," much of the conflict in most band and tribal societies is generated because of contests over the *means of reproduction* (Chagnon 1979).

Let me make one thing perfectly clear at this juncture. I am *not*

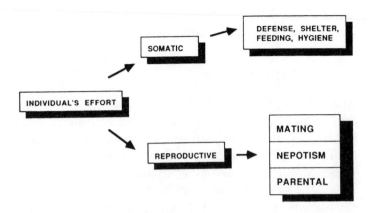

Figure 4.1: Model of Individual Life Effort from a Darwinian Perspective. Individuals expend basically two kinds of effort during their lifetimes: Somatic Effort and Reproductive Effort. The former has basically to do with the survival of the organism as such, while the latter has to do with costs, benefits, risks, etc. associated with mating, nepotism (aiding non-descendant kin), and parenting.

claiming that all conflicts of interest in band and tribal society derive from conflicts that are reproductive in overall quality, nor am I claiming that conflicts over material resources are not found in such societies. I am simply arguing that conflicts of reproductive interests occur commonly in band and tribal societies and that these often lead, as indicated above, to intergroup conflicts that we traditionally consider to be warfare. I accept (and have always accepted) explanations of specific band and village warfare patterns in which demonstrable and convincing evidence indicates that shortages of material resources are directly implicated in the genesis of the conflicts. I will return to this below.

The category "reproductive effort" in my model is advised by and basically derived from the post-1960 theoretical developments in evolutionary biology. Reproduction entails getting copies of one's self into subsequent generations. This can occur in more than the single obvious way we normally think of reproduction: begetting and successfully raising offspring. Since related organisms share identical genes by immediate common descent, organisms can advance their reproductive interests by engaging in activities and behaviours that affect, in a positive way, the reproductive efforts and accomplishments of relatives with whom they share genes. Thus, while the original Darwinian perspective viewed success in terms of fitness measured by numbers of immediate descendants (offspring), the new Darwinian perspective views success in broader, more encompassing terms. What is significant is the number of copies of one's genes that are perpetuated in subsequent generations.

This draws attention to the enormous importance of W. D. Hamilton's now classic papers (1964) defining "inclusive fitness." Individual Egos can pass on their genes by direct acts of reproduction (having children) and by aiding genetic relatives, who, by definition, share genes with Ego in proportion to the degree of genetic relatedness between them. If the aid enhances the relatives' reproduction, Ego "benefits" in a reproductive sense by having more copies of his/her genes enter the gene pool of subsequent generations – through the reproductive accomplishments of those relatives.

The study of "reproduction" becomes, then, more than merely the collection of genealogical facts and reproductive histories of individuals. It entails the study of all social interactions that potentially affect the reproductive success of the individual and those with whom he or she is interacting. Such interactions include, for example, taking risks to protect a kinsman in a mortal duel, sharing a piece of food, tendering aid in clearing gardens, and reclassifying a covillager from the kinship category "sister" to "wife" (Chagnon 1988b).

The study of reproduction also entails the study of both the "rules" and violations of the rules, injunctions, moral prescriptions, etc. (Alexander 1979, 1987), which can and often do lead to conflicts and fighting. Thus, failure to give a piece of food might possibly reflect an immediate shortage of food and have, therefore, relevance in a purely somatic context. At the same time, it can reflect a *reproductive* strategy on the part of an individual to enhance his or her political esteem and authority – to insult a reproductive competitor, for example. It thus has relevance in a purely reproductive context as well, often in the absense of resource scarcities. Such affronts are common in meat distributions among the Yanomamö, for example, where there is a chronic struggle among men to establish individual reputations for authority, prestige, esteem, productivity, generosity, and matrimonial success. The "rule" is to give portions of large game away first to the "big men" and then to the lesser. A meat distributor can strategically conduct his distribution to indicate to the assembled that he doesn't consider a particular individual in the group to be as "important" as he himself and others might consider him to be. This can be done by deliberately giving him an unacceptably small portion, an undesirable portion, or presenting a portion after first acknowledging that others are more important than he by distributing to them first. He might even go so far as to give him no portion. This is, of course, remembered and noted by all . . . and adds to all those other factors that accumulate eventually into smouldering inter-individual hostilities and conflicts that eventually explode and are expressed in arguments, club fights and, occasionally, homicides.

Reproductive efforts, then, includes a more comprehensive set of variables than traditional anthropological concepts embrace. It can conveniently be partitioned into several broad sub-categories (Figure. 4.1): parental effort, mating effort, and nepotistic effort (Alexander 1985). Parental effort deals primarily with those factors we are familiar with in our more traditional views of reproduction: all those costs and risks required to rear one's children successfully and, by extension, grandchildren and great-grandchildren, i.e., descendant relatives. Mating effort includes the study of all those variables that affect the success that individuals enjoy in attracting (obtaining) a mate; guarding the mate from the seductive attempts of others (cf. Dickemann 1981; Flinn, 1988); and keeping the kin of that mate satisfied in terms of the expectations that they have regarding bride price, bride service, food sharing, etc. Nepotistic effort includes all those social activities entailing costs and risks that are expended in order to aid non-descendant relatives. These individuals, by virtue of receiving such beneficence, are in a position to translate it into reproductive consequences that ultimately enhance the "inclusive fitness" of the original helper, i.e., by producing additional copies of the helper's genes through their own reproductive accomplishments.

LIFE EFFORT MODEL

Figure 4.2 summarizes the model of "Life Effort" that my proposed approach is based on. Historically, the development of the "life effort" approach goes back to at least the time of Fisher (1930), but the most extensive and elaborate use of the life effort model for interpreting human social behaviour can be found in the works of R. D. Alexander (1985; 1987) on whose version my own is largely based.

By thinking of an individual's life time as a series of efforts entailing costs and risks on the one hand and benefits on the other, one can more clearly identify the factors that are likely to be significant in terms of the

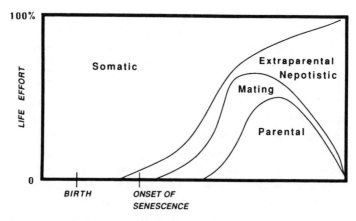

Fig 4.2: Allocation of Life Efforts During an Individual Lifetime (Redrawn from Alexander, 1985). Early in life organisms expend most of their efforts at growth and development to reach reproductive age. Nepotistic efforts begin before reproduction in most human societies and often take the form of "baby sitting" or aiding other relatives and continues throughout life. Mating and Parental effort can only begin after the point of reproductive maturity. After the birth of a child, parents expend efforts for both somatic goals (survival) and reproductive goals.

individual's attempts to be successful as both a member of society and as an organism constrained by societal rules. One can see how culture and cultural success is relatable to biology and biological success (Irons 1979; Borgerhoff Mulder 1987). The myriad factors that potentially or actually lead to conflicts of somatic and reproductive interests and, ultimately, fighting and warfare can also be appreciated.

By focusing on individual level conflicts of interests, we can more clearly see how the patterns of escalation, found widely in tribal societies, grow in such a way as to enable us to trace the sources of the conflicts back to the individual level and relate them, where possible, to reproductive versus somatic conflicts. This is particularly important for understanding warfare in band and village societies where the initial conflicts are almost always at the level of individuals. The "causes" of specific "wars" in such societies are bound up in complex, often vague, issues that transpired months or even years before the specific raid by "Group A" on "Group B" which we traditionally identify as "war" actually occurs. In contrast, by starting with the "group" as our initial

85

level of analysis (because we usually define warfare as mortal contests between groups), we lose sight of the anterior patterns and are forced to interpret the group level phenomena as having started there.

The focus on individuals not only makes the conflict genesis clearer, it also compels us to consider the history of the conflict and how initial conflicts over one particular cause evolve into newer, more encompassing conflicts that are perpetuated by secondary causes. Thus, a clubfight might be precipitated by an act of marital infidelity and result in a homicide in Village A. This leads to a village fission and the subsequent development of alliances with other groups by the two newly independent communities: "A" subdivides into A1 and A2. A1 develops alliances with neighbours B and C, while A2, does the same with neighbours Y and Z. The new alliances, in turn, involve these more remote and formerly non-belligerent villages in mortal, intergroup raiding, groups that were not involved in the initial conflict. The ensuing raids lead to mortalities among the formerly neutral allies (e.g., B and Z) who are then motivated to perpetuate the war to avenge deaths of their kinsmen.

ASSUMPTIONS ABOUT CARRYING CAPACITY AND RESOURCE ABUNDANCE

While both somatic and reproductive conflicts are commonly found in most human societies, it would be reasonable to say that anthropological theories about primitive war, particularly cultural materialist theories (Vayda 1969a; Harris 1984a, 1979b; Ferguson, 1984a, this volume; Johnson and Earle 1987), have either emphasized or focused exclusively on conflicts over material resources. In one sense, this is not surprising in that anthropologists come from societies where military conflicts are generally over such issues and these factors have always been significant in the written historical documents of our society. Scientifically, of course, material conditions of survival and well-being are important and are, under many circumstances, well worth fighting over.

They are not the only causes of conflicts, however, and empirically we know that to be successful, organisms must not only survive, they must reproduce. The natural history of all organisms must be taken into consideration in order to understand the nature of the behavior we observe among them, even in those environments that are now novel –

such as our own industrial world. Certainly it would be preposterous to suggest that today's remaining band and village societies live in the pristine social and material environments within which human behavior and morphology evolved (see Haas, this volume). Nevertheless, it is reasonable to say that they represent the only remaining approximations to human ancestors who did live in those kinds of environments. These are the only situations in which we can make behavioral observations on individuals with an attempt to understand the causes of conflict and warfare in pre-state societies and attempt to document and analyze them.

The traditional emphasis in studying and explaining primitive warfare has been on conflicts of somatic interest of whole groups (villages, bands, communities) with an attempt to identify the particular limiting resource(s) over which group contests are waged. The theoretical inspiration for this approach stems, in part, from an earlier theoretical biology, particularly ecological theory, where the relative numbers and densities of people are examined with respect to the life-sustaining material resources on which the group (culture) depends and to which it is "adapted." Thus, "man–land" ratios figure prominently in such studies, and conflicts are usually explained in terms of scarce material resources, documentation for which is often unavailable and, therefore, often simply asserted. Where some documentation exists, it is often in the form of qualitative assessments of resource abundance from which only circumstantial cases can be made. In any event, the state of the art in explaining primitive warfare in "scientific" terms focuses on the material conditions and seems to proceed from assumptions about carrying capacity that can be, but are almost never, documented with detailed ecological studies.

The point I want to make here is a very simple one and has to do with the probable variation that exists today and has existed in the past with regard to carrying capacity and human conflicts.

CARRYING CAPACITY

Figure 4.3 shows a typical logistic growth curve for population increases over time. As a population enters a new niche, one that is free from conspecifics who might be competing for the same resources, the population begins to grow at a high rate: the curve climbs steeply. Over time, as resources become scarcer and/or more difficult or costly to

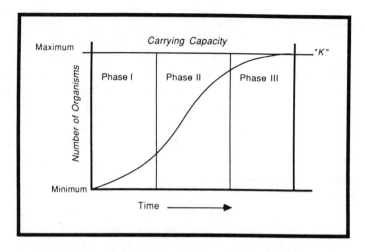

Figure 4.3: Modified model of Carrying Capacity. Population growth in this modified model is shown as taking place in three "phases" of the population's history in the ecological niche. In Phase I, life-sustaining material resources are relatively abundant compared to the situation in Phase III. Such conflicts as might occur between individuals in this phase are likely to involve reproductive resources rather than somatic resources. In Phase III, as the population approaches "K," conflicts of interest are more likely to revolve around life-sustaining material resources in most species and in egalitarian human societies. Conflicts of interest in all phases can, of course, revolve around both reproductive and somatic resources and it cannot be assumed on first principles that they will always occur over resources in only one of these categories.

obtain, and when "hostile forces" (density dependent diseases and parasites) begin checking growth rates (fertility and mortality rates begin to converge), the population growth rate slows down and the population eventually approaches its theoretical upper limit: K, or "carrying capacity."

I have modified the traditional graphic expression of the carrying capacity model by indicating three possible "phases" in a population's history in any particular ecological niche. More phases could be suggested, but three are sufficient for my present purpose. Phase one represents the early phase of the population's history in the niche. Growth rate is very high and it is presumed that the individuals are expending relatively more of their efforts at reproduction rather than in somatic efforts (Williams 1966). Conflicts, if they occur, should be expected to be primarily over reproductive issues. In phase two, the population continues to grow, but is beginning, toward the end of the phase, to slow down. Here we can expect conflicts to be more or less equally distributed between reproductive and somatic issues. Finally, in phase three, the population is nearing carrying capacity and one should expect that conflicts will become increasingly dominated by somatic issues, although reproductive conflicts will also occur. In a word, individuals fight for mates when resources are abundant, and fight for the means to acquire mates when resources become scarce.

It cannot simply be assumed, as appears to be the case in many materialist works, that all human populations are in phase three of their history in any particular niche (viz. Harris and Ross 1987; Ferguson, this volume). The materialist preoccupation with explaining warfare in terms of scarcity of resources appears to be based on precisely this assumption. At the same time there is an attempt to convey the message that this is the only "scientific" way to explain warfare, particularly in band and village societies. If it is to be truly scientific, then its proponents should make the effort to empirically document that populations are at or near carrying capacity. Otherwise, we have simply an elaborate tautology: war is a contest over scarce material resources; evidence that resources are scarce is the existence of war. Short of actually conducting elaborate, expensive and time-consuming studies that lead to the assessment of a niche's resource abundance, there are a number of practical, time-saving and reasonable considerations that can be taken into account. These include such things as extremely low population densities coupled with high growth rate being a probable reflection of a condition in which resources are not a limiting factor and that competition for them is not a very persuasive explanation for such conflicts as might be occurring. By contrast, extraordinarily high population densities and other information, such as native assertions that they are short of land or other material resources, help make a persuasive case that conflicts, if they occur, probably do reflect material resource shortage and one need not engage in the expense, time and effort required to document the obvious.

An appropriate and scientifically acceptable perspective on the relationship between carrying capacity, resource abundance and conflicts between individuals and groups requires a more realistic and empirically demonstrated assessment of a culture's ecological circumstances than is found in most contemporary materialist formulations. It simply cannot be assumed that conflicts in band and village societies must necessarily be driven to the level of allegedly scarce material items, the search for which ends in futility where groups are in phase one of their expansion. This has as much application in archeological studies of conflict as it does in contemporary ethnographic studies of band and village societies (Haas, this volume).

VARIATIONS IN INDIVIDUAL POTENTIAL FOR SURVIVAL AND REPRODUCTION

Anthropological textbooks at both the introductory level and advanced level make the point that, in general, individuals in band and village societies live in a condition of relative egalitarianism. This is usually stated to make the point that in state-organized societies one's place and influence in society is largely determined by factors that are not found in kinship-organized society, such as inherited rank and privilege on the one hand, and wealth and the power that wealth confers on the other. To paraphrase Morton Fried, one of the well known anthropological experts on "egalitarianism," in such societies there are as many positions of prestige as there are people capable of filling them (1967). One's position and status in egalitarian societies are determined primarily by age, sex and whatever personal charisma one happens to possess.

Considering the overall evolution of culture and the vast differences in the nature and kinds of components and variables that lead to status differentiation in industrial compared to kinship-dominated societies, Fried's assessment is heuristically useful for broad comparative purposes. When one must focus on and use the individual as the basic unit of analysis, however, as my approach requires, this notion of status is neither very useful nor very accurate.

When one begins to examine the differences in authority, influence and sheer "presence" between individuals in particular kinship-organized societies, the above notion of "egalitarianism" is, in fact, misleading (Chagnon 1979b; 1982). Being organized by kinship and dominated by nepotistic interactions, many so-called egalitarian societies include individuals who vary along an axis of "funds of kinship power" that has enormous implications for their survival and reproductive interests. The abducted woman from a distant village has no

90

kinsmen in her new home. If she is abducted with a dependent infant, that infant has only one relative in the village. Her subsequent children, at best, have only about half as many kin as their peers. The headman's son, on the other hand, may be related to virtually everyone in the village.

The age and sex of one's relatives are also important. Someone with many adult male relatives has an advantage in some contexts compared to another with many adult female relatives. Descent group membership is also important. Having many relatives is less important for some somatic and reproductive purposes than having fewer, but mostly agnatic, relatives. In a word, the kinship environment within which one is born, grows up and strives has a potentially large effect on survival and reproduction in most so-called egalitarian societies. In this sense, one's status is in fact a product of *inherited* attributes, the kinship nexus one inherits at birth (Chagnon 1982). In a word, people differ dramatically in their ability to influence others and impose their wills on them in kinship-organized societies. The reason they are able to do so is because some individuals have a larger nexus of coresident kin they can depend on. An example, drawn from my studies of village/kinship variation among the Yanomamö, is provided in Figure 4.4

RELATIVES PER PERSON IN A TYPICAL YANOMAMÖ VILLAGE

What Figure 4.4 shows is that a few people have almost no coresident kin (Quartile 1), many have substantial numbers of kin (Quartile 3), and some are related to nearly everyone in the village (Quartile 4). In addition to relative numbers of kin, it is important to know the kinds of kin people have (agnatic, matrilateral, ascending generation, etc.) and how this affects their decisions to take sides in disputes, tender aid to others, and, in general, develop social strategies of interaction that potentially affect their somatic and reproductive interests (Chagnon 1979a; 1979b; 1980; 1982). The study of conflicts in band and village societies must begin, therefore, with a comprehensive knowledge of genealogical and matrimonial relationships, for a large number of conflicts of interest begin at this level of bio-social relationship.

It should be clear from the discussion of the components of reproduc-

91

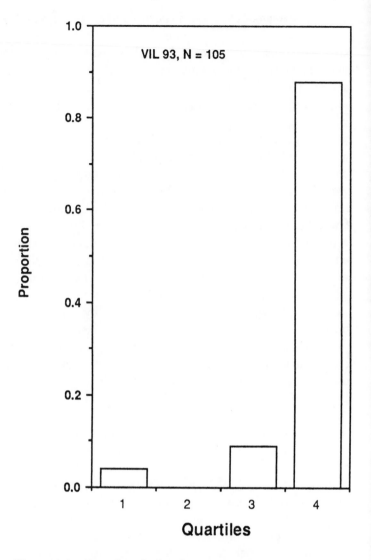

Figure 4.4.: Quartiles of relatedness in a typical Yanomamö village.
Quartile 1 = fraction of the village members related in at least one way to 25 percent or less of the village members; Quartile 2 = fraction of the village members related in at least one way to 26 to 50 percent of the village members; Quartile 3 = fraction of the village members related in at least one way to 51 to 75 percent of the village members; Quartile 4 = fraction of the 105 village members (0.88) related in at least one way to 75 percent or more of the village members (data from Chagnon, 1988a, p. 987).

tive effort described above that kinship relatedness is an important variable in understanding not only conflicts of interest, but the relative abilities of individuals to draw on and exploit their neighbors in many social ways. Kin selection theory (Maynard Smith 1964; Hamilton 1964), one of the fundamental components in new Darwinian approaches to understanding social behavior, requires an assessment of the individual's distribution of kin of varying degrees of relatedness. Therefore, the study of conflicts and conflict resolution necessitates at the outset a comprehensive study of genealogy and reproductive accomplishments of all individuals as a background matrix against which choices in individual actions can be assessed. "Kinship" in this context does not mean only what people "call" each other or the ideas they have about proper behavior vis-à-vis some relative. It also requires an understanding of the probable biological (genealogical) connections between individuals and the extent to which their patterns of sharing, helping, contending, etc. are consistent with their overlapping genetic (genealogical) interests (cf. Chagnon and Bugos 1979; Chagnon 1981).

Indeed, one can proceed in a study of nepotism with just the information about genealogical relatedness and be completely ignorant of what people call each other or say about how they should treat particular kinds of relatives. Inversely, it would be impossible to make a meaningful study of nepotism knowing only what people call each other irrespective of or in spite of the genealogical connections that might obtain between then. Kinship as commonly discussed by anthropologists is not the same thing as genealogy, and "kinship studies" can be (and frequently are) made with no reference to genealogy. Studies of nepotism and kin selection *cannot* proceed in that fashion. Ideally, one should have both genealogical data and kinship classification/ideology data, for the connections between them can be shown to be relevant for many kinds of behavior (cf. Chagnon 1988b).

STRIVING FOR ESTEEM AND PRESTIGE

Kinship and genealogy become significant in understanding conflicts for a variety of reasons. They are as a result central variables in understanding the causes, development and escalation of violence in kinship-organized band and village societies. However, in addition to the variations in one's relative influence in his/her society as determined by the size and structure of one's kinship nexus, individuals are significantly different in their ability to achieve prestige and status through chronic or episodic acts of competition in various arenas of social life. There is marked variation from one society to another in the extent to which there is competition among individuals (viz. Benedict's classic work on patterns of culture [1934]). In some, it is so negligible that ethnographers insist that it is irrelevant or does not occur at all (see Gibson and Gregor, this volume).

This is one area in which we must do more work. Inter-individual conflicts of interest presumably exist in all societies and individuals must therefore resolve them somehow and, we would predict, in fashions that benefit *them* rather than others. In some societies, it might be very difficult to distinguish the effects that kinship power confers on individuals from those attributes of esteem and prestige that are achieved apart from or in spite of the kinship nexus. Among the Yanomamö, virtually every village I have studied is led by headmen who invariably come from the largest descent groups in the village. Yet in a large number of villages there are men from distant, essentially unrelated villages who, through their individual skills and political abilities, rise to high levels of esteem in spite of their comparatively small number of relatives (see Chagnon 1983 [1968b], discussion of the man named Rerebawä). In many societies, competition for or striving for high esteem and prestige is obvious and often spectacular.

The benefits for achieving high esteem in most band and village societies normally entail polygynous marriage and/or a more desirable position in the food/labor exchange networks, which can ultimately be related to differential access to mates and differential reproductive success. Among humans, prestige leads to influence and power, and power appears to lead to high reproductive success. Betzig (1986) has convincingly demonstrated this in her analysis of a larger number of "despotic" societies, but the extent to which this is true, statistically, in a significant sample of egalitarian societies must yet be established. The correlation has been demonstrated for the Yanomamö in several of my own publications (Chagnon 1979b; 1980; 1988a). Large numbers of ethnographic descriptions of tribal societies suggest that polygyny, one spoor of high reproductive success, is usually associated with leadership or other positions of prestige, but none of them document statistical differences in reproductive accomplishments of polygynous versus nonpolygynous males. Indeed, variations in male reproductive success have been documented in only a few instances for *any* species.

94

Striving for prestige entails taking risks that lead to greater or lesser amounts of success for particular individuals: there will be winners and losers. Those who lose are all the more anxious to establish or reestablish their position. As a result, conflicts and fighting arise, often over issues that appear to have no obvious direct relationship to either somatic or reproductive interests. Whether or not they ultimately do can usually be established by documenting variations in survivorship among the offspring of the successful, as well as differences in numbers of mates and numbers of offspring among the losers and winners, and the comparative reproductive success of the adult offspring of the esteemed (Chagnon and Hames 1983). Among the Yanomamö, and many other similar societies, the individuals with the highest esteem are the headmen. One demonstrable attribute of headmen is the significantly larger number of wives they have (or have had) and, as a consequence, the larger number of offspring they sire (Chagnon 1979b). While the kinship nexus of headmen is favorable to their attempts to achieve high status, who among several eligible adult brothers wins the headmanship is decided principally on the basis of differences in their personal abilities.

There are clearly several routes to prestige and esteem among the Yanomamö and, presumably, in other egalitarian societies as well, and these can lead to differential reproductive success. A recent analysis of marital and reproductive correlates of Yanomamö men who are *unokais* (those who have killed someone) indicates that they, compared to same-age non-*unokai*, have over twice as many wives and over three times as many children (Chagnon 1988a). Whether or not *unokais* have other attributes such as greater industriousness in gardening, more skill in diplomacy or trading, greater adeptness at oratory or shamanism, etc. is not clear at this point. I believe that it is safe to say, however, that headmanship and being *unokai* are prestigious statuses among the Yanomamö and they are correlated with both striving and differences in reproductive success.

EXAMPLES OF CONFLICTS AND WARS GENERATED FROM CONFLICTS OF INDIVIDUAL INTEREST

Manipulating kin classification for reproductive advantage

Rather than present a lengthy catalogue of all the possible reasons and conditions that illustrate the above argument, a few examples will suffice. Individuals in most band and village societies will have kinsmen who are of an age appropriate for marriage; however, for reasons having to do with age at first marriage, age at first reproduction of males and females, and duration of reproductive life-span by sex, these kinsmen will fall in a genealogically defined generation that makes them an ineligible mate. By contrast, one's "genealogically eligible" potential mate might be 25 years older or, perhaps, yet unborn (Chagnon 1982; 1988b).

In Yanomamö society, these chronic problems are resolved by constantly manipulating kinship classifications to keep age and generation in relative harmony. People reclassify kin and move them "up" or "down" in generation. It is not done randomly and, as one might expect from evolutionary theory, the pattern seems to be such that the manipulators are reclassifying kin in such a way as to increase their reproductive opportunities. Men reclassify ineligible females (aunts, sisters, nieces, etc.) into cross-cousin categories (eligible as wives and mates) more than would be expected by random chance (Chagnon 1982, 1988b). While this is interesting in and of itself, it also has implications for conflict and violence, and ultimately, the development of warfare between groups.

When an individual male decides to reclassify a 15-year old girl from the "correct" category "niece" to an "incorrect" category "wife" with the intent of marrying her, he is in fact threatening a marriage possibility of another male who is legitimately related to that same girl as "wife." (The reclassifications are usually initiated by male ascendants rather than by the young man himself.)

In 1960, a few years before I began studying the village of Bisaasi-teri, such a manipulation took place and eventually led to the fissioning of the village into two independent groups. The reclassification led to an illegitimate marriage (from one point of view, the loser's) and this deprived someone of an eligible and legitimate mate in a society where females are scarce and competition for them rigorous. The man who initiated the reclassification was very prominent as he was one of the leaders from the largest descent group in the village (Chagnon 1968b, 1988b). In other words, he had a good many predictable and dependable supporters who took his side in the ensuing fights and arguments. At least some of these gained directly in reproductive potential as a consequence by being then eligible to marry hitherto prohibited women. Several marriages by his sons resulted from that manipulation.

Once separated by the fission, other conflicts of similar genre developed. Today (1988), the two groups are on semi-hostile terms and on the verge of mortal violence as a consequence of the latest incident contributing to their bad relations – a rape that occurred in 1986 involving men from one of the groups and a girl from the other. Thus far, one man has been shot in the leg with an arrow, and nearly died from the wound. Several men have been shot from a distance with shotgun blasts, none being fatal. Both groups have verbally threatened to kill any member of the other group should he come into the other group's village. While they live only a half-mile or so apart, their political relationships are quickly developing into one of out-and-out shooting. One of the groups, although it has a nearly new shabono and new gardens, is beginning to clear additional gardens at a site much further away and plans to move there as soon as practicable. Once the move is completed, it will take very little additional provocation to precipitate killing, i.e., intervillage warfare.

While it would be misleading to simply claim, if a "war" develops, that it was caused by a kinship reclassification, it would be equally misleading to argue that reproductive striving is irrelevant to understanding the development of that war.[1] And it would be meaningless to engage in a pursuit for some allegedly scarce material resource that "must" lie behind the war.

Status and leadership can be shown to vary with size, extent and structure of one's "fund" of kinship power in the local community. People cannot do much to change the luck of the draw that birth conferred on them (see below). Though for the Yanomamö, they can elect to fission away from a larger group and create a village whose kinship composition is more congenial to one's somatic and reproductive interests (Chagnon 1974; 1979a; 1982) or, as just described, redefine some kinds of relatives as other kinds (Chagnon 1982; 1988b). But individuals among the Yanomamö, and many other societies, strive to enhance their reputations and defend them jealously. They do this not only for their own prestige, but ultimately for the benefit of close kin and preferred neighbors.

An enormous amount of intimidation and "status testing" goes on in Yanomamö society (Chagnon 1966; 1968b; 1974). Individuals, particularly men, attempt to improve their position in what might be considered to be a complex dominance hierarchy of prestige and power.

While there are many kinds of routes up this hierarchy, dissent can be provoked by failing to constantly defend one's position, even over the most trivial of matters or incidents. I mentioned how one can diminish a peer during a meat distribution by simply altering the order in which the meat is distributed, or by giving a slightly less desirable portion to a prominent competitor. Verbal insults are common, and "bad mouthing" someone is a way to diminish them before others. Clubfights and chest-pounding duels are frequently provoked when one group hears that another has been accusing them of cowardice.

To a larger extent, the prestige and independence of a village is a function of the prestige and coercive abilities of its political leaders. Political leaders strive to maintain their reputations for many reasons, one being that quickness of response depresses a would-be intimidator's willingness to escalate insults and demands (Chagnon 1988a). An uneasy peace is preferable to either a costly war or acquiring a reputation that invites predation. It should be noted that men of prestige also enjoy the highest levels of polygyny and reproductive success (Chagnon 1974; 1979b; 1988a). Thus, political leaders gain in several ways by being quick to demonstrate their willingness to fight and take mortal risks. In such a milieu fights and wars are provoked largely by acts of intimidation and status testing that get out of hand and end in unanticipated fatalities. An example is in order, one that, as in the previous one, entails a long history of earlier conflicts between the groups.

A headman's prestige and reaction to insult

In about 1980, a particularly devastating war developed between the village of Bisaasi-teri, the group I described in my 1968 monograph *Yanomamö: The Fierce People*, and the village of Daiyari-teri, a smaller neighboring group described by Lizot (1985) in *Tales of the Yanomami*.[2]

The war was provoked by a trivial incident in 1981 that amounted to a gross insult of the Bisaasi-teri headman, but its ultimate origins go back to the mid-1950s. The Daiyari-teri are members of a larger population bloc that includes a village called Mahekodo-teri. The Bisaasi-teri had just recently fissioned from their parent group, the Patanowa-teri, and were attempting to establish themselves as an independent, viable village. To this end, they were cultivating alliances with unrelated villages to their south. Unfortunately, their erstwile allies invited them to a feast and treacherously massacred many of the men and abducted a number of their young women. The survivors fled to and took refuge among the Mahekodo-teri (Chagnon 1968b). The Mahekodo-teri, acting from a position of strength, took further advantage of them and appropriated a number of their young women. At the same time, they also tendered them sufficient aid to enable the Bisaasi-teri to recover and regain their independence by making new gardens further away from their enemies. The Daiyari-teri, congeners of the Mahekodo-teri, eventually located their village at a site within a day's walk of the Bisaasi-teri. For the next decade or so, relationships between the two groups varied from friendship and amity to neutrality to overt hostility verging on warfare. In 1965, for example, the Bisaasi-teri spread rumors that the Daiyari-teri were cowards. The Daiyari-teri responded by demanding to have a chest-pounding duel with the more numerous Bisaasi-teri to show them – and the world at large – that they were valiant and would not tolerate insults to their reputations. From that point until about 1980, relationships between the two groups were strained, but the Daiyari-teri were not powerful enough to threaten the Bisaasi-teri militarily. Eventually, visiting between them resumed and they became allies, albeit suspicious allies.

   In 1980, the Bisaasi-teri headman decided to take his village on a camping trip up the Orinoco river, near the village of Daiyari-teri. Since they were allies, this headman decided to visit their village and ask them for plantains, a commonly expected courtesy between allies under such circumstances. When he reached the village, there were a large number of Daiyari-teri children and youths playing in the water. They began pelting the headman with mudballs and sticks, harassing him in that fashion all the way into the village – an insult of the first order. What apparently made matters serious was the fact that the Daiyari-teri adults neither scolded the youths nor prevented them from continuing their abuse. The Bisaasi-teri headman left, angry, and without plantains. He moved his people back to the village and cancelled the camping trip.

   Some time later, perhaps a few weeks, a large number of Daiyari-teri men visited the Salesian Mission at the mouth of the Mavaca river, immediately across the Orinoco from the Bisaasi-teri village. The Bisaasi-teri spotted them immediately, and challenged them to a fight. They attacked them first with clubs and, ironically, pelted the Daiyari-teri men with lumps of hardened cement that had been discarded from a house-construction project on the mission side of the river. Considerable injury to the Daiyari-teri resulted, and they left for home, bleeding from their numerous wounds, threatening to get revenge. They eventually sent word to the Bisaasi-teri that they wanted to settle their dispute in a chest-pounding duel. The Bisaasi-teri enthusiastically accepted the challenge and went to their village to feast and fight. In the ensuing duel, two young men were killed. The Bisaasi-teri departed immediately, but were intercepted by Daiyari-teri archers who managed to wound one of them with an arrow. Shortly after, the Daiyari-teri raided and wounded a Bisaasi-teri man.

Some weeks later, one of the young men in Bisaasi-teri went on a fishing trip with an employee of the Venezuelan Malarialogia service. He was warned not to go on the trip because it was too close to the Diayari-teri village. He went anyway. While they were fishing from their canoe that night, a party of Daiyari-teri men discovered them and killed the young man with a volley of arrows, three of which struck him in the neck. The Bisaasi-teri recovered his body the next day and, in the ensuing weeks, mounted several unsuccessful raids against the Daiyari-teri, who had fled inland to escape retaliation. The Daiyari-teri eventually returned to their village.

The Bisaasi-teri called on their allies to join them in a raid. One of the allied groups, Iyawei-teri, attacked a day before the main group. The Bisaasi-teri raiding party reached the Daiyari-teri village a short time after the Iyawei-teri raiders had struck and fled, leaving two Daiyari-teri men dead. The Bisaasi-teri and their allies, armed with both arrows and shotguns, surrounded the village and set it ablaze, forcing the inhabitants to flee to the bank of the Orinoco river. There they took cover in a large pit they had dug into the ground in the event they were driven from their village by raiders – as they were. They were bombarded with volley after volley of Bisaasi-teri arrows, shot into the air and descending, like mortar rounds, into the open pit. Those who raised up to return the fire were shot with both arrows and shotgun blasts. A number of the adult males were killed; at least two women were deliberately shot as well, and an undetermined number of children and infants were accidentally wounded by the volleys of arrows and random shotgun pellets some of whom later died. One of the fatalities was a woman who was a sister to the Bisaasi-teri headman and had been appropriated when the Bisaasi-teri took refuge with the Mahekodo-teri in the 1950s.

The survivors fled to an allied village when the raiders left. They solicited aid from the Mahekodo-teri and several other villages to mount revenge raids and eventually managed to ambush a young Bisaasi-teri couple who were on their way to the garden one morning, killing both of them. The Bisaasi-teri were satisfied that they had taught the Daiyari-teri a lesson and have no further interest in raiding them. However, they say they have every intention to exact revenge on the Mahekodo-teri for the two most recent killings and are presently waiting for the most opportune time to do so.

Discussion

In both of the above examples, the notion of prestige and status figure prominently and must be taken into consideration in explaining the conflicts. Moreover, the conflicts are not simply isolated incidents, provoked by a specific single act. They are continuations of smouldering antagonisms that originate in a multitude of previous acts, some involving seduction and male/male competition for women, others involving reactions to insults or testing of resolve and status, and others are purely vindictive and motivated by vengeance. Among the Yanomamö, it is relatively easy to relate all of these variables to reproductive striving, for a village that fails to respond to aggressive acts, even verbal ones, soon finds itself victimized by stronger, more assertive allies who translate their advantage into appropriating reproductively valuable females.

For the leaders, the reproductive rewards for aggressiveness are even more obvious. The above Bisaasi-teri headman, for example, has had 8 wives during his lifetime and has sired 25 children by them (not all survived). At present (1988), he has two wives, one of whom is still young and able to produce his children. Finally, the followers, who take risks on behalf of and at the instigation of leaders, benefit in both somatic and reproductive terms as well. By complying with the suggestions and directions of the leaders, they contribute to the reputation of the village, as well as to their own reputations as individuals. By thus establishing the credibility of their claims for being valiant and aggressive, they also manage to prevail in a milieu of chronic aggressive threats and enjoy relatively secure and predictable somatic and reproductive opportunities compared to those who fail to make such demonstrations.

101

The overall aggregate of groups comprised of competitive status-seeking individuals has its social costs as well. The most obvious one is a domestic condition fraught with relatively constant stress and bickering, particularly in larger groups whose kinship composition might favor factionalism. The chronic fissioning of larger groups along lines of close kinship (Chagnon 1974; 1979a) is a response to this internal social stress and competition whenever external threats are sufficiently low to permit them.

SUMMARY

A synthesis of the most useful attributes of cultural ecological theory from anthropology and selected aspects of new Darwinian theory can be developed to shed light on the genesis and ontogeny of conflicts and intergroup warfare in band and village societies. Such a synthesis is not only possible but necessary, given that the traditional materialist approaches to the study of primitive warfare have failed to take into consideration all the relevant factors that generate conflict in such societies. They have unnecessarily demanded that conflicts, warfare in particular, be viewed as emanating, ultimately, from conflicts about the material conditions that affect the survivability of whole communities or groups.

While many specific insights from recently developed theory in evolutionary biology are germane to the proposed synthesis, several in particular have been presented here as departure points in the development of the synthesis. First, evolved conflict – warfare – should be viewed in terms of its developmental history, which often traces back to conflicts of interest between specific individuals. Warfare is thus seen as only a sub-category of the more comprehensive category labeled, simply, conflict. Second, individuals are viewed as striving to maximize their well-being, esteem, and biological success, with the latter considered to be the ultimate goal of evolved organisms in any species. To this end, they are viewed as developing lifetime social strategies that affect their decisions and now they allocate their efforts. Efforts, in turn, are analytically partitioned into two basic categories: those that pertain to survival as such, and those that pertain to reproduction.

Since no two individuals are genetically identical (save, of course, for identical twins), there will always be conflicts among individuals for somatically and reproductively useful resources and opportunities. Individuals strive to appropriate both, either for themselves, or for their immediate kin or those neighbors with whom they share overlapping reproductive interests. Kin selection theory predicts that individuals will, in most circumstances, favor kin over non-kin, and close kin over distant kin depending on the costs and benefits, measured, ultimately, in inclusive fitness terms. Non-kin will be favored to the extent that their cooperation enhances the benefactor's inclusive fitness interests, as would be the case, for example, in favoring actual or potential wife-givers or resource-givers.

Resource abundance and the model of carrying capacity must be more carefully considered in order to arrive at a reasoned and informed position regarding the extent to which competition is generated principally or predominantly over scarce material (somatic) resources, or whether it is more reasonable to seek the causes of conflict elsewhere. In the absence of empirical data that describes the quantity, quality, accessability and predictability of material resources, one can and should consider additional evidence that sheds light on possible resource issues. These may include population growth, population densities, time and effort expended in obtaining material resources, comparative health of individuals, etc. This kind of more comprehensive research strategy is preferable to simply advocating on first principles alone, that conflict ultimately entails contests over scarce material resources.

Status differentials among individuals are more numerous and dramatic in so-called egalitarian societies than many contemporary theoretical arguments from anthropology assert. These are, in part, inherited in a very real sense. One's fund of kinship power is fixed largely at birth. One cannot, for example, pick his or her parents or descent group, nor alter the reproductive facts of the ascending generations, i.e., how many kin of what kinds or degrees of relatedness he or she will be surrounded by at birth and among whom he or she grows up and must interact socially with on a daily basis. An individual can, as he or she matures, modify the "luck of the kinship draw" (Chagnon 1982) in a number of limited ways, but all of them require the cooperation of others (Chagnon 1980; 1981). One way is to produce children, but Ego must first find a mate, i.e., have elders who will find a mate for him or her. Another way is to "manipulate" kinship classifications and move people in kinship categories that are socially and reproductively more

103

useful, an act that requires the "endorsement" of co-villagers who will go along with the manipulation by altering their own kin usage to conform to that initiated by the original manipulator (Chagnon 1988a). A third way is for particular men to lobby for a village fission that will divide the larger group into smaller ones permitting Ego to surround himself with a mixture of co-resident kin more congenial to his social and reproductive interests (Chagnon 1981; 1982). One's ability to influence others, make demands, coerce, garner cooperation, etc. is often a direct function of the individual's kinship nexus and the kinds and numbers of kin-defined allies he or she can draw on to enforce his or her will. Conflicts of interest emerge and develop in a kinship matrix in most band and village societies, necessitating an understanding of genealogical relatedness, reproductive and marital histories, and other features of kinship and descent. In addition, high status and esteem usually confer advantage in matrimonial striving and, therefore, in reproductive success. It thus should be expected that individuals will compete over and have conflicts about relative degrees of esteem, conflicts that may, on the surface, reveal no obvious relationship to either somatic or reproductive resources. Measurements of relative status and relative degrees of reproductive success should be made to determine if there is a positive correlation between them.

An effective synthesis of the two bodies of theory is only now developing. What appears to be clear, however, is that the emerging synthesis is more capable of including a wider variety and larger number of specific variables that can be shown to be implicated in the genesis of conflict, violence and warfare. It can also provide explanations for them, as well as explanations for the institutional and behavioral means whereby humans cope with them and manage to live in a condition of relative harmony.

Notes

1. I subsequently learned that the two groups temporarily settled their differences in a club fight.
2. Lizot (1989) gives 1979 as the date of this war in a criticism of my 1988a publication where this war is briefly mentioned in a footnote. I will address Lizot's criticisms in a future publication.

5

Uneasy peace: intertribal relations in Brazil's Upper Xingu

THOMAS GREGOR

Tell the Americans about us. Tell them we are not wild
Indians who club people. Tell them we are beautiful.

SHUMION MEHINAKU

In 1884 the German explorer Karl von den Steinen descended the
Kuleseu River in Central Brazil to become the first European to visit the
tribes of the Upper Xingu basin. The peoples he discovered spoke four
different languages (Trumai, Tupi, Carib and Arawak), but longstanding political and social contact had created a remarkably homogeneous
Xinguano culture that endures today. The ten Xingu villages remain
separate and politically autonomous communities, with a strong sense
of their own uniqueness and positive qualities. Although the villages are
in some respects opposed to and suspicious of their neighbors, they are
intensely and elaborately involved with them through trade, intermarriage and intertribal ritual.

What is striking about the Xinguanos is that they are peaceful. During
the one hundred years over which we have records there is no evidence
of warfare among the Xingu groups. To be sure there have been
instances of witchcraft killings across tribal lines, and rare defensive

105

reactions to assaults from the war-like tribes outside of the Xingu basin. But there is no tradition of violence among the Xingu communities. In fact, the value systems of these communities are "antiviolent" in nature. Supernatural sanctions inhabit the expression of aggression, prestige is awarded to men who avoid conflict, and methods of socializing children discourage displays of anger. The entire pattern of intense, peaceful relationships between communities speaking different languages is rare if not unique in native South America and other culture areas of the world. This paper examines the puzzle: Why are Xinguanos peaceful?

AN APPRECIATION OF THE XINGUANO ACHIEVEMENT: THE SCARCITY OF PEACE

If by war we mean organized violence between separate communities, then humans are a warlike species. In attempting to compare the Xingu data with other similar societies I have been frustrated by the minimal numbers of peaceful peoples. Other researchers, who have combed the literature more systematically than myself, have reached the same conclusion. Thus Richard Sipes notes in his study of war and combative sports: "Relatively peaceful societies are not easy to find. I had to investigate 130 societies to find eleven, of which five were rejected because of insufficient information" (1973: 68). Similarly, Otterbein (1970) found only four peaceful cultures among the fifty in his study of the evolution of war. Turning to advanced, state-level societies the searcher for peace becomes even more disheartened. Thus Arthur Westing in a study of high fatality wars during the last eighty years, finds that on the average three such wars were occurring simultaneously, and that there was only one year in which none was being waged. He concludes: "The sad, but seemingly inescapable conclusion that I draw is that war remains as a routine, typical, and thus, in fact, normal human activity" (1982: 263).

In constructing a sample of peaceful cultures I have adapted the criteria of David Fabbro (1978), who has written one of the few comparative studies of peaceful societies. A peaceful society is one that is not involved in internal collective violence; one that exhibits relatively little interpersonal violence; one that provides no special roles for warriors; and one that has values and sanctions precluding violence as a means for resolving conflict. It is disheartening to realize that very few societies meet these criteria completely. Even those that do so in a

106

reasonable fashion, such as the Kung Bushmen (the "harmless people" of Elizabeth Marshall's popular account) are themselves perpetrators and victims of armed violence.[1] Peaceful societies are rare, and even when they are found peace is seldom, if ever, absolute. As shall become clear further on, this same caveat applies to the peoples of the Upper Xingu.

The societies that come closest to fitting the model of the truly peaceful culture are small in scale and primarily hunters are foragers. This conclusion is in keeping with research on war by Wright (1965: 68), Borch and Galtung (1966), Russell (1972), Eckhardt (1975: 56), Wiberg (1981: 114) and others who have positively associated war with community size and cultural development. Peaceful peoples also tend to be geographically isolated. Otterbein (1970), for example, finds that societies lacking in military organizations, such as the Copper Eskimo, the Dorobo and the Tikopians, live on islands, mountain tops, arctic wastelands and plateaus surrounded by malaria infested jungles. In some cases this isolation is a strategic adaptation to dealing with more aggressive societies that surround them. In most instances, however, peaceful societies appear to achieve their status by evading rather than solving the problems of intertribal relations. The tribes of the Upper Xingu are of special interest precisely because they do not conform to the profile of the typical peaceful society. Unlike most peaceful peoples they are sedentary with fairly advanced economies based on slash and burn horticulture (a system that is often associated with warfare [Vayda 1961]). The isolation characteristic of many peaceful societies is also not typical of the Xinguanos. Indeed, the unique feature of the area is the intensity and the richness of intertribal relations.

PEACE IN THE UPPER XINGU

The historical developmental of the Xingu system

How did the Xinguanos reach the compromises and make the social changes needed to create the culture of the region? At the moment, in the absence of systematic archeological data or an historically accurate oral tradition in the Xingu, we have only educated guesses. The first derives from Galvo's (1953) belief that the Xingu basin has served as a refuge for peoples menaced by more aggressive tribes to the north. We may speculate that the refugees, unwilling to stand their ground and do battle, were uniquely amenable to assimilation into a peaceful inter-tribal system. The geographically isolated Xingu basin may have thus filtered out warlike peoples. In opposition to this theory is Carneiro's (1961) intriguing hypothesis that the Xingu tribes were once warlike and organized at the chiefdom level. Malaria, introduced in the sixteenth century by the Europeans, depopulated the region, reduced competition for the now abundant land, and eventually produced the stable intertribal system we see today.

Although the origins of the Xingu peace remain uncertain, we can occasionally glimpse the past in today's social life. One of the major puzzles of the Xingu system, for example, is its tendency to assimilate other societies. The Xingu region is an area of "native acculturation," which has expanded to peacefully include tribes from four different language groups into a remarkably homogeneous Xingu culture. The Txicão, a Carib speaking tribe, is in the initial stages of joining the Xingu system and provides us with clues to how the process occurs. The Txicão village, formerly a single house in a clearing, is currently designed like the Xinguano communities. The Txicão cut their hair like Xinguanos, wear arm bands and earrings in the Xingu style, and carry on Xingu rituals. These changes have largely occurred within the last few years, and are all the more remarkable since the Txicão initiated contact with the Xinguanos by raiding their villages.

The events that led the Txicão to participate in Xingu culture began with a series of retaliatory raids by the Xinguanos against the Txicão. These raids, combined with epidemic disease, left the Txicão in such a desperate state that it became in their interest to establish peaceful relations with the Xinguanos. This process was facilitated by the tendency of all the Xingu villages to expel men accused of witchcraft. Two accused witches, using kinship ties to the Txicão established through previously kidnapped Xinguano children, are now living with Txicão wives in the Txicão community. They are agents of "Xinguification" and are systematically teaching their rituals, music and mythology. The Txicão do not yet clearly perceive that their own culture is in jeopardy. Rather they view what they are learning as a beautiful and interesting addition to their traditional culture. But it is also clear that if the process continues the Txicão will be full members of the Xingu system within a relatively short period of time. The Xingu system thus has a tendency to expand and bring unrelated groups into its orbit.

The structure of the Xingu peace and the system today

Peace in the Upper Xingu is a bimodal process which organizes tribes and individuals in enduring relationships, but at the same time sets them apart and keeps them at a social distance. Fundamental to this process are values that define the identity of individuals and tribes while setting expectations for participating in the system. My account of these values and institutions is primarily based on field work among the Mehinaku, but it is supported by research in most of the other communities, and by recent (1985) interviews with informants from all of the other language groups on the specific subject of war and peace.

In ancient times, according to one of the Xingu origin myths, the Sun created three races of humankind, including Xinguanos, "wild Indians" and whites. Recognizing the warlike nature of whites and wild Indians, he assigned them to separate worlds and even separate afterlives, well away from the headwaters of the Xingu River and the "Village in the Sky" above it. Ideally, according to the villagers, things should have remained this way, since the Xingu system was self-contained and autonomous. All the villagers' needs, whether for trade goods, spouses, or ritual participants, were met within the system. But the wild Indians and the white man came to look for the Xinguanos, out of a desire for plunder, trade, and sex with Xingu women. As a result, the system is more open than it has ever been before, with regular contact with both Brazilians and non-Xingu Indians. But these relationships are a source of profound ambivalence to the villagers, who look forward to a day (which may actually come fairly soon) when they can once again seal off their reservation from contact with the outside world.

Seen from within, the Xingu world is divided into ten single-village tribes, each of which is intensely engaged with its fellows. The total population is approximately 1200 persons, most of whom can personally recognize each other at least to the extent of identifying tribal and kinship affiliations. To a degree, social interaction is structured by membership in the four major language groups, with the most frequent contact occurring between members of the same group. Each language group is regarded as having a unique culture, and even a unique physical appearance. From the perspective of the Arawakan tribes, for example, all of the Carib tribes are described by one term ("Yanapukwa") and all are said to be alike in their language, their appearance, their penchant for rudeness, and even their preference for

109

barely cooked fish. Similar stereotypes label the other linguistic groups, and are reciprocated by them. At heart, however, the values of this peaceful intertribal system are cosmopolitan in character. Thus one of the Mehinaku villagers explained that to him the Carib language once resembled the barking of dogs and the slobbering of pigs. "But then I ate their food, had sex with their women, and learned their words.[2] Now I think their language is beautiful."

The values and institutions of peace

In June of 1985, I took the Mehinaku chief, who was then visiting Rio de Janeiro, on a tour of the city zoo. Each time we examined an unfamiliar animal, such as a giraffe or an elephant, he posed the same question: is it peaceful ("awujitsi") or is it ferocious ("japujaitsi")?

In the Xingu, this is the overriding moral question about individuals, relationships, and cultures. Above all, the concept of what is good is tied to peacefulness. The good man is circumscribed in his behavior, he avoids confrontations, and he rarely shows anger. In Mehinaku, his peaceful comportment is "ketepepei," a word that is also applied to a well-made craft object, suggesting a beauty and balance.[3] The good citizen is peaceful because he responds to the feelings of others. He refrains from injuring them because he would "feel sad" and sense their pain as if it were his own. The violent man lacks the requisite sensitivity, and kills and maims others, often without motive. He beats and torments his children, and "it is for this reason that his children do not sense others' feelings when they are adults." The difference between the peaceful Xinguanos and the warlike Indians and whites is lack of empathy.

If pressed, informants will offer additional reasons why peace makes good policy: "The peaceful man is treated peacefully by others; after death, only the peaceful man lives in the [paradisiacal] Village in the Sky." But in fact, peace as a philosophy is not substantially developed as a positively defined concept. The value of peacefulness in the Xingu appears to be a "terminal value," one that is at the apex of a pyramidal structure of instrumental and specific rules of conduct. As is common with such fundamental values, its rightness is taken for granted. Question a villager about the reasons for peaceful interaction, and he is more than likely to leave aside an abstract discussion of values and turn to the relationships that connect the Xingu tribes.

110

Intertribal relations: trade

The earliest observers to the Upper Xingu noticed that each of the tribes of the region made goods that they exported to the others: shell belts and necklaces, stone axes, salt, cotton, fish spears, hard-wood bows and ceramic pots. Some of the tribes maintained effective monopolies in these items, so that good trading relationships and peaceful relations was a necessary part of subsistence. Today, the monopolies persist, even though the system has been significantly eroded by the introduction of steel axes and aluminum pots.

Some of the specializations are ecologically based. The high quality clay used by the Waura for their ceramic pots is available primarily on their traditional territory. The shells used for necklaces and belts by the Carib speaking tribes are mainly accessible in areas near their villages. Other trade specializations are grounded in special knowledge or in substantial investment of labor. The Waura ceramic monopoly is the best example of the former, and the Mehinaku salt works, with its large, labor intensive plantings of water hyacinth[4] is an instance of the later type of monopoly.

What is particularly intriguing about the specializations is that none of them is fully defensible as a monopoly. Knowledge of ceramics diffuses across tribal boundaries as a result of intermarriage and visiting. Clay and shells could be obtained outside of Carib and Waura territory. The labor needed to make salt or other products is potentially abundant in all of the Xingu villages. The puzzle of the monopolies deepens when we consider that the trade goods are highly valued by the Xinguanos. Shell belts, necklaces and ceramic pots are the measure of a man's wealth. They are used to pay shamans in medical treatments and are public offerings for important rituals. Why not make these things at home?

When this question is put to villagers from different tribes, they respond with a list of sanctions that protect the monopolies. The men do not dare to get shells and make necklaces because they are fearful of Carib witches. The women would not make pots because they would be ridiculed by Waura women who are masters of the craft. No one would make salt for export because that would anger the Mehinaku. Thus put, the trade system seems to depend on institutions which separate villagers rather than those which bring them together. But in fact, the villagers also value the positive impact of intertribal relations. Trade means trust, since the items offered may not be reciprocated for several months or more. Trade means mutual appreciation, since craft objects, unlike our manufactures, are an extension of the self which the maker hopes will be admired. Trade is a social relationship that is valued in and or itself, and is a conscious reason for maintaining the monopolies. As one of my informants explained to me: "They have things that are really beautiful, and we have things that they like. And so we trade and that is good."

Intermarriage

All of my informants agreed that no one likes to live in villages other than his own. When, due to the extension of the incest taboo and the small size of the Xingu communities, a man can not find a suitable mate in his own community, he will marry into another village. Approximately thirty-five per cent of Xingu marriages are of this type, and given the reception of a typical in-married spouse it is a wonder that the percentage is that high. The first problem such a spouse faces is that of the language. The Xinguanos are proud of their languages which are the major maker of tribal distinctiveness. They are intensely ashamed when they try to speak a language they do not know. Consequently the villagers develop a passive understanding of the language of their spouses' community long before they speak it themselves. "You should not," explained one of my Mehinaku informants, "speak the language of your father-in-law."

An equally significant barrier to intertribal marriage is the pattern of hazing the in-married spouse. The villagers maintain that such a person "robs" them of potential mates, and properly he must pay a price by being made to suffer. Presently, in the Mehinaku, one young man is being tormented by his wife's lovers. His hammock has been filled with ashes, his canoe hidden and submerged deep in the swamp outside the village, and his garden has been vandalized. The level of ridicule and practical joking to which he is subject has reached such a pitch that he avoids the men's house and the center of the community: "I don't dare go there at all."

Finally, the in-married spouse must overfulfill his obligations to his in-laws. Onerous enough at home, in the host community these duties can amount to servitude. As one young man explained to me as I interviewed him in his father-in-law's house: "Each day I fish for my father-in-law, work in his garden, or build him a canoe. Today's work is done, but I can not lie in my hammock and seem to be lazy. I have to sit on this bench even though my back and shoulders ache."

The shame regarding language and the pattern of hazing is evidence of the centrifugal, oppositional nature of the Xingu villages. Intertribal marriage transcends the social distance by extending kinship across tribal lines and eventually producing bilingual children who can move fairly freely from one community to the other. These individuals are crucial links between the Xingu villages in establishing new marriages, in extending bonds of fictive kinship between the tribes, and in facilitating visits, rituals and trade. The result is that loyalties are divided along lines of kinship and residence and the barriers between the tribes are semi-permeable. In a conflict between persons from different communities kinship overrides common residence. The quarrel is simply not perceived as a community affair, and the disputants count only on the active support of their kinsmen.

The centripetal potential of intertribal marriage for producing one common Xingu society is most nearly realized in the Yawalapiti village, which now has more speakers of Carib and Tupi than Yawalapiti. For some of the villagers in other communities this is an unfortunate arrangement, which they compare to a noisy flock of birds of different species, none of whom can speak each other's language. But for all of the Xinguanos, intertribal marriage is a major source of peaceful contact with each of the Xingu villages.

The role of the chief

"One word from the chief and everyone does whatever they want" was John Cooper's summation of the chiefly role in societies of the South American lowlands. Among the Xingu societies the chief also has minimal authority (see Dole 1966), and yet he has a substantial expressive role in rituals, in making public speeches (Gregor 1977: 80–3), and in organizing trade sessions (Dole 1956–58). The most visible enactment of his special position occurs during the major intertribal festivals in the fall of each year. The focus of the rituals is the inaugural of new chiefs and the commemoration of chiefs who have died. The rituals require the participation of all the tribes, and are perceived by the villagers as an explanation of the peaceful nature of the Xingu system: "We don't make war; we have festivals for the chiefs to which all of the villages come. We sing, dance, trade and wrestle."

THOMAS GREGOR

Within the communities, the chief embodies the values of generosity, hard work, lawfulness, and peacefulness. Ideally, he never displays anger, never engages in gossip, never makes witchcraft accusations, and never participates in witch killings, no matter how severe the provocation. Psychologically, among the Mehinaku, he approximates the idealized father in that he represents prosocial values· and the repression of antisocial impulses. The villagers explain that the chief "takes care of," "provides for," and "gives food to his people," who are often referred to as "his children." Like the father of a family, the chief is said to be responsible for the moral tone of his community. He lectures "his children" in the evening and at dawn, correcting their behavior "the way a father lectures his son." According to the villagers, communities that split into rival factions (as has recently occurred to the Carib speaking Kalapalo) or lose ancient traditions (as has happened among the Trumai) have not heeded their chiefs, or have not had a chief worth heeding.

The role of the chief in the Xingu is not entirely limited to ceremony and speeches. With the advent of the Brazilian administration the tribes have moved much closer together, and increasingly interact in informal situations unstructured by the traditional rules of affinal kinship and ritual. On occasion, this contact has led to friction between groups of young men in different tribes who chop down trees on the paths between the villages and "borrow" other tribesmen's canoes and bicycles. The chiefs play an active role in negotiating a quick settlement to disturbances of this kind. More serious disagreements, such as allegations of theft and witchcraft, are beyond the scope of the chief's formal authority and must be resolved by the disputants themselves.

What strikes the observer of the Xingu chief is that despite his role as a negotiator, the status is elaborated far beyond what might be expected from societies with an essentially unstratified political system. The elevation of the chieftainship, particularly its ceremonial component, appears to be a means of celebrating the peaceful intertribal system rather than the chief's local authority.

As expressed in institutions, the Xingu peace system is based on mutually rewarding ritual participation, the exchange of trade goods and spouses, and a conscious appreciation of the values of a peaceful culture. But in fact this is only half the picture. The Xingu peace relies heavily on institutions that separate the tribes and preoccupy the villagers with thoughts of death and violence. If we question a villager

114

about the benefits of peace, he quickly turns to the dangers of unusual but socially important events, such as witch killings, battles with wild Indians, wife-beatings, rapes, physical punishment of children, and the sadistic killing and torture of animals. In an important sense, the Xingu peace is negatively defined, emerging with greatest clarity in the culture of aggression and violence. This culture stands as a foil against which the Xinguanos forge a self identity, and aim their behavior towards the ideal of peace.

NEGATIVE PEACE: BLOOD, WITCHES, AND WILD INDIANS IN THE XINGU CULTURE OF VIOLENCE

Anger, aggression, violence

Anger is a disturbing and even frightening emotion for many of the Xinguanos. In Mehinaku, the term for anger ("japujapai") is applied metaphorically to things that are completely out of control, such as a raging fire, a thunderstorm, venomous wasps and a species of pepper so hot that it leaves anyone foolish enough to eat it writhing on the ground in agony. The villagers explain that they are not angry people, because they avoid foods that produce aggression: "We don't eat animals with blood or hot foods. Our food is 'tasteless' and so our bellies are never hot with anger."[5] When the villagers do become angry, they can release their feelings harmlessly: "When we are angry we wrestle; and then the anger disappears. The wild Indians don't know how to wrestle and so they club people instead." Finally, the villagers claim they are peaceful because of their unique culture: "In ancient times the Sun gave us ceramic pots, hoes and fishing arrows. He gave the wild Indians clubs, spears and arrows for killing men."

Blood

The villagers' attitude towards violence finds its expression in a logically developed set of ideas that are rooted in a theory of human biology, and shared by at least the Arawakan and Tupian tribes. Above all, blood is defiling. Most game animals are considered inedible because they "have too much blood." Fish are served well-cooked so that their blood is not visible. Persons who are bleeding – from serious wounds, ritual incisions or menstruation – are ritually impure. Killing is wrong, in part,

115

because the killing produces wounds and blood, and especially a bloody corpse, which is an object of fear and revulsion. Such a corpse is buried in a shallow grave outside the village, and its soul will never ascend to the Village in the Sky. The killer is also contaminated. The blood enters his body where it enlarges the face and abdomen, darkens the skin and produces a characteristic foul smell. Xinguanos who kill witches use special garments and medicines to distance themselves from the task, and when it is completed, they attempt to remove the defiling blood from their bodies by consuming medicines made from anatto. But, like Lady Macbeth who could never cleanse her hands of Duncan's blood, these "fiends for killing humans" cannot wholly wipe away the moral stain. Considered repulsive, they are deprecated as village leaders and rejected as lovers.

The "wild" Indians

Each of the Xingu languages has a word for non-Xingu Indians. In each language the term conveys emotions that range from fear, to distaste and contempt. The term, which my informants often translated as "wild," condenses in a single powerful symbol what the Xinguano is not and strives not to be. According to my Arawakan informants, the wild Indian is ugly. His skin is black and he rubs it with rancid pig fat. His hair is slick with grease. He wears lip disks and slobbers when he talks. He sleeps on the ground like an animal. He sits on the prow of his canoe and defecates into the water he drinks. He never bathes and has a foul smell.[6] He eats rats, toads, pigs and snakes.

Above all, the wild Indian is violent: "He beats his children. He rapes his wife. He shoots arrows at the white man's planes. He splits peoples heads with clubs. He kidnaps children and burns villages. He kills his own kin. War for him is a festival." Why is the wild Indian so violent? The answer is tradition: "It is because their grandfathers were violent." My informants also cited legends in which the Sun presented the wild Indians with weapons and a violent culture, and other origin myths in which some of the wild Indians were the offspring of a bestial union between a woman and a venomous snake (see Gregor 1985: 56–7). When I pressed further, they would explain the propensity for violence as deriving from their steady diet of bloody animals, and their inability to wrestle like the Xinguanos.

These answers are genuine explanations for the villagers, but

116

ultimately, the wild Indian is violent because that is his nature: "That is the way it is with them. Wild Indians are not people." It is for this reason that their outrages are described with an almost detached tone, as if they are so beyond the human pale that one can expect no better of them. In fact, in terms of cultural symbolism, the wild Indian approaches the status of an animal. Like an animal, he sleeps on the ground, defecates in the water, fornicates in strange positions, crawls with vermin, and reeks with foul odors. Like an animal, he attacks unpredictably, and without provocation.[7]

The Xingu villagers themselves have been the victims of unprovoked aggression from the wild Indians, most recently the Suya and Txicão. These raids (in which Xinguanos were shot and kidnapped and communities ransacked) precipitated violent defensive reactions. In one such assault approximately thirty years ago, individuals from several communities teamed up with a Brazilian to kill many Txicão men, women, and children. In explaining this departure from the normal pattern of peacefulness, my informants exphasized that the Txicão had attacked first and that they would attack again unless destroyed. Moreover, the moral gulf between the wild Indians and the Xinguano made it permissible. Nonetheless, the successful warriors took no trophies and received no special honor upon their return. According to some of my accounts, they had to consume medicines to rid themselves of the enemy's defiling blood before they were accepted in their villages. These defensive raids clearly show that the Xinguanos are fully capable of organized armed violence. Such warfare, however, is regarded by the villagers as a moral exception to the normal pattern of peaceful relations, and in fact seems to have been historically unusual.

Nowadays there is little daily contact between most of the Xinguanos and the wild Indian. Nonetheless, he is in their thoughts, their myths, and (among the Mehinaku) in their dreams as an image of now not to behave. "Keep still," a mother will say to her child as she attempts to remove his head lice, "or you will crawl with vermin like a wild Indian." Aggressive individuals find themselves compared to a lip-disked Kayapo Indian who the villagers find especially repulsive, and who has allegedly killed more than one hundred Indians and whites. The wild Indian thereby provides a dramatic moral counterpoint for the ideal of peaceful behavior. Contrary to appearances, he plays a role in the Xingu peace.

117

The witch

In ancient times, claim the Mehinaku, a malignant spirit fell to the ground. His body parts and adornment were apportioned among some of the villagers who discovered that they could use them as fetish objects to cause illness and death. These first witches passed their skills on to their sons by scarifying them with snake fangs and scorpion stingers. Gradually a culture of witchcraft developed, which allegedly persists in each of the Xingu villages. It is witchcraft, the personal malevolence of individual villagers, that causes death, disease, crop blights, windstorms, and plagues of mosquitoes.

Why are some villagers thought to practice witchcraft? Ultimately, the reasons are the same as those which motivate aggressive animals and wild Indians: "They don't have feelings for others; they are not people." But there is also an important difference between witches and wild Indians. The wild Indian, like an animal, has no social relationship with his victims. The witch, on the other hand, is a kinsman, a fellow villager, or another Xinguano. His motives for attacking others include revenge for the theft of his possessions, anger at sexual advances towards his wife, the affront of being left out of a distribution of fish, or almost any imagined slight. Nursing his grudge, the witch assembles a variety of fetishes charged with magical power. These include tiny bows and arrows, splinters of wood from ancient objects, potsherds believed to be from mythical times, and the hair clippings, clothes or personal effulvia of the victim. After the appropriate spells and magical acts, the victim falls ill and soon dies.

Both the literature on the Upper Xingu and my own research persuade me that witchcraft is seldom if ever actually practiced. The fear, however, is palpable in all of the communities in which I have worked. Among the Mehinaku, where I have lists of witchcraft accusations from more than half the adults in the village (Gregor 1977: 207–9), every adult male is suspected by a least some members of the community. It is small wonder that at night children may be called in so that they will not be shot with invisible arrows. The doors are locked, and fearful householders sometimes construct crude alarms of tin pot lids. By day, the village gossip network is alive with rumors and accusations of specific individuals. After a death, highly paid professional sorcerers and witch hunters (see Gregor 1977: 340–344) provide further support for the system of belief by identifying the witch and exhibiting his fetishes (which they themselves have secretly created for the occasion).

If the alleged victim of witchcraft is a young man, the accused may be executed by the kin of the deceased. Such executions occur approximately every two to three years in the Xingu (the last instance in 1984), and are a major limitation on our classification of the Xinguanos as truly peaceful. The killings themselves are brutal affairs, in which the victim is taken by surprise and slaughtered with arrows, machetes and rifles. Such executions are possible in an essentially antiviolent culture because of the killer's absolute conviction in the justice of his action, and the use of devices that separate him from his daily role as a peaceable Xinguano. These include a variety of magical spells and objects said to give him courage for the task, weaken his victim, and remove the polluting effect of the blood.[8]

The political impact of witchcraft beliefs and witch killings on Xinguano political institutions cannot be overemphasized. The most significant is the veneer of courtesy that marks ordinary relationships. Persons who despise one another seldom show anger. They are fearful of their enemy's witchcraft, and equally frightened of being held responsible as an alleged witch if he falls ill. Between tribes (especially from the perspective of Arawakan and Tupian groups), the pattern of false good manners is even more marked. The most dangerous witches are often said to live in other tribes, so it is well to receive them with courtesy when they visit. Those who are cautious avoid all informal (nonritual) visits to other tribes, limiting intertribal relations to relatively predictable and circumscribed ceremonial occasions.[9]

Perhaps the most interesting effect of witchcraft beliefs on the Xingu political system is to limit the power of the chief. Despite the symbolism of the peace-loving chief, his role is a threat to the balanced nature of the Xingu intertribal system. As things stand, he can only command the loyalty of his dependent kin. A dispute between him and members of another tribe is seen as a disagreement between the parties involved, not as an intertribal dispute. Were he able to command the loyalty of an entire community, an interpersonal quarrel between two local chiefs could evolve into a full fledged war. But even a powerful Xingu chief knows he must tread softly in exercising his limited authority.

The chief is the point man in the political system, and as such he is inevitably the target of jealous accusations by the community at large. In the midst of his noncontroversial, self-depreciating public speeches, he imagines his rivals' resentment. When he has actual control of individuals and resources (as is becoming increasingly true of two of the chiefs who are linked to the Indian agency administration) he lives in chronic anxiety: "Let us say that I distribute gifts. I keep nothing for myself or my family, but there is still not enough to go around. I explain to those who received nothing that there is no more left. They say 'fine, that is all right, we understand.' They say the right things, they speak beautifully. But at night they sort their fetishes and plan to murder me and my family." Thus the imagined witch curbs the power of the chief, retains the essentially egalitarian basis of local organization, and preserves the symmetrical and balanced relationships among the different tribes.

But at what a price! Within the villages the apparent good fellowship of everyday life masks murderous intent. Today in the Xingu villages there are individuals who are marked for execution. During my last field trip in December of 1985 two of them were too frightened to leave their own houses. Others moved erratically from village to village in the vain hope that they would be accepted elsewhere. An even larger group now live off the reservation among the wild Indians and on backwoods Brazilian farms and ranches – completely cut off from their kinsmen and their traditional culture.

The cost of witchcraft beliefs can go beyond openly accused witches to include virtually everyone, no matter how well established as good citizens, no matter how well protected by large numbers of male kin. Such is the system among the Mehinaku, and I believe in the other villages as well, that everyone will from time to time be gossiped about and come under suspicion. As one man explained: "I am not a witch. But I am frightened that people think I am. Have you noticed that children will not come close to me? It is because their parents have said that I am a witch."

Witchcraft beliefs have the potential of dragging the Xinguanos into an abyss of accusations, killings, and ultimately a Hobbesian war of "everyone against everyone." But even though the villages smolder with anger, only rarely does the violence degenerate into a vengeful feud. I have documented a few instances in over fifty years of Xingu witch killings where the conflict continued to spiral after the initial execution, but in no case was there more than one additional death. In general, wider conflict is restrained by the careful choice of the victim. Though apparently selected magically, he is killed only when he and his kin are substantially outnumbered by the killers. If he is too strong, they may employ a sorcerer to kill him magically, or they will simply seek revenge through malicious gossip.

The villagers are conscious that the system of revenge is atavistic and violates the essential Xingu value of peacefulness. One of the most powerful individuals in the Xingu communities, a man whose own father was killed as a witch, is presently conducting a personal crusade against the killings. He belittles false shamans, and uses the gossip network to discredit their accusations. "I would not kill a witch even if he killed my sons," he explained. "There is no way to know with certainty who is guilty. Most of those who have been killed were needlessly killed. Their deaths were ugly affairs." Conscious awareness of how the system functions thereby limits the violence in the Xingu, and offers some hope for an evolution towards a more rationally based political system.

WHY ARE XINGUANOS PEACEFUL?

War makes rattling good history; but peace is poor reading.

THOMAS HARDY

Peace theory

Comparative research on the cause of war and peace is based on the hidden premises that peace is an expectable state of affairs in human relationships were it not for conflict. Peace is the absence of conflict, and it is conflict that needs to be explained (cf. Haas, this volume). My own perspective is the reverse. Political systems are so volatile and war is so contagious that its existence should occasion little surprise. It is peace that needs special explanation. But it is here that social science lets us down, since peace is seldom studied much less explained. A case in point is the *Journal of Peace Research*, the foremost interdisciplinary journal devoted to peace studies. Despite its title, the *Journal* is mainly dedicated to the study of conflict, conflict resolution and the causes of war. Thus the editor sadly notes: "It turns out that of the approximately 400 articles [published in the *Journal*] over seventeen years, a single one has been devoted to the empirical study of peaceful societies with a view to find out what seemed to make them peaceful" (Wiberg 1981: 113).

With few ethnographic examples to study, peace theory is a highly speculative and essentially intuitive sector of social science research. The simplest of the theories are those of "negative peace" (Galtung

121

1968: 487). Negative peace in a pure form is based on minimal relationships: "Good fences make good neighbors." The classic form of negative peace is deterrence, a conscious political policy that goes back at least as far as ancient Greece and remains an active part of military doctrine. The efficacy of deterrence in non Western societies is attested to by a substantial number of anthropological studies, such as Evans-Pritchard's (1940) examination of the "ordered anarchy" of stateless societies.

Positive peace depends on the exchange of goods, services and peoples. One of the effects of exchange is to create loyalties which are divided by both territory and bonds of interest, such as kinship and economics. These competing allegiances attract a natural constituency in favor of maintaining peaceful relations (Colson 1953, Gluckman 1955, Murphy 1957). Moreover, exchange leads to the creation of a common culture. Parallel institutions in different societies can generate a consensus of values and stimulate the kind of diffuse emotionally meaningful relationships that would inhibit violence (Galtung 1968: 491).

Although all of these theories are intuitively reasonable, none of them survives the test of the cross-cultural data. Trade and culture homology, for example, are actually positively associated with war (Teft 1975). Intermarriage, which should lead to the most solid kind of alliances based on kinship also fails the test of cross-cultural comparison: intermarriage, kinship and war are actually positively correlated (Teft 1975: 701). Just as interpersonal violence often occurs in close relationships, the most intense conflicts seem to occur between polities that are similar in structure and intensely engaged with one another.

Peace theory is at an embryonic stage of development, but the apparent failure of the basic theorems of deterrence, exchange and cultural homology is surprising and counter-intuitive. A partial explanation of the failure may be that the theorems are to a degree contradictory. Those who champion cultural homology and exchange maintain that closeness, positive affect and diffuse attachment are the keys to peace. Promoters of the institutions of negative peace, on the other hand, see peace emerging from distance, fear, and even hostility. There is a possibility that both are partly correct. Intimate association and similar values mean that there are commonly valued objects to fight over, and that the fights will be internecine and vicious. Cultural distance and the mutual fear, however, create a highly volatile system in which a minor breach of the peace leads to a major conflict. We can conceive of a system – and I believe that the Xinguanos are a rare example – which is balanced at a stable midpoint between the institutions of positive and negative peace. At this point there is meaningful homology and exchange, and yet at the same time members of the system will be sufficiently concerned about the dangers of aggression to avoid any breach of the peace.

Why then do the Xinguanos live at peace? They do so because of their unique history in an ecological abundant and isolated region of South America. They maintain that peace because of the institutions and values which bring them together in meaningful relationships, including trade, intertribal marriage and the institution of the chieftainship. In an ideal world, this would be enough. But political life inevitably generates resentment, antagonism and fear. Among the Mehinaku these tensions have been built into institutions that may actually preserve the peace. Thus linguistic ethnocentrism and hostile stereotypes keep the Xinguanos at home and limit interaction between the tribes. The compelling images of violence and blood are constant reminders to the villagers of what they must avoid. The aggressive "wild Indians" stand as symbols of who they must not be. The beliefs in witchcraft are a powerful sanction that enforces courtesy among the villagers and limits the role of the chief. The irony of the uneasy Xingu peace is that the institutions which curb conflict are also those which painfully express fear and anger.

Notes

This paper is based on field research among the tribes of the Upper Xingu during the summer and fall of 1985. This work was supported by grants from the Harry Frank Guggenheim Foundation and the National Science Foundation.

1. Richard Lee (1979: 370–400) documents a long history of 22 feud-like killings among a small population of Kung. Although the demographic impact of such battles is hard to qualify, it would seem to account for at least as high a percentage of the death rate as war in our own society (about 1–2% of all deaths). The social and psychological impact of violence within Kung society may even be higher. If these are our measures of what constitutes war, then even "harmless people" qualify.
2. Speech, sexual relations, and eating are all closely connected activities in the conception of the human body.
3. The concept and importance of peacefulness is roughly similar to

that of "ifutisu," the term used by the Carib-speaking tribes in the Xingu system (see Basso 1973: 12–14).

4. Foliage from this plant is burned and the ash is leached with water to produce potassium chloride, the salt of the Xinguanos. As the villagers describe it, the Carib tribes' specializations in shell belts and necklaces should also be considered labor intensive monopolies, since they involve long and dangerous trips to find the shells, and arduous work to craft them into the final product.

5. All of the Xingu tribes eat fish, monkey, and a number of species of birds, avoiding most game animals.

6. The villagers are far more acutely attuned to odors than we are, and will often spit to reduce the sensation of a bad smell. In accounts of interaction with both wild Indians and forest animals (with whom wild Indians are believed to share a great deal in common) the Xinguanos often remark on the fetid smell.

7. Some of the Xinguanos claim to have seen a tribe called "The People Who Live Inside Trees" some distance to the east of their reservation. The tree people purportedly live in tree trunks, eat uncooked birds, wear no clothes, and speak in hoots and grunts. Symbolically, this cultureless tribe fulfills an animal-like potential which other wild Indians only approximate.

8. In 1972, I witnessed the killing of an Xingu Indian who was hacked to death with machetes as we tried to hold off his assailants in a room at the Indian Post. After the execution, the killers exhibited an icy calm. One approached me, pointed to the corpse and the wailing relatives and said: "You can take photographs now."

9. These findings are based primarily on my work with Tupi and Arawak speaking informants.

6
Raiding, trading and tribal autonomy in insular Southeast Asia

THOMAS GIBSON

In this paper, warfare in insular Southeast Asia is examined through the comparison of three groups of highland shifting cultivators.[1] The thesis is that the current social evaluation of violence and aggression within each group is the result of differing historical experiences within a loosely integrated regional political economy dominated by the institutions of slave raiding and coerced trade. Those groups positively disposed toward bellicosity are those which played a predominantly predatory role in the region, while those which are negatively disposed toward violence in any form were primarily prey. There is, however, nothing deterministic about the argument, for each concrete example represents only one of a number of logically possible responses to a given sequence of historical events. All three groups still retain a significant degree of autonomy over their internal political and ideological systems, and each must be seen as creatively responding to a changing set of external political and economic forces.

In the first part of the paper, a brief outline is provided of the general historical context in which these three societies have developed. In the second part, an overview of each society is given. In the third part, their respective attitudes toward violence, social ranking and indebtedness are

125

compared and contrasted. The paper concludes with a look at some of the implications of asking questions about human violence in the contexts of exploitation and of ritual attitudes, as opposed to those of aggression and competition for scarce natural resources.

SOUTHEAST ASIA AS A LOOSELY INTEGRATED REGION

Southeast Asia is a region in which the sea serves as the major means of communication and the land forms the major impediment to it. It is often easier to sail long distances from one island to another, than to walk across the smallest island (Reid 1984: 151). Dense rain forest and rugged mountains provide a natural barrier behind which tribal populations have been able to preserve a remarkable degree of autonomy into the modern era. This autonomy should not mislead us into assuming, on the one hand, a complete lack of contact between tribesmen and state systems. On the other, extensive trade also should not lead us into treating tribal areas and states as belonging to a single, tightly integrated system. It is precisely the importance of trade in the history of the region, associated with a pattern of predatory raiding, which has allowed the complex articulation of fundamentally diverse cultural and political systems. Violence and commodities are truly inter-cultural phenomena, which can have very different meanings for neighboring populations, and at the same time exert decisive influences on the development of each trading and raiding partner.

Scott (1986) gives an illuminating account of the political economy of the coastal Philippines at the time of Spanish contact. His account may serve as a model of one of the simpler forms of maritime economies in the region. The Philippines remained peripheral to the major international trade routes until relatively late. Even then it was primarily Chinese ships which traded into the islands, and not Philippine ships which sailed to China. As far as domestic Philippine trade is concerned, however:

Every community traded with other communities, and most of them did it by boat . . . the total impression is one of continual movements of rice, camotes, bananas, coconuts, wine, fish, game, salt and cloth between coastal barrios – to say nothing of gold, jewelry, porcelain and slaves . . . [Raiding] was the esteemed occupation of the able-bodied male who could afford it . . . Although raiders took booty both ashore and afloat when they could, their real object was

126

slaves . . . It is to call attention to . . . the mixed merchandizing of [this] commerce [that it] is here referred to as "trade-raiding." Potential customers for this trade in the Philippines were legion because the purchase of slaves was an ordinary means of investing surplus wealth . . . Filipino communities supplied most of their own slave labor by usury and penal action, but always preferred aliens for religious purposes – that is, sacrifice. (Scott 1982: 87–91)

Trade in the western parts of the achipelago had long been more sophisticated. The Sri Vijayan state dominated regional trade between the seventh century and 1025, when it was destroyed by the Chola dynasty of South India. Its rulers had been "content to provide a neutral commercial facility for the exchange of Western, Chinese, and Southeast Asian products" (Hall 1985: 210). In later times, local rulers of coastal states began to supplement their position as mere port custodians, servicing the ships of Chinese or Indian traders, by attempting to secure local products from their hinterlands for the international market. Prior to the fourteenth century these products were in large part gathered in the forests of the interior (items such as camphor, sandalwood and benzoin), or from the sea (items such as pearls) and had to be acquired from autonomous groups of shifting cultivators and huntergatherers (see Reid 1980: 236). After the fall of Sri Vijaya there followed a two hundred year period in which Arab, Indian and Chinese traders attempted to trade directly with the producers of the spices and forest products for which there was a growing demand both in south China and in Europe. However, according to Hall:

By the 13th century Asia's internal trade was back in the hands of Southeast Asians, as foreign merchants found it once again expedient to deal with Southeast Asia-based intermediaries at major international entrepots rather than attempting to deal directly with the people who controlled the sources of supply. (Hall 1985: 24)

One aspect of this process insufficiently emphasized by Hall is the fact that human labor power itself became a "local product" to be acquired from the hinterland for sale in the entrepots along the coasts.

Before indentured labor was developed in the nineteenth century, the movement of captive peoples and slaves was the primary source of labor mobility in Southeast Asia. Typically it took the form of transferring people from weak, politically fragmented societies to stronger and wealthier ones. The oldest, and demographically most important movement was the border raiding against animist swidden-cultivators and hunter-gathers by the stronger wet-rice cultivators of the river valleys . . . There seems little doubt that the majority of the Southeast Asian urban population prior to about 1820 was recruited in a captive state . . . Slavery was an important means whereby animistic peoples were absorbed into the dominant Islam of the city and coast. (Reid 1983: 28–29, 170–171)

Warren (1981) has amply documented the explosive growth of the Sulu state during the eighteenth and nineteenth century, a growth that was based upon a system of extracting forest and sea produce, by means of slave labor, for trade with Canton. The labor was itself "produced" by raiding the poorly defended populations of the Bisayan islands and Luzon. Again, Endicott (1983) provides a useful summary of what is known concerning slave raids against the Orang Asli of the Malay peninsula. Throughout the area it is clear that slave-raiding has gone hand in hand with international trade from the earliest times. The forests and mountains which protected the tribesmen of the interior from day-to-day control and routinized exploitation by the coastal states, also left them militarily weak and unable to resist the organized slaving expeditions which were periodically launched against them. Shifting cultivation in the tropics requires a low population density and is most efficient when the population is evenly dispersed. This is not to say that shifting cultivators were themselves innocent of slave-trading and slave-holding. Among the Ngaju of south Borneo and the Maloh, Melanau, Kayan and Berawan of central Borneo, for example, a class of aristocrats was freed from subsistence production for long-distance trade by its ownership of a class of hereditary slaves. The Iban also took captives as well as heads from their enemies for ransom, sale or adoption.

The relative underpopulation of Southeast Asia also had consequences for lowland societies in the area. One of the chief aims of warfare for both coastal and inland states was the capture of prisoners to supplement the domestic work force (Reid 1980:243; Tambiah 1976: 120).

The key to Southeast Asian social systems was the control of men. Land was assumed to be abundant, and not therefore an index to power (with the partial exceptions of Java and Central Thailand in relatively modern times). It is this that distinguishes traditional Southeast Asian states from feudal ones. Society was held together by vertical bonds of obligations between men. (Reid 1983: 8)

These bonds of obligation could take the form of voluntary loyalty to a lord, indebtedness to a creditor, or outright ownership by a purchasing master. Chattel slavery was only the endpoint of a continuum of dyadic relations of dependency.

128

The prominence of debt and judicial sentence as sources of slavery appears to be distinctive in the Southeast Asian pattern. Since inability to pay a judicial fine may be taken as a variation on inability to pay a debt, we may safely regard debt as the most fundamental source of Southeast Asian slavery. (ibid: 159)

In lowland societies as well, then, trade goes along with slavery, although in a rather different way. In the first place, prosperity derives so much from trade that all social relationships become mercantilized, and any inability to maintain one's creditworthiness soon leads to one's becoming a commodity oneself. In the second place, centralized state power was usually so weak that semi-autonomous wealthy merchants were able to surround themselves with virtual armies of slaves to defend themselves and their possessions. Privately owned slaves constitute a limitation on the power of the monarch and tend to disappear where central power is greatest (ibid: 18). But in the great trading cities along the coast, monarchs tended to be weak, and real power was in the hands of a merchant plutocracy.

Crudely speaking, Southeast Asian societies can thus be grouped into at least four types as regards their experience of slavery. First, there are the weak, fragmented societies of the highlands which served primarily as a source of goods and slaves for the lowlands. Second, there are the larger, more organized societies of the highlands which maintained their own class of slaves for ritual purposes and to free a small aristocracy for long-distance trade. Third, there are the predatory trade-raiding societies of the coastal areas who regarded slaves primarily as a commodity to be traded on to large urban centers. And fourth, there are these urban centers themselves. There is a fifth type of society represented by Bali and the Toraja which seems to have generated internally a large volume of slaves for export during certain periods (van der Kraan 1983; Bigalke 1983). Relatively dense populations dependent on fixed-field, wet-rice agriculture were necessary for this somewhat unusual situation to arise.

It is inevitable then, that the highland societies which managed to maintain their autonomy from lowland states should give a great deal of prominence to those same lowland states in terms both of practical measures of resistance and of symbolism. Violent raiding, coerced trade for jungle products, and debt bondage are all problematic areas to which some sort of response is required by their insertion in the regional political economy.

129

THOMAS GIBSON

RAIDING AND TRADING IN SOUTHEAST ASIAN CULTURES

The preceding discussion of the loosely integrated regional economy of insular Southeast Asia has defined the context in which the societies now to be described have had to operate. In the following discussion of three groups of shifting cultivators, I shall focus on the moral and symbolic values attached to activities in which raiding and trading are involved.

The Buid

The Buid are one of a number of highland groups in Mindoro known collectively to the lowlanders as "Mangyan," a term which has strong connotations of inferiority, wildness, and even slavery. It should be pointed out, however, that the lowlanders have begun to use *sandugu*, "one blood," or "blood brothers," as a term of reference and address for the highlanders. The implication of, and reason for using this term, is that the lowlanders would like the highlanders to feel bound to the lowland speakers by ties of artificial kinship. These ties should obligate the highlanders to treat the lowlanders with affection and gratitude, but above all to trade and to pay their debts. The highland Buid reject the term as presumptuous, for they view the lowland traders as a necessary evil, whose view of society as made up of moral and material debtors and creditors is the direct antithesis of their own.

In the Buid value system, violence is only the ultimate outcome of a whole series of negative forms of interaction which begins with boastfulness (*buagun*) and quarreling (*garisugan* "reciprocal aggression"). *Isug*, " aggression," connotes all that has a negative value in Buid social life: the uncontrolled expression of individual emotion and the assertion of egotistic desires, the attempt to dominate others, and, ultimately, physical violence and murder. They regard *maisug*, "aggressive" behavior, as being typical of their lowland Christian antagonists, who they continually hold up as a negative example. This word has a wide distribution in the Philippines. Among the Tausug Muslims, it refers to all that is positively valued in men: virility, courage, and the ability to stand up for one's honor (Kiefer 1972: 53). The Buid, by contrast, have no word for "courage," in the sense of a positively valued aggressive attitude in the face of physical danger. There are many words for fear of

130

and flight from danger, neither of which is seen as being reprehensible. Indeed, they are the only rational response to danger. It is recognized that Buid may on occasion act in an aggressive manner, but such behavior is attributed either to a weak mind, unable to control the emotions of its soul and body, or to affliction with a *fangarisugan* "spirit which causes aggression." I am aware of only one homicide occurring within a Buid population of one thousand in a ten year period, and that was carried out by a man with a fearsome reputation as a sorcerer.

Rather than compete in performing acts of courage, Buid youth are most likely to spend their time learning love poems with which to court young girls. The southern Buid and the neighboring Hanunoo have preserved a script which was used throughout the Philippines in ancient times. The main purpose of this script is to record and memorize poetry. The sort of prestige one can acquire with one's knowledge of poetry, and the sort of "conquests" one can make are the very opposite of those acquired through "bravery" and violence. Seduction is not associated with aggression among the Buid as it is in other cultures which value aggressiveness in men. The poems themselves are full of gentle imagery.

In addition to their categorical aversion to aggressive behavior of any kind, the Buid place an extremely high value on individual autonomy. This is taken to such an extreme that even parents are reluctant to interfere in the behavior of their children more than is necessary. They strive instead to substitute the dependency of small children on specific adults with their dependency on the adult community as a whole. Between adults, there should be no hint of dependency, either emotional or material. Such attitudes account in part for the extremely high rate of divorce among the Buid. While the optimal economic unit in Buid society consists of one adult male and one adult female, and virtually all adults belong to such a couple at any one time, there is a high rate of turnover in the composition of couples. A divorce is almost always caused by one partner deciding to marry a new spouse. The abandoned partner receives a sum of mutually agreed compensation and then begins his or her own search for a new spouse, often setting off a chain reaction. Children soon learn to accept whatever step-parents come their way. (Elsewhere I have described in detail Buid attitudes towards dyadic relations of dependency [Gibson 1985].)

In order to maximize individual autonomy and mobility, some mechanism must be found which allows people to detach themselves from their present set of companions and attach themselves to a new set

131

without much trouble. This mechanism is what I call "sharing," and was first clearly identified in the study of hunting and gathering societies. It is based on the principle that "entitlement does not depend in any way on donation" (Woodburn 1982: 441). Individuals are obligated to share certain goods and services with the rest of the community. Among the Buid the most obvious example is again meat, which is only butchered on ritual occasions, and which must be shared out in portions which are identical in both quantity and quality among all those present regardless of age or sex. Performing these rituals is no route to augmented status, for they are only carried out in response to illness or death within the sponsoring household. Their performance is thus a demonstration not of the wealth and vitality of the sponsors, but of their misfortune. No one is obliged to receive a portion of meat, and no one is obliged to repay the individuals whose sacrifices they have attended in the past. The only obligation is on the giver.

I have argued elsewhere that the characteristic manner in which Buid conduct conversations, help each other work on their fields, and, indeed, marry and divorce may best be described as the sharing of speech, labor and sexual intercourse (Gibson 1986: 44–48, 83–84). The underlying principle is that strictly dyadic relationships are likely to lead to either competition and aggression, or to dominance and indebtedness. If each individual sees himself or herself as interacting only with a undifferentiated social group, the possibility of losing one's personal autonomy is minimized. Sharing prevents ties of personal dependency from arising by making the individual dependent only on the group, and so ensures both autonomy and equality within the group.

Buid ritual activity is also carried out on a cooperative basis, and no individual adopts the role of specialist with privileged access to the spirit world. All adult men possess spirit familiars, and mystical power derives from large numbers of men chanting together.

Constant participation in obligatory collective ritual, in which the legitimacy of religious belief derives from personal experience of the spirit world, and not from tradition as interpreted by elders or specialists, from a sacred text, or from the privileged experience of a charismatic figure, provides the Buid with a shared core of belief and a deep conviction of the reality of invisible powers. (Gibson 1986: 148)

Buid view themselves as the prey of a host of evil spirits who feast on them when they die in the same way that the Buid feast on their own pigs. Quarreling within the human community is believed to render people more vulnerable to attack by these evil spirits. In the religious sphere, then, aggression is associated with violence, killing, and in the case of the most dangerous evil spirit, cannibalism. The most feared spirit is the *fangablang*, a giant said to resemble a Christian lowlander.

The Buid may be said to have an economic system which maximizes a married couple's ability to be virtually self-sufficient, and a political system which maximizes people's ability to form and dissolve social relationships. It eliminates competition for power and prestige by restricting any form of dyadic interaction. The two institutions which I have said constitute the main forms of interaction between neighboring societies in Southeast Asia, raiding and trading, are both assigned negative symbolic values and referred to the exterior of the society. Buid acquire lowland trade partners and put up with the exploitation they suffer because they must (cf. Gibson 1986: 16). But the concepts of debt and dependency on which this trade is based are not allowed to operate within Buid society. Raiding is a matter of suffering predation by evil and aggressive outsiders in the material and mystical worlds, but counter-raiding is confined to the imaginary world of spirit medium-ship. Flight, and quick integration into new communities through the institutions of divorce and sharing, are the main defenses against raiding in the material world.

Put more abstractly, one can characterize the Buid and other groups of people like them as having an ideology of ascribed equality: people are considered equal no matter how successful they are in various activities.

The Ilongot

The Ilongot of northern Luzon resemble the Buid in their egalitarian values and assertion of individual autonomy. They differ from the Buid primarily in terms of their attitudes towards violence and competition. Scott (1979), who has worked out a classification of "unhispanized" Philippine societies according to class structure, includes the Ilongot with the Mangyan in his "classless" category. Despite their fondness for headhunting, Scott resists placing them in his category of "warrior societies" because they do not "practice coup counting which might produce a warrior elite." They also lack a class term for accomplished warriors "which distinguishes a category of men with shared status, privilege and responsibility in the community" (1979: 156). While including the Ilongot and other violent, classless societies with peaceful, classless societies is perfectly legitimate given the purposes of Scott's classification, I require for my own purposes a classification which privileges attitudes toward violence, aggression and dependency.

The motivation for engaging in violence among Ilongot youth is precisely to *achieve* equality with adult men. The Ilongot do possess a form of ranking, but it is of the simplest sort: that between youth and age. Where the Buid are uncomfortable with and play down the dependency of children on adults, the Ilongot emphasize it and play around with the opposition between the passion of youth and the knowledge of age.

> Inside the house men *tuydek* [command] women, who in turn pass their commands on to children, and children are quick to *tuydek* those who are younger than themselves. The dynamics of *tuydek* tend ultimately to permit all adults the orderly poise of the platform – while requests for betel, food, tools, and water set children in almost continuous motion across the relatively unordered floor. (M. Rosaldo 1980: 72)

The impetus toward violence comes from the fact that young men must prove their passion, or aggressiveness, in order to acquire a wife and gain the respect of other adult men.

> Of course, in daily life, unmarried youths are the subordinates of their established seniors. Though free to move and to resist requests that contradict their plans and wishes, young men lack wives and gardens of their own and so are subject to "commands" (*tuydek*) by senior kinfolk in whose households they reside. Adult men may decide to "lend" the labor of their sons, and thus affirm their ties of kinship and concern with their adult fellows. (M. Rosaldo 1980: 155)

> With marriage as with beheading, the youth transforms his social self by demonstrating that he is an "equal" – dependent on no other man, and equivalent, in "angry" force, to all. (Ibid: 165)

Among the Ilongot, then, courting is associated with aggression. In line with the cultural idealization of males as warriors is a relatively greater elaboration of gender symbolism, in which the sexual division of labor is more explicit, and the inability of women to scale the same heights of achievement as men is stressed.

Michelle Rosaldo (1980) points out that the ideal of autonomy among the Ilongot applies less to individuals than to households. Divorce is rare and a cause for violence (pp. 8, 171). Women are exchanged in marriage by men, and are always under their authority (p. 84). Ilongot men must acquire control over a woman to become autonomous, and until they do they are dependent on the men who already control women. This notion that one must gain control over women leads to a reluctance to relinquish control over them, unless it be in return for control over another. Thus Ilongot youths react aggressively to the suitors of their sisters.

Because marrying, like beheading, provides young men with terms that will define their adult status, all men of a cohort may find themselves caught up in fights concerning women – and it is not surprising that Ilongots often allay the *liget* ["passion" or "aggression"] sparked by marriage with an "exchange" of maiden "sisters" . . . (p. 170)

The notion that marriage is a strenuous achievement, rather than a natural result of physical maturation, parallels the need to achieve equality with adult men through acts of bravery and violence.

The Ilongot economy is built around a symbolic opposition between the "collective" activity of men in hunting, meat distribution and pollarding the trees in swiddens, and the "individual" activity of women in planting, weeding and harvesting rice in swiddens (R. Rosaldo 1981). While women probably cooperate with one another as much as do men, "women's cooperative labor is seen as casual and informal, deserving neither celebratory feasting nor other public note" (M. Rosaldo 1980: 133). The Ilongot hold a "cultural view of rice as private produce, the fruit of individual effort in a private field" (M. Rosaldo 1980: 133). Hunting, on the other hand, even though it is often carried out by individuals for the private sale of meat in the market, is always bound up with the public domain; game is either traded with outsiders or shared within the group: it is never intended for consumption by a single household.

And the reluctance of Ilongots to talk about inequality of skill among hunters is rooted in a view of game as a collective product, publicly appropriate and consumed. (Ibid: 118)

Adults both refused to boast about how much game they had bagged, and persisted in maintaining their doctrine that no man was a more gifted huntsman than another . . . Men who found themselves again and again compelled to cooperate on short-term projects felt they could not enlist the aid of men who stood above or below them upon any imagined ladder. Only equals, as they saw it, could work together in improvised and coordinated harmony. (R. Rosaldo 1980: 145–46)

This brings us to what I see as the peculiarity of the Ilongot among all the Southeast Asian societies so far described, and which disposes me to place them in a class on their own. They place enormous stress on

135

achievement and competition, and yet they regulate these types of behavior in such a way that inequality does not result. That is, for the Ilongot, achievement is not a matter of "more or less," but of "whether or not": whether or not a man has taken a head, acquired a wife, provided meat for the settlement. Having acquired the status of adulthood, there are no further statuses to be attained, only the one to be maintained. For not only must equality be achieved in the first instance, it is a fragile thing which is constantly being put in question.

A daily world in which autonomous and equal adults engage in cooperative interaction is shown, through oratory, to be as fragile as it often is . . . (M. Rosaldo 1980: 220)

Oratory is the domain in which the Ilongot play around with the notion of dyadic exchange and the danger of imbalances between equals which may result from it. Oratorical negotiations are one of the chief cultural mechanisms used by the Ilongot to define and create equality between men. They are designed to move from a situation in which negative reciprocity obtains between feuding groups, through the balanced reciprocity of negotiation to the generalized reciprocity of the kin group. They require two balanced groups to even be initiated: if one group is much stronger than its enemy, it simply absorbs it or hounds it out of existence.

Formal covenant appears, in short, to require an equality of difference, strength, and "anger" . . . Although covenants by themselves do not necessitate further dealings, marriages over time provide the grounds for future visits and cooperation; as such, they constitute a sort of transition from a state of difference and balanced opposition to one of mutuality and acknowledged bonds. (Ibid: 210–11)

It is as if Buid-type rules of sharing and the repression of aggression are followed within Ilongot *bertan* (literally, "groups of people of one kind," labeled by the Rosaldos' "bilateral descent groups"). But where the Buid oppose the operation of these values within their own society to the contrary values operative in lowland Christian society, the two value systems operate in different social situations within Ilongot society. Aggression, exchange, and potential debt are not evil per se in Ilongot society. They are inevitable characteristics of a stage in the male Ilongot's life cycle, as he seeks to acquire a wife, prove his ability to defend his autonomy, and cooperate with adult men as an equal. They are balanced by the knowledge, mutuality and acknowledged equality of adults.

Raiding, trading and tribal autonomy

The Ilongot have an economy which stresses the autonomy of the household as opposed to the individual or the community more strongly than the Buid. Their political system also binds an individual to his "kin" group by opposing it to other potentially hostile "kin" groups. Where the Buid see competition as leading to the eventual domination of one party over the other, and so necessarily evil, the Ilongot view competition as a necessary stage in the achievement of equality.

It may be noted that the Ilongot live at the headwaters of the largest river in Luzon, as far from the coast as one can get. Slave raiding was not the persistent threat in this area that it was throughout the Visayan islands to the south. The only society in northern Luzon which possessed chattel slaves was the Benguet, where they were employed for mine labor. Raiding throughout the highlands of northern Luzon was always more ritual and political than economic in motive: it was heads and revenge that warriors desired, not prisoners to keep or trade as slaves. It is also possible that trade has not played as important a role in Ilongot history as it has in societies closer to the coast. Aside from scattered references to the sale of game, the Rosaldos make little mention of trade, or dependency on trading partners. In sum, I would argue that the Ilongot represents a society which has not developed the same absolute rejection of violence/raiding and debt/trading as have the Buid, and that there is less evidence of the presence of the state in their symbolic life, due to their relative isolation from the maritime world.

The Iban

The Iban are vigorous traders and raiders, as their history attests (Pringle 1970). As Sahlins (1972: 224–226) has argued, they are unusual for "tribal" people in keeping an exact account of labor exchanged between households, and in limiting the sharing of staple food surpluses. This is because the latter must be stored up for trade with outsiders. Aside from other functions, the acquisition of prestige goods such as jars and gongs in trade also serves as a buffer against a poor rice harvest:

Each season, some families succeed in producing a surplus, while others find themselves with a deficit; families exchange gongs for [rice], or [rice] for gongs. Jars (*tajau*), though to a much lesser extent, are used in the same way. Again, money – obtained from the marketing of forest produce – is often used to purchase rice . . . (Freeman 1970: 267)

137

The Iban method of shifting cultivation is such that the labor of young men is only required for two or three months a year. The domestic group, or *bilek* usually contains enough women and older men to free young men for the activities of trading and raiding, or *bejalai* (Freeman 1970: 222–24).

The Iban live along large, navigable rivers and possess a fair degree of maritime skill. This meant that they are likely to have been more intensively involved in maritime trade than mountain dwellers, and are thus somewhat more sophisticated. But it also gave them the ability to mobilize much larger numbers of people than shifting cultivators inhabiting rugged mountain terrain. At the same time, they had to adopt more aggressive tactics in their own defense. In the nineteenth century they were able to put thousands of warriors to sea in war boats holding 60 to 100 men each. They are reported to have served as mercenaries in Illanun war fleets, the most feared slave raiders in all of Southeast Asia, although later they became their bitter enemies (Pringle 1970: 50–53, 76).

They have gone from being the must successful and expansionist warriors of Sarawak, during the nineteenth century, sweeping all other shifting cultivators before them, to being widely traveled migrant traders and laborers in the twentieth:

For Iban young men then (and particularly since the cessation of headhunting), going on journeys is the greatest and most consuming interest life has to offer . .
the most powerful incentive is the very considerable social prestige which a much-traveled man can command . . . Above all, it is only after having accomplished many successful journeys that a man begins the performance of the series of elaborate rituals (all based on the institution of headhunting) which confer prestige in middle and old age. (Freeman 1970: 222–24)

Traditionally,

When he had taken a head, and only then, was an Iban male entitled to have the back of his hands tatooed. With this achieved, his prowess was on constant display. . . A successful young head-hunter, it is said, could have his pick of the most desirable young women, and was much sought after as a husband. In contrast, a man who had never taken a head, or who was known to be reluctant in battle, would be told by the women he courted: . . . "First scale the posts of an enemy long-house; first bedeck your hair as does he who has taken a head." (Freeman 1979: 238)

Violence and aggression were directly linked to courting, and head-hunting itself was preliminary to a ritual intended to secure both fertility

138

and prestige for its male sponsor. These head-hunting rituals are "occasions for the celebration of the preoccupations and the narcissism of men" (Freeman 1968: 388).

The Ibans are known to have taken their enemies captive for sale or ransom, as well as merely taking their heads. But there was no place in Iban society for a class of hereditary slaves. Freeman presents convincing arguments that war captives were not incorporated as a permanent stratum in Iban society, but were either ransomed or adopted into a *bilek*, the fundamental corporate group, as equal members, with equal rights to inheritance.

The custom of ritually enfranchising and adopting captives taken in war, which was integral to the traditional society of Iban, is a striking expression of their egalitarian values. (Freeman 1981: 47; cf. Rousseau 1980: 59)

One must not get carried away, however, in extolling Iban "egalitarianism" simply because unequal statuses were not, in principle, hereditary. *Bilek* units maintained careful accounts of labor credits and debits between each other, and if an individual or his *bilek* could not repay a debt, he might be obliged to pay the debt "in part or in whole by the labor of himself or others of his *bilek*" (Freeman 1981: 49). At the other end of the ladder of achievement, was the *raja brani*, literally, "rich and brave man":

Once he had succeeded in taking a trophy head, a warrior was entitled to tattoo on the backs of his hands, and thus adorned he could, if he had also amassed sufficient wealth, come to be recognized as *raja brani*. This, however, was not the end to an ambitious individual's quest for reknown, for there was also in Iban culture an ascending sequence of complex rituals, or *gawai amat*, specifically associated with the cult of headhunting, that he could, *if he chose*, perform. These *gawai amat* (lit. true rituals) were always performed by individuals . . . Such rituals, the more complex of which (lasting for four or five days) demanded extensive resources, were performed before and after major raids, with the celebrant taking the invocation (*timang*) a stage further on each occasion until, over a span of forty or more years, the sequence was complete. (Freeman 1981: 40)

Even ritual life, then, is characterized by a hierarchy of achieved statuses. Shamans fall into three classes: "raw" or novice, "ripe" or fully initiated, and "transformed" or transvestite. Freeman described the boasts of one master shaman, and his denigration of the abilities of all others (Freeman 1967: 320).

Although skill in rice cultivation was important to a man's prestige, it is primarily success in competitive and violent endeavors away from the longhouse that is the measure of prestige within it. Internal ranking is the result of mastering an external realm of activity. The Iban see themselves as predators of the outside world: of neighboring tribes, whom they raid for heads; of the environment, whose virgin forests they cut down; of the regional economy, in which they earn wages for brief spells before returning home. They stand in marked contrast to the Buid, who see themselves as the prey of the outside world.

In short, while the Buid got the worst of the regional system of trading and raiding, the Iban thrived on it. The Iban may be said to have a political economy which maximizes the autonomy of a domestic group (*bilek*), frees men for raiding and trading by assigning most of the agricultural labor to the female members of the *bilek*, and allows for the temporary organization of large groups of men under charismatic individuals, who lead their followers on trading expeditions, migrations to new river basins, and on headhunting expeditions (Freeman 1981: 35–36). The over-all ethos is one of achieved ranking. Every individual is expected to prove himself, but there is a finely graded ladder of achievement, with the ranking of individuals according to merit the ultimate goal.

SUMMARY AND COMPARISON

To summarize: the Buid reject any form of violence, aggression, or even competition. Among the Buid, even quarreling is thought to have mystically dangerous consequences for the vitality of both humans and crops. The Ilongot and the Iban stress the competitive achievement of status by typically engaging in sporadic, violent assaults on members of neighboring societies in order both to demonstrate the virility of their male members and to acquire mystical vitality by obtaining heads. The stress on individual achievement also lends a rather cyclic character to violence in these societies. Raiding parties are organized by ambitious individuals more or less according to whim (M. Rosaldo 1980: 139; Freeman 1981: 36). As a result, members of these societies have historically acquired a great deal of notoriety as headhunters.

All these societies represent specialized adaptations to the regional political economy. All lack instituted hierarchy. The extreme emphasis on individual autonomy and rejection of super-household authority evident among them must be seen as a rejection of the political values of their predatory lowland neighbors. Far from constituting primordial classless societies, they must be seen as political groups which have been able to maintain significant degrees of autonomy only by developing special social mechanisms for evading control by the lowlands. They are neither pristine tribesmen, nor are they, to borrow a phrase from Fox's argument concerning South Indian hunter-gathers, mere adjuncts of agrarian states (Fox 1969).

Fox and Gardner (1966) argue that the central features of South Asian hunter-gatherer societies are attributable to their enclavement within agrarian states. These features include highly migratory individuals, a stress on individual autonomy, and a value system which condemns aggression and competition. These features make them clearly comparable to the Buid. Fox and Gardner go on, however, to characterize these societies as non-cooperative and as lacking sharing or reciprocity between family groups. This seems to be rather an exaggeration, for as among most hunter-gatherer groups, even in South India, meat which is not traded is shared out equally among all members of a camp, while gathered vegetable foods are retained within the family (Gardner 1972: 415; Morris 1977: 231; Roy 1925: 69–88). Nevertheless, it remains possible that the exposure of the South Asian hunter-gatherers to a dense, fixed-field agricultural population has placed them under greater inter-cultural pressure than the Southeast Asian highlanders exposed only to the sporadic interventions of the coastal trade-oriented states. One result of such pressure might be a necessity to further intensify individual mobility and to further diminish the size of sharing groups.

Mobility and sharing are mutually reinforcing institutions and serve as a highly effective means of evading control by neighbors who cannot be resisted militarily. As I have argued above, sharing is characterized by a radical disconnection between giver and recipient. It is this characteristic lack of strong *dyadic* bonds which has led writers like Gardner to characterize members of societies organized around sharing as "atomistic." But if one looks at sharing in terms of the moral bonds which unite the individual to the group, this characterization appears inadequate. These bonds are often emphasized in collective rituals, which act out the mystical dependency of the individual on the group.

There are many instances of societies in highland Southeast Asia whose members are repeatedly described in the literature as being systematically cheated of the market price of the produce they bring to trade, and as being permanently indebted to lowland traders. Indeed, these forest dwellers are often called by a term which means "slave" or debt slave, e.g. *Sakai* for the Orang Asli, *Ata, Aeta* or *Agta* for the Philippine Negritos, and *Mangyan* for the highlanders of Mindoro. Since the lowlanders already regard the members of these groups as debt slaves, it would be fatal for those people themselves to acknowledge the principle of debt. These societies thus reject, often explicitly, the most fundamental principle of lowland state societies: dyadic dependency phrased in an idiom or moral and material indebtedness.

Individual mobility and a system of sharing which allows people to enter into immediate social relations without regard to past transactions are two essential features of Buid society. But the rejection of attempts to acquire prestige through acts of violence or through feast sponsorship sets the Buid off from the Ilongot and Iban as well. Among the Buid, the symbolic equation of violence and dominance with life threatening external forces is so complete that the central life generating rituals of the Ilongot and Iban are negated: headhunting and the competitive sacrificing of large animals. Where animal sacrifice is carried out, it is done in as non-aggressive a manner as possible.

The Buid share with the Ilongot and Iban a refusal to grant political power to any individual or office in their respective societies. It has been remarked again and again that the most "conservative" cultural groups are those which lack internal stratification: finding no point of application within the enclaved society on which to apply pressure, external agencies must try to control members of the former one by one. Colonial states confronted with such a society, tried to create "chiefs" where none had existed, usually with little success (see, for example, the appointment of Iban *penghulu*, "headmen," by the Brookes [Pringle, 1970: 157]). In the extreme case of the Buid, even boastful behavior is seen as immoral. It is quite inaccurate to characterize members of such cultures as "submissive": they do not respond to attempts to dominate them with violence as do Ilongot and Iban, but they are just as insistent on the maintenance of their personal autonomy. Buid will often resort to suicide if imprisoned by the state, or even threatened with imprisonment. They will not voluntarily work for wages, disliking being placed in a position where they must obey the will of another. They will, however, at times render labor at absurdly low rates of remuneration as a sort of tribute to lowland patrons who furnish them some protection against the more violent elements of the lowland population.

It is when groups of highlanders engaged in a subsistence system such

142

as hunting and gathering or shifting cultivation are brought into unavoidable confrontation with the members of aggressive state systems that one is most likely to find Buid-type systems developing. The mode of subsistence must be compatible with a certain degree of mobility, and the highlanders must inhabit a terrain sufficiently resistent to easy penetration by subjects of lowland states to make this cultural adaptation feasible. It is not unlikely that all the formerly autonomous societies in similarly exposed geographical locations which had an internally ranked structure have long since been incorporated into the hierarchical state systems of the lowlands, and that the autonomous groups which have survived have done so because they possessed an ideology which rejected any form of dominance.

CONCLUSIONS

The argument of this paper is that any explanation of the role of violence and domination in the social lives of insular Southeast Asia shifting cultivators must be sought in terms of their relations to the regional political economy. This relation is influenced by their geographical situations, and their consequent degree of exposure to the trading and raiding economy of the region. But it is impossible to argue that their ideologies are "caused" in any sense by their own subsistence economies or by their role in the larger regional system. It is possible to argue, however, that their continued existence as autonomous political and cultural groups can be explained in terms of their development of ideologies appropriate to that end, given their different geographical situations. Groups which failed to develop appropriate ideologies were either absorbed into lowland states or eliminated. There remains an urgent need to understand the interaction of societies with autonomous ideologies and value systems in a common regional economy, without either reducing these ideologies to epiphenomena of the wider system, or ignoring the real effects of commodity relations and military force upon the component societies in the regional system.

The argument in this paper addresses the question of the "causes" of war and peace in Southeast Asia in a manner very different to the many of the papers in this volume. In conclusion, I would like briefly to indicate some of the areas of disagreement, and the implications these have for our understanding of human violence and war in general.

Some writers view war as a natural phenomenon, susceptible of

143

explanation in terms of universal laws, rather than of particular historical developments. Their tendency is to look for pan-human drives to
maximize either inclusive fitness (Chagnon, this volume), or access to
natural resources (Ferguson, Carneiro, Haas, this volume). These
attempts to treat a socio-historical phenomenon in naturalistic terms
have familiar effects: since war is assumed to always derive from the
same essential cause, it is treated as a single, unitary phenomenon,
easily identifiable across time and space. What is needed, rather, is an
attempt to differentiate types of inter-group violence, and to recognize
that each type may require an entirely different sort of theory to account
for it.

As Ferguson (this volume) notes, questions about war and violence
vary depending on the broader theoretical context in which they are
asked. If they are asked in the context of individual motivations or
sentiments, such as aggression, there will be a tendency to concentrate
on either biological or psychological issues, which have a timeless
universal quality. If they are raised in the context of a struggle for scarce
resources, between evenly balanced opponents, there is a tendency to
view it as a game between players who begin as equals and only end as
"winner" and "loser." There is a reduction of inter-group violence to
timeless questions of tactics and strategy, of "game theory." Focusing on
aggression and focusing on scarcity are both conducive to a view of
violent conflict as somehow pathological, the product of maladaptive
personality or social structures. Violence is both an inevitable and an
evil part of the human condition.

In this paper, violence has been discussed in relation to exploitation
and to ritual. This approach highlights the role of violence in what is
perhaps its most prevalent and significant form since the origin of states
and classes: the exploitation of a weaker group – class, gender, ethnicity,
nation, race – by a stronger group. In this view, violence and war are not
"about" natural scarcity or individual sentiments, but "about" socially-
produced surpluses (for some) and scarcities (for the others). Occasional
clashes between the ruling elites operating two parallel systems of
exploitation, which is the normal subject of investigations of "war," may
then be seen for what it is: a subsidiary and intermittant form of
violence. Furthermore, for the group which profits from the violence
built into a system, violence will be seen as anything but a negative
phenomenon. It will, on the contrary, be celebrated and glorified. This
brings us to the question of ritual. Violence in any society will be

144

assigned a value, and it will have different values in different situations. Very rarely is it seen as evil in all situations, although the Buid provide a rare case in which it is. In political economies based on the coercive extraction of surplus value from neighboring societies, inter-group violence may even be fetishized as a product of mystical vitality in itself. Thus violence is neither a necessary part of social life, nor is it necessarily seen as an evil: there are societies which systematically devalue it, just as there are societies, or ruling groups within societies, which view it as the ultimate good when exercised in appropriate contexts against the right opponents.

Notes

1. This paper is based on research carried out among the Buid in the field from 1979 to 1981, and again in 1985, and on library research conducted in 1985–86. The second period in the field and the library research was funded by the Harry. Frank Guggenheim Foundation. Different versions of this paper have been presented at the conference on the Anthropology of War held at the School of American Research, at the Seminar on Equality and Inequality held by the London School of Economics Department of Social Anthropology, and in the Colloquium of the Department of Anthropology of the University of Rochester. This draft has benefited from comments by participants in all these meetings, and from detailed comments by William Henry Scott, Maurice Bloch, and Jerome Rousseau. My thanks to all of them. While I have not always followed their advice, I have always found it stimulating.

7
The Snake Warriors – Sons of the Tiger's Teeth: a descriptive analysis of Carib warfare, ca. 1500–1820

NEIL LANCELOT WHITEHEAD

Scholars describing and analyzing warfare among the non-state societies of South America, such as the Caribs, have largely confined themselves to a handful of easily available historical and ethnographic accounts of particular instances of conflict. The extremely limited nature of this data base undermines the general veracity of analyses of warfare in this region.

By contrast, the use of the archival and manuscript material can partly offset the fact that, aside from a few celebrated cases such as the Yanamamö (see Chagnon, this volume) or the Jivaro (see Ross 1984), the martial societies of this region have all been "pacified."

For both these reasons, the accurate historical modelling of past patterns of Carib warfare requires that the data base include the extensive unpublished archival material. Doing so will radically alter our appreciation of those sources on which most commentators have exclusively relied.

In the case of the Caribs such considerations are particularly relevant. Failure to appreciate the limitations of the data with which all authors have previously worked has led to confusion over the actual identity of the Carib, with a consequent serious misapprehension about the nature of Carib warfare. The "Caribs" (*Karinya* or *Galibi*) need to be clearly distinguished from the so-called "Island Caribs" (*Kalinago*). Although these two groups showed some similarities in their social organization and were close trading and military allies (Kalinago men used a special traders' and warriors' dialect based on Karinya loan words), the "Island Caribs" were, in fact, *Arawakans* (Taylor 1954a, 1954b).

This confusion arose from the Spanish use of the word *caribe* as a political category, not just as a cultural term, to describe those Amerindian groups that most fiercely resisted conquest (Whitehead 1984). The misnomer passed into the usage of subsequent commentators through an uncritical and almost exclusive reliance on the authority of Spanish sources. The resulting legend of conflict between "caribes" and "aruacas," in which the mighty Carib are supposed to have driven the peaceful and noble Arawak from the Antilles to the mainland of South America, described, initially at least, no more than a tradition of raid and counterraid among the Arawakan-speaking *Lokono* (*aruacas*) and Kalinago of the Antilles, Trinidad and Guayana coast.

An accurate portrayal of Carib warfare is needed because all previous accounts have failed to appreciate the consequences of this cultural distinction for our image of Carib "fierceness." Their descriptions are constructed from wildly incompatible source material or in apparent ignorance of the actual range of material available. Moreover, given the frequency with which the Carib case is referred to in regional discussions of warfare – particularly the associated practice of cannibalism – the theoretical consequences of this reevaluation will be relevant to many broader discussions of warfare.

The first consequence would be to bring into question the possibility of arriving at a common causal explanation of an illusory phenomenon, "Carib warfare." Close historical analysis reveals that only some Carib groups were persistently warlike. In turn, the origins and purpose of warfare among these more militant groups itself varied considerably over time.

A second consequence is that the colonial context of Carib combat needs to be stressed, since it is necessary to examine systems of conflict on a regional level. Any attempted explanation of the incidence of conflict must directly address the extent to which contact with the Europeans induced or reduced such conflict. Without some attempt to make this assessment little reliance can be placed on possible explanations of war or even of specific wars in the Carib area.

A third consequence of reevaluation will be to allow for more comprehensive explanations of Carib warfare. Conflict in Amazonia and the Guianas is unlikely to result from one determining factor. Previous discussions of warfare in this region, however, have tended to look for a single overarching explanation, at least for specific incidents of conflict. As will be apparent from the Carib case, previous commentators have often confused the pretext for war with its "causes." Two factors will eventually serve to explain warfare: the identification of what may stand as a pretext for war in any given society; and the study of the total social milieu from which that society has historically arisen.

The purposes of this paper are accordingly twofold: first, to provide a detailed and accurate description of Carib military tactics and weaponry, as well as the social and ideological context in which they were deployed; and second, to analyze the effects of European intrusion on these same aspects of Carib society.

The Caribs are today represented by remnant communities living in Venezuela, Guyana (*Karinya*), Surinam, and French Guiana (*Galibi*), and have long played a central role in the history of colonialism in this region of the Caribbean and South America. Despite some regional dialect differences these groups are as linguistically homogeneous today as they were in the sixteenth century (Hoff 1968). They have also displayed exceptional tenacity and longevity in their resistance to European domination and maintained their independence from the colonial state for more than 250 years.

The perpetual militancy that resulted from their resistance exaggerated and altered many of the traditional features of Carib life. The martial orientation of their society, however, is evident from the earliest of contact with the Europeans (*palanakali* or spirits-from-the-sea) and from the legends of other Amerindian groups. For example, both the Warao and Saliva Amerindians, northern and western neighbors of the Carib, share a similar tale of the origins of Caribs. To wit, they say that the Carib arose from the rotting body of a giant snake (the anaconda), which had been killed by them following its seduction of their wives. The Achagua, another neighboring group, said simply that the Caribs were *chaviani* or "sons of the tigers teeth".[1]

Such Amerindian legends, first noted by the early missionaries José Gumilla and William Brett in the eighteenth and nineteenth centuries, neatly dovetailed with existing European images. From the time of Columbus the Carib were seen as a bloodthirsty, cruel and ruthless nation addicted to the capture of slaves, the joy of battle and the eating of human flesh. The political value of fostering such a stereotype, in terms of justifying military action against Carib settlements and socially and economically isolating Carib traders, was well understood by the Spanish from the beginning of their occupation of the New World. It was also assiduously employed by them throughout the pacification of the Orinoco basin (Whitehead 1988). However, in the colonial experience of the English and Dutch, while losing none of the more lurid attributes in many descriptions we have of them, the Caribs emerge as invaluable military allies and trading partners. This fact particularly disturbed the Spanish vision of conquest on the Orinoco. In 1638 the Corporation of Santo Tomé, Spanish capital of Guayana, left the King in no doubt as to consequences of this situation:

One grieves for so many women and children who are yet awaiting death at the hands of such inhuman savages, eaters of human flesh and heretics, enemies to our Holy Catholic Faith from whom God was pleased to deliver this town following its capture by the Caribs and Dutch, on the 22nd July, the Feast of St. Mary Magdelene. (BL-V.P.XI, 15)

Later, in the eighteenth century, the Caribs were to form the core of the slavehunting militias for the Dutch colony of Essequibo. In April 1764, immediately following the Berbice slave rebellion, the Director-General of Essequibo wrote the following to the Directors of the Dutch West India Company (DWIC);

. . . affairs, God be praised, are beginning once more to take a tolerably satisfactory turn there [Berbice], to which end our Caribs, both from these rivers [Essequibo & Demerara] and even Barima, have loyally done their best and are yet doing it, constantly roving about between the two Colonies . . . having been so successful in all their expeditions as to have lost none of their own people. (PRO-CO. 116, 34)

The Spanish opinion of the Carib was not without some justification for they were, on occasion, ruthless warriors and slavers. However, the historical context and motivation of these activities is complex and cannot be understood in isolation from the European presence, which itself forced certain lines of Carib social development. The creation and persistence of this particular image of the Carib expresses an important fact of Carib history. The Carib were a critical factor in the success or failure of colonial schemes throughout the Guayana area. Furthermore, this central role, over a period of nearly three centuries induced the Caribs to approximate more and more closely the very stereotype that European fears and insecurities had so gratuitously assigned to them. Even the Prefect of the Capuchin Mission, Fr. Benito de la Garriaga, felt obligated to acknowledge the effects of this process: "this trade in Poytos[2] has so completely altered the Caribs that now their only occupation is constantly going to and from war, selling and killing the Indians. . ." (AGI.C. 258-9/6/1758). The Director-General in Essequibo also noted a pattern, and remarked to the DWIC in 1746 that the trade in *poitos* had now become the activity "from which alone that nation derives its livelihood" (PRO-CO 116,39).

This paper then traces the course of the relations between Carib and European to show how Carib warfare (*oreku*: literally "wounding"), was recruited to and changed by European colonial priorities. To fully explicate this process the nature of Carib combat and warfare at earliest contact will be examined first, followed by a consideration of the changes that encompassed the Snake Warriors as they became inextricably enmeshed in the European economic order.

CARIB COMBAT

Traditional Carib weapons of war were the poisoned arrow and the club. According to eyewitness testimony such weapons were highly effective. For example, the Dutchman, A. Cabeliau, reported the following in 1597 concerning the Carib use of the bow (*akapra*) and envenomed arrows (*purewa*);

. . . if anyone is hit by them, so that blood flows, he must perforce die within twenty-four hours: his flesh dropping from his bones: so that the Spanish greatly fear that nation and their arrows (Jonge 1862: 153–60)

Carib technique in using such arrows was described thus:

. . . They shoot all their arrows into the air with such accuracy that, though not taking direct aim at a body, they know that they will hit it . . . of those that are wounded by them, few recover. (Van Berkel 1695: 32)

Antidotes to arrow-poison were known to the Amerindians, but were kept a close secret from the Europeans to maintain that strategic advantage which Cabeliau noted. Thus when the small grandson of a war chief inadvertently showed the traveller Jean Mocquet the plant from which the antidote was derived,

150

. . . I would have plucked up some of this Root but this little boy would not suffer it. And besides the Indians who were with him, seemed to be very angry he had showed me this Plant, which they prised and esteemed above all others. (1696: 57)

The Europeans were equally impressed with the efficacy of the Carib war club (*aputu*). The following judgement, brutally simple in its explanation, was made by the mercenary soldier John Gabriel Stedman, who personally led Amerindian levies against the black rebel slaves of Surinam: "One blow from this club, which is frequently fixed with a sharp stone, scatters the brains" (1796:I:396). Finished clubs were richly carved with various symbolic devices, including images of women, and the number of "kills" achieved (see Whitehead 1986).

In the high savanna country there is evidence that the spear (*amara*) or sword (*macana*) and shield (*maluana*), favored weapons of the Lokono and Yao, were adopted. In 1607 Robert Harcourt sent musketeers to the aid of the Yao chief, Ragapo, in the Sierra Lombarda, Brazil. The following is Harcourt's report of their action, that King James I "might note the factions among the Indian nations, the discipline and order they hold in warre."

. . . in the Front he [Ragapo] first placed our foure Englishmen, by two in a rank, next to them two Indians armed with wooden Swords and Targets [shields]; then two Archers; and after them two men with sharpened staves, instead of Pikes; and in like manner ordered and ranked all his company. Being thus prepared hee marched against the Caribs who (neere at hand) were comming in the same order towards him; but when they approached, and (unexpected) perceived our Englishmen amongst the Yaios, they were amazed and made a sudden stand. (Harcourt 1613)

Harcourt adds that, the Caribs "presently agreed to peace by reason of our mens presence [which] in time will much avail us, being well observed and rightly applied, according to occasion" (1613: 22–3).

More usually the forest and river were the scenes of Carib combat, and the war canoe (*kanawa*) the base from which such attacks were launched. This vessel might hold up to 50 warriors, who paddled the craft, being ranged on twelve benches, two abreast, along each side. The sides themselves were protected by a raised wooden rail, running right round the craft, from which shields might be hung as a further protection against enemy arrows. Gumilla (BM.V.XX-13, 24/10/1733) and Pelleprat (1965: 164–95) add that the skulls and smoked limbs of courageous enemies (*itoto*) might also festoon the kanawa.

Judging from sources such as these, it seems that ambush, raid, and set-piece battle were all part of the Carib warrior's repertoire. In defense of his village he might be summoned to arms at a moment's notice by the blowing of a conch. For a planned raid, the organizing war chief would send knotted-cords out to allied villages to indicate when the raid would take place. Then he would have the women prepare a great feast at which he would present his reasons for proposing the attack.

Once assembled, the war chiefs, who formed a distinct group, would discuss strategy and tactics as well as who was best fitted to lead the raid. This would not necessarily have been the one who proposed it. Meanwhile the assembled warriors drank, danced, and acted out mock-battles as the women harangued them to be cruel to their enemies and avenge the dead.

A special form of manioc-beer (*paiwarri*), containing the brain, liver and heart of a tiger, an anaconda and vanquished enemies, was consumed at these ceremonies. These organs were thought to promote, respectively, cunning, courage and energy during the coming fight. Their arms and clubs would also be smeared with a salve made from the worms collected from the buried teeth and claws of the tiger – echoes of the Achagua tale of their origins quoted above.

The dances that were performed, perhaps rehearsals of the co-ordinated movements of Carib battle-formation, were designed to awaken the Snake-Spirit and Tiger-Spirit. A Snake Dance aroused in the warriors the spirit of Anaconda (*kiliu*), silent and invisible, capable of strangling and swallowing even the Tiger. Its force was felt to be an indispensable element in the psychological armour of the warriors. Appropriately so, when one recalls that, according to both the Saliva and Warao, it was the womb of their nation.

The Tiger dance was intended to awake *Kaikusi-yumu*, the Tiger-Spirit himself, who, on taking possession of the warrior, enabled him to kill as the tiger kills. However, he only relinquished possession of the warrior's spirit on tasting the blood and flesh of a dead enemy that the warrior had killed. Penard and Penard (1907:I:66–7) quote a Carib warrior's explanation of his dance:

I growl. I hiss, I swing the club just like he does when he crushes his prey with one blow of his terrible claws. And when I have killed my enemy I must also drink his blood and taste his flesh that the spirit that impels me to do this deed will be assuaged . . . When the Tiger is in the man, the man becomes like the Tiger.

It is in this context that reports of Carib cannibalism should be interpreted – a means by which the warrior could distance himself from the trauma of killing. An ideological theme whose importance is attested to by the fact that it still persisted even in the period when Caribs were being paid by the Dutch to hunt down runaway-slaves. In April 1768 the Director-General of Essequibo wrote to the DWIC:

Tampoko came down river yesterday evening with his body of Caribs. When the canoes arrived we thought there were some negroes in them because some of the Caribs had completely covered their heads and faces with their *salempouris* [cloaks]. This custom was quite unknown to me. When they came on shore I asked Tampoko what it meant and he told me that these were men that had killed negroes; this is their custom and they must go like this for a month (PRO-CO 116, 36)

The size of these Carib raiding parties was highly variable, and dependent on the purposes for which it was formed. Even the earliest reports, however, indicate that a force of 300–400 warriors, comprising a flotilla of around 20 vessels, was typical. Based on an estimate of "average" size at around 400 persons, this suggests a level of political and military alliance which incorporated four or five villages. Contemporary estimates of the scope of the authority and influence of a local war chief are also at least of this order (Whitehead 1988).

Nonetheless, leadership did not derive from the prestige of the war-chiefs alone. Leaders also exercised shamanistic authority as exemplified by *piaii* in Carib societies. The role of piaii is difficult to discern in early times, though it probably declined further as the whole framework of the aboriginal warfare collapsed, following the European invasion. Nonetheless the piaii were certainly originally consulted on questions of tactics and strategy, as well as the general propitiousness of the particular enterprise in hand. Mocquet was told that Camaria, "King of the Caribs" in eastern Guayana, practised divination of his enemies' movements. When Camaria, who ". . . had but one eye, and was mighty Crafty and Treacherous . . .",

. . . had a mind to know anything Concerning their Wars against their Enemies, he made a hole in the ground pronouncing some certain Words and then came something[3] up with a horrible thundering noise, which spake to him, and instructed him, giving him notice what their enemies were doing at that time. (1604: 110)

Mocquet adds that on this occasion Camaria correctly divined an imminent attack by the Yaos. In addition, since attacks were sometimes

153

abandoned on the basis of unfavorable omens, even within striking distance of the enemy village, it is probable that the advice of the piaii was taken throughout an expedition. Thus Biet (1664: 369, 380) mentions that just prior to an attack, the war shields would be placed in a line. From the manner in which they fell to the ground the piaii would divine whether or not the battle would go well.

At a more general level the piaii were intimately involved in the selection of war-chiefs. It is clear that duties and obligations to the latter, even if expressed within the idiom of kinship, were heavily dependent on the ability to successfully prosecute a raid and control its political consequences (see Whitehead 1988). This should not be taken to imply that such leadership was "weak," but that accession to the rank of war-chief was arduous. Under the direction of the piaii, candidates submitted themselves to various ordeals, primarily a long period of fasting on manioc and water accompanied by the periodic drinking of large quantities of tobacco-juice. It was also expected that such candidates already would have killed many enemies. On his own death the bones of the war chief were preserved and rubbed with red-dye (*anatto*) and might be hung in the trophy-hall of the warriors, which once dominated the center of the larger Carib settlements.

As has been indicated, the war chief was responsible for supplying basic foodstuffs for the raiding party. In the first instance this need was met by advance preparation of large quantities of cooked manioc, both by his own wives and by the other women of the village. Smoked meat might also be carried or fish caught en route. Alternatively the war-chief's political influence might ensure hospitality among allied groups that lay on the way to enemy settlements. This situation was probably tense at the best of times but must have become particularly precarious in the eighteenth century, as the orbit of Carib raiding came to include previously allied villages:

. . . to their allies they say that they are not at fault for burning or capturing a given settlement, since had that settlement shown them hospitality and traded provisions for their expedition, then they would not have harmed them; however, having had their weapons confiscated with such discourtesy and having been shown less hospitality than had been shown to others, they [the Caribs] now wished to punish them. This is the ruse by which they lay the ground for an attack the following year. (Gumilla 1745: II,324)

Either way, the problem of victualling Carib raiding-parties, with easily 400 warriors, formed a natural and inherent limit to the scope and flexibility of military ambitions.

At the same time, the possibility often remained open to make peace. For example, on March 22nd, 1624, a large Aricoure war-party, from the Cassipour River in Brazil, stopped at a Yao village on the Oyapock, en route to attack Carib settlements at Cayenne. The Yao intervened, as they were "common friends of the two." They secured a peace between the Caribs and the Aricoures, but only "on condition that the Aricoures should ask for it":

> Their ceremony was as follows; the Caribs obliged them to wait on the seashore with their arms and as the Caribs fitted the arrow to the bow, ready to let fly, the Aricoures took water and poured it on their heads. This done, the Caribs, throwing down their arms, rushed into the canoes of the others and embraced them. On the occasion of this peace the Yaos entertained them together for eight days, peace having never been known between them before. (BL-Sloane: 179b)

Barrére, some 130 years later, reported a similar procedure[4] whereby one of the opposing war-chiefs would approach the enemy with a small band of warriors declaring that they wished friendship. If this proposition was well received then both parties would array their forces in battle-order and start singing, recounting the past capture of women and the death or cannibalism of relatives. Following these declarations both sides would throw down their arms, rush to embrace each other and then retire to one or another village for a feast (1743: 174–5).

However, when an attack was pressed home, the general aim was to capture young women and boys and to kill enemy warriors, taking various portions of their bodies for the ritual purpose of expunging the Tiger-Spirit. In the case of set-piece confrontations, as in the upland savannas and the llanos, the combatants would first face each other at a distance and dance. They then released poisoned arrows, and followed up with individual combat with clubs. The Orinoco Caribs are said to have preferred this kind of attack, as opposed to the night-time or surprise raid, since it enhanced their military kudos by demonstrating contempt for their enemies (Depons 1806: 49–50). The Orinoco Caribs were also noted for their extreme reluctance to allow their dead or wounded to fall into enemy hands: ". . . in order to regain them, they will expose themselves to a whole range of dangers and on many occasions lose more men through this desire than in actual battle" (Pelleprat 1965: 70).

Following the attack the warriors retired to practice cannibalistic rites. The sources indicate that there were preferred places for such purposes with river mouths and islands favoured. Sparrey (1625) mentions the island *Taroo* in the Orinoco, while the shell-middens of the Barima/Waini river mouths appear to have been used for the same purposes – Brett (1868: 424–40) and Im Thurn (1883: 410–21). Indeed, these practices may have persisted in just a few sites over many generations, since it was reported in 1597 to the King of Spain that the Orinoco Caribs and their Kalinago allies from Dominica and Grenada were already accustomed to go to the mouth of the Barima,

. . . where they are on terms of peace and friendship with other Caribs, and where they go to divide their spoil and offer sacrifices, and eat those Indians that they have captured. (BM-V.P. IV,15)

Following such ceremonies the warriors would disperse to their home villages, with human-trophies or those captives (*poitos*) to be incorporated as village members. Their arrival, in turn, might lead to a fresh bout of celebration. The practice of bringing home captives to live in the village was in contrast to that of the Arawak (Lokono), whose captives were tortured to death by both women and men in the settlement itself (see Van Berkel 1695). This also seems to have been the case among the neighboring Tupi of Brazil (see Knivet 1625, Lerius 1625, Staden 1557, Forsyth 1983). The Caribs, however, firmly segregated the killing of enemies from village life, although the human-trophies that they took, such as bone flutes, belts or hair, and dried heads, were originally made and displayed in the village. By the eighteenth century, however, many of these articles were being traded to tourists in Paramaribo as "Indian Curiosities" (Whitehead 1986).

Generally, increasingly close relationships with the Europeans, and in particular the development of habitual slave-hunting for the Dutch, brought new strategies and tactics, including the use of small scale military units in Carib warfare. Such innovations directly threatened the survival of traditional patterns of leadership. As described above, these required at least an inter-village level of consensus if an effective military force was to be recruited. The central factors in the new pattern of war were a wider access to fire arms and a more permanent state of militancy among the Carib warriors as reasons for raiding increased. This situation in turn may be traced to the chronic instability of Dutch control and authority over their slave populations coupled with a limited but steady demand for Amerindian domestic servants (*poitos*).

Moreover, in the eighteenth century the determined efforts of the Spanish on the Orinoco to find a final solution to the "Carib problem" forced even the most isolated and pacific Carib villages to evolve some response to the rapidly changing conditions in the Orinoco area. Chief among the changes was the sudden population loss that inevitably accompanied the advance of the Spanish missionaries as they evangelized the densely settled villages of the Orinoco flood-plain. With depleted populations, traditional lines of leadership were further weakened. The opportunities offered through service to the Dutch, in turn, encouraged some Caribs to become more and more involved in hunting slaves, both black runaways and red "domestics." In 1767 the Director-General of Essequibo informed the DWIC that:

. . . I have had a great deal of trouble with the Caribs because they spoke to me only of killing and it is only with a lot of effort and promises of double payment that I have got them to agree to catch the runaways and bring them back alive, (PRO-CO 116–57, 8/3/1771)

Accounts of Carib attacks on rebel black settlements in Essequibo and Demerara make it clear that quite small parties of Caribs could be extremely effective. Similarly, raids on isolated Amerindian villages in the interior, to take and sell captives rather than taking trophies, could be easily achieved by relatively small numbers of men, especially if equipped with firearms. Brett comments:

If a party can muster eight or ten stand of fire-arms, it will fight its way through all the mountain tribes, though at open war with them, and by the rapidity of their marches, and nightly enterprises [ambushes], they conceal the weakness of their numbers, and carry terror before them. (1868: 145)

Inevitably, in response to such changed conditions of warfare, some villages, notably those of the Arawak (*Lokono*) and Akawaio, evolved defensive measures such as palisading and the laying of poisoned traps along the approaches to the village. These were techniques that had, in some cases, already been learned in the seventeenth century.

However, as was suggested above, the alleged "ethnic war" between Carib and Arawak was an example of European intervention in the face of overwhelming Amerindian numbers. It had always been European strategy to attempt to exacerbate and exploit any existing tensions that they found amongst the Amerindian population. The conflict and vendettas between Carib and Arawak emerged largely due to the various alliances that different villages or networks of villages had with the

European powers. This conclusion is further confirmed by evidence that much of the early Amerindian resistance to the Spanish was without regard to "tribal" differences (Whitehead 1986). As Ralegh's discussion (1596) of his attempts to raise a general Amerindian rebellion against the Spanish in Guayana shows, traditions of raiding between groups implied a mutuality between them. This mutuality could, under different circumstances, involve military cooperation, as occurred, for example, in 1618 when Arawak, Carib and Warao united to attack the Spanish capital of Santo Tomé (BM-V.P. VIII, 16). Nor should it be forgotten that it was the usual fate of any female and child captives to be fully integrated into Carib society. Only under European influence, which encouraged the sale of such captives, was the stability implied by such local and habitual conflicts upset.

It was therefore the historic role of the Europeans to shatter such relationships, producing a steady hemorrhage of captives from the cycle of exchanges that had defined the aboriginal Amerindian polity. In the Carib idiom, it was as if *Kaikusi-yumu*, the Tiger Spirit, had been released from his magic constraints, to become a constant force in the consciousness of the Carib warrior.

THE EUROPEAN INTRUSION

Perhaps the single most striking fact of Carib history between 1500 and 1820 is that, despite a continual presence at the margins of their territories, it was not until the 1770s that the Spanish can be said to have effectively "pacified" the Caribs of the Orinoco basin. The reason for this was not just the tenacity of Carib resistance to encroachments on their political sovereignty but also their pivotal role in the colonial conflict of the Dutch and Spanish in this region. This is made clear by a letter of April 6th, 1766, from the Director-General of Essequibo to the Directors of the DWIC:

I continue to have good look-out kept on all the movements of the Spaniards . . . In such matters we can fully rely upon the assistance of the Caribs. The deep-rooted hatred and enmity of that nation towards the Spaniards is so great that there is little probability of a reconciliation between them, and although that nation has lost many of its old characteristics, this still continues to be one of its innate peculiarities. (PRO-CO 116, 34)

Accordingly, although it was the Spanish who were responsible for definitively breaking Carib power on the Orinoco, the influence of the

Dutch on Carib society, throughout the seventeenth and eighteenth centuries was just as significant. Though the Spanish had defined *"los caribes"* as the paramount enemy as early as 1503 (Whitehead 1984: 70), it was only in the context of Dutch colonial ambitions that the Caribs were able to mount widespread resistance to their presence on the Orinoco. Nor was this just because both Dutch and Caribs had coinciding interests in expelling the Spanish. It was also due to the mutual economic benefits involved in the trade in forest products that developed via the various Dutch outposts situated along the Wild Coast in the early seventeenth century.

By the beginning of the eighteenth century, however, Dutch economic priorities had radically changed. The emphasis was on plantation products, primarily sugar, from which derived the increasing demand for black slaves and Amerindian servants. As a result Dutch colonial policy was re-oriented to achieving a détente with the Spanish of the Orinoco. They had to since the capital and labor intensive plantations were far more vulnerable to attack and disruption than the relatively anonymous trading posts had been. As we shall see, this change in economic and political priorities drastically affected Carib groups, even beyond the immediate orbit of the Dutch colonies.

Nonetheless, Carib leaders made impressive achievements in assembling and maintaining widespread alliances, not only of far-flung Carib groups, but also of such non-Caribs as the Saliva, Warao, and Arawak. Such alliances were ultimately rooted in the virtual monopoly of Dutch trade goods that the Caribs possessed. However, they could also be activated for wider political ends, as is clearly shown in the way the Caribs resisted Spanish power on the Orinoco for over two centuries. Even in the eighteenth century the Spanish were still faced with chronic and widespread rebellion. In 1750 the Prefect of Capuchin Missions on the Orinoco reported to the Commandant of Guayana concerning the failure to pacify Amerindians:

. . . and not only the Caribs of the forests but even those of the missions participate in these wars, without our being able to control them in any way and whenever we make an effort to do so, they immediately desert us in great numbers. (BL-V.P. XXV, 1)

By the 1770s, as the full impact of European diseases was felt, the Caribs appear to have accepted much of the mission regime. This was a tenous "conversion," however. When these missions collapsed due to the depredations of the Venezuelan War of Independence at the turn of the eighteenth century, they were instantly and almost universally deserted. This suggests that at least some of the old patterns of Carib village leadership still survived, notwithstanding the vast population losses of these mission villages, and all the concomitant consequences for the endurance of the underlying kin network.

There is, therefore, a useful distinction to be drawn between the period up to the eighteenth century and thereafter. It is also necessary that the main features of the growth of Carib power in Guayana in the seventeenth century should be outlined before its defeat and retrenchment in the eighteenth century can be properly examined.

THE RISE AND FALL OF THE CARIB HEGEMONY IN GUAYANA

As outlined above, the key feature of Carib combat and warfare was its inherently limited nature, until the beginning of sustained intercourse with the Europeans. There were restraints of ideology, as expressed in beliefs that human violence and aggression are of external origin (i.e. from *Kaikusi-yumu*, the Tiger Spirit) and potential enemies and captives are part of the world of affines [see note 2]. These in turn were coupled with constraints of opportunity, imposed by logistical considerations and a social context in which infinite accumulation of the spoils of war (women and/or labor power of the *poito*) had no practical rationale. Such factors combined to make aboriginal warfare an endemic and persistent, yet socially-controlled event. One has only to think of the highly ritualized confrontations that are reported from the early seventeenth century to realize that there was a large measure of agreement between opposing forces as to what behavior was appropriate to such occasions.[5] The introduction by Europeans of distinctly different ideology of war, exemplified in the famous formulations of Thomas Hobbes, inevitably disrupted Amerindian assumptions and practices as to the permitted scope and purposes of armed conflict. The rise of Carib power in the sixteenth and seventeenth centuries is to be directly related to their obvious ability to adapt to these novel conditions.

Such an alteration in the custom and practice of warfare was experienced directly by Carib warriors through their employment as a local militia by the Dutch. Indirectly, it was experienced through the

160

new political and economic ambitions engendered by their ease of access to European goods, derived from their many trade partnerships with the Dutch. In consequence, they had the rationale to expand the scope and frequency of their raiding expeditions, which in turn signaled an irreparable fracture in the pre-existing consensus as to the rules and procedures of warfare.

The steady stream of war captives drained out of the circuit of Amerindian societies, into the hands of the Europeans, greatly unbalanced the traditional relationships between groups. Because of this loss of captives from the Amerindians polity, any rough parity between traditional enemies was unlikely, even in the longer term. Furthermore, a practical monopoly on the distribution of European goods could result in a rapid increase in the economic and political status of any of the groups so privileged. Broadly, this is what happened to the Carib in the seventeenth century, as it happened to the Lokono (Arawak) and Kalinago in the sixteenth century.

Until the seventeenth century, Carib groups were not at the forefront of contact with the Europeans, and various Carib groups experienced contact at different times throughout the seventeenth century. However, to paraphrase Cook and Borah (1963: 4) it took place uniformly with a steadily increasing violence of effect. Most obviously this "violence of effect" was meted out by firearms and artillery, with the psychological impact of such weapons being well established. As one missionary succinctly put it to Humboldt: "They do not hear the Voice of the Gospel where they have not first heard the sound of gunfire" (1852:ii: 219).

Despite such advantages the Spanish strategy on the Orinoco was often defensive in the face of extensive Carib hostility. The following description of a mission stockade that the Spanish Govenor considered to be particularly well-designed shows the pattern.

Close to the Padre's house there is a large tower . . . in which they have placed two or three swivel guns. The said tower, house and church are defended by a hedge of stakes, a sufficient wall to keep off the Caribs, unless they come accompanied by the Dutch, against whom the swivel guns are useful – if there is anyone in the village who can manage them – and their noise too frightens off the Caribs, so that they do not venture to come near the village or the stockade which protects the tower where the women and children and Indians are, if the enemy are in superior force or give no opportunity for them to mount a defense with their arrows. (BL-V.P. XXVII,2, 15/12/1763)

Not being faced with the colonial necessities of population control and territorial defense, until the eighteenth century, the Dutch were able to more fully exploit by pacific means the traditional conflicts they found among the Amerindians. They also reaped the benefits of their greater mastery of the complexities of Amerindian politics (stemming from the prolonged presence they maintained in this area) without frequent recourse to military measures against the native population.[6] The Spanish were aware of these differences in Amerindian policy between themselves and the Dutch:

. . . the Indians embrace their company [the Dutch] because they imitate the barbarity of their lives and allow them to enjoy full liberty without the constraints of tributes, labour or the sweet yoke of the Gospel, heavy in their opinion (BL-V.P. XI, 6, 19/11/1637)

In this context it is not surprising to find that the founder of the first permanent Dutch trading post in Essequibo, Aert van Groenewegen, took a Carib wife to ensure both his safety and prosperity in this region.

Subsequent Dutch, as well as various English and French, attempts to settle Guayana also invariably involved the construction of local alliances with the Amerindians and with groups of the interior as well, if trading operations were to be profitable. It was the need to trade with the interior groups that resulted in the development of Carib preeminence throughout the Guayanas since they acted as middlemen between the Dutch and the interior Amerindians.

The western and southwestern limits of this zone of Carib trading power were defined by a number of groups with whom the Carib had a series of sharp clashes in the late seventeenth and early eighteenth centuries. These included the Manoas, Maipures, Caberres, and Guaypuinavis. Such conflicts themselves were symptomatic of the political instability that resulted from the influx of European goods and the outflow of Amerindian captives. To the South, south-east and north, the Portuguese and Spanish blocked the old lines of trade. But within this vast and loosely circumscribed area, the Caribs heavily dominated the distribution of Dutch goods.

They maintained their pre-eminent role in this distribution not just by acting as guides and intermediaries for Dutch traders but also by producing native goods themselves, especially dye-woods, for which the Dutch paid well. In such a context a new rationale for the accumulation of labor power quickly emerged, since the processing of dye in particular was a labor intensive activity. In turn this reinforced the tendency to a purely economic trade in war-captives initiated by the Europeans on their arrival.

Evidence as to Carib involvement in this early slave trade is ambiguous. The ambiguity is particularly evident given probable differences in the interpretation of native patterns of kinship and social relations. On the one hand, the Europeans saw the Caribs as engaging in the open "sale" of their "sonnes and daughters of their own bretheren and sisters, and for somewhat more, even their own daughters" (Ralegh 1596: 39). The Caribs on the other hand may well have envisioned instead that the giving of kin to the strangers would obligate them to become involved in a cycle of exchanges over an extended period of time. Disappointment in this regard, particularly with the Spanish, seems to have been a major factor in the development of Carib attitudes towards the Europeans.

Such anyway was the situation until the eighteenth century, when the DWIC switched to the intensive cultivation of sugar. Thus as the European population of the Dutch colonies increased, a new market was created for the war-captives the Caribs were accustomed to using in the production of dye. The precise scale of these activities remains to be determined. The most widely quoted estimates of the effects of Carib slaving are those of the missionaries, for whom the charge of slave-taking, like accusations of cannibalism, functioned politically to justify the conquest and pacification of the Caribs. Suffice it to say here that missionary claims that tens of thousands of Amerindians were sold into slavery to the Dutch are in no way borne out by the evidence of the Dutch archives. This is not to deny that there was a dramatic decline in Amerindian numbers in the eighteenth century but it was the missionaries themselves who introduced epidemic diseases among the peoples of the Orinoco. If not actively engaged in concealing these tragedies, they were at least blind to these particular consequences of their evangelizing efforts. Nonetheless, trade in "red-slaves" brought great kudos to some Carib leaders and drew them into direct conflict with the Orinoco missionaries, for whom exclusive access and control over the Amerindians was paramount.

A good example of the relation between the Caribs and missionaries was the career of the Barima war-chief, Taricura, who reportedly had thirty wives, ". . . each one of a different nation" (Gumilla 1745: 135). The general dominance of the Barima Caribs was developed through the long succession of colonizing attempts made by the Europeans generally in this area. However, the close proximity of the established Dutch trading colonies of Pomeroon and Essequibo, as well as attempts to directly colonize the Barima, between 1670 and 1730, undoubtedly underwrote the social wealth of Carib groups in this area. The clearest evidence that such new-found opportunities were being fully exploited by Carib leaders is given by the large scale raids against the Jesuits led by Taricura and his father Araguacare from the 1680s to the 1730s. As contemporary records make clear, these raids were prompted by the advances the missionaries had made in disrupting regional Carib trading relationships (BL-V.P. XX-2,8, 13/XXXI-3,5).

Although his father dramatically terminated the Jesuit presence on the Orinoco, Taricura in fact failed to dislodge the missionaries. This indicates the extent to which the Spanish had learned from their experience of the 1680s and, indirectly, the limits of Carib military power. Taricura, despite having built a considerable web of alliances, was not actually in a position to militarily dominate the Spanish on the Orinoco indefinitely, in the context of the wider Amerindian rebellion against the missionaries, the sources of his power among the Orinoco Amerindians sprang from his trading relations with the Dutch, particularly the illicit trading of guns. It was this trade in firearms, however, especially to Caribs on the fringes of the Dutch colonies, that the DWIC severely curtailed in the eighteenth century under the pressure of Spanish threats of retaliation as well as the fear of overweening Carib power itself. With just these kinds of considerations at the front of his mind, the Director-General of Essequibo wrote to the DWIC in 1770 (the last free Caribs on the Orinoco having sent a deputation to him to ask for support against the Spanish raids being made against their settlements) that he had been unable to accede in urgent Carib requests for firearms.

Within the Dutch colonies themselves the situation differed somewhat, since Carib warriors were used as a bush-police against the black slaves. However this usefulness of the Caribs to the authorities did not survive under the British administration which supplanted the Dutch in 1803. When the Carib chief, Mahanarva, entered the capital in 1810, seeking to continue the trade that had been established by the Dutch, ". . . on the refusal of the Govenor to accept a fine slave, dashed out the brains of the slave and declared, for the future, that his nation should never give quarter" (Hilhouse 1825: 29).

In contrast, some of the Orinoco Caribs in this same period joined with Patriot forces of Simón Bolívar to fight the Spanish Crown. They formed a special group who operated in support of the cavalry on the eastern llanos, where a number of critical victories were won by the Patriots:

> . . . 'Sotillo's Men', as they were proud to be called, or 'Sotillo's Bloodhounds' as their enemies called them. Each was equipped with his bow and a quiver of arrows – suspended over his back as well as shouldering a lance . . . [their] only clothing a narrow strip of cloth and the lap. (Lance 1876: 154)

These new developments in the relationship between the Caribs and the authorities in Venezuela and British Guiana only tend to underline the contrast with earlier times when the Snake Warriors were able to virtually dictate their own terms to the Europeans. In the words of Major John Scott, the absence of Carib support for nascent colonies ". . . did occasion their mouldering away to nothing" (BL-Sloane 3662). But having accepted and served the ways of the white-men they were no longer in a position to resist them.

In some respects the legacy of this close Carib involvement in European affairs lived on, despite the fact that many groups withdrew into the interior of the old Dutch territories. According to the Govenor of Essequibo, the Caribs withdrew ". . . because they got no encouragement, received no presents, and obtained no sign of that esteem and friendship on which they prided themselves in being held by the Dutch" (Govenor of Essequibo to British Colonial Office PRO C0 III/4–2010).

As has already been mentioned the mission settlements in Venezuela were also deserted. In the context of massive population loss, however, and the social instabilities of the Venezuelan War of Independence and British indifference, the Carib groups were left with a situation in which violence and aggression were still socially generated. However, there was no longer a means of expression, other than within the shrinking circle of neighbors and kin. Quite simply, the collapse of a pan-Amerindian tropical forest society meant that the most basic Carib assumptions about raiding and the taking of captives were no longer tenable. The Moravian missionary, Zander, records the following words of a Carib war chief from the Maroni, in the early eighteenth century:

> I asked a Carib chief how many nations there were in Orinoco. He took a handful of sand and asked me if I could count the grains, when I said that I could not he replied that, "So many are the nations in Orinoco." (Staehelin 1912: I, 95)

By the end of the eighteenth century the Caribs had themselves experienced a 90 per cent population loss, and the "nations in Orinoco" had all but disappeared, as a result of epidemic disease. As a consequence of this sudden isolation and the decline in traditional patterns of leadership, Amerindian societies experienced social crisis, resulting in the emergence of both apocalyptic spiritual movements (see Thomas 1982: 146) and vengeance cults, or *Kanaima*.

The latter, dedicated to *Kaikusi-yumu*, the Tiger-Spirit, emerged in the latter half of the nineteenth century. Brett encountered one such assassin on the Demerara in the 1840s:

Two Indians passed us in a very light canoe. One was unadorned; but the man who steered wore a handsome tiara of feathers, and had his skin covered all over with bright red spots, like those of the jaguar, save in colour. His eyes gleamed wildly through circles of the same paint; and both himself and his companion were paddling with all their might against the stream. (1868: 288)

Assassination according to the code of the *Kanaima* specified that the victim was first to be immobilized and only then to be killed, ideally by grasping the throat and forcing the fangs of a venomous snake through his distended tongue. Significantly, in the context of what has been said in the preceding section about Carib rituals of cannibalism, the practitioner of *Kanaima* could only be released from the Tiger-Spirit which possessed him if the liver and blood of the dead man were tasted. Failure to observe this injunction, just as a failure to kill the intended victim, involved dire consequences. The *Kanaima* would not find release from *Kaikusi-yumu* and would thus be condemned to wander as a social outcast:

An Indian, reduced almost to a skeleton, and in a dreadful state of exhaustion, was picked up in the forest by some Arawaks [*Lokono*] and brought to the Pomeroon Mission. He had lost a portion of his scalp and had his lower lip torn down at each corner . . . Those wounds were in a most loathsome condition. The Acawaios at the mission took care of him at first, but afterwards judged, from his refusing certain kinds of food and other signs, that he was a devotee and victim of an unappeased Kanaima, and . . . we had some difficulty in getting him nursed till his strength had returned, as they feared lest they should become his future victims. (Brett 1868: 359)

In the Venezuelan territories where the Caribs had not already become incorporated into the lowest ranks of the new nation-state, it was said: "Though pretty well broken, they [Caribs] retain features of their former character, having resisted the forced levies [Venezuelan army] and, in some instances, united into predatory bands." (Hamilton 1820: 276). So too, as Caribs increasingly conceded their independence to national loyalties, they developed among themselves and others identities as either "Spanish" or "English" Caribs (see also Whitehead n.d.). An old Carib made the following statement in 1897, the year of his death:

> When we were captured by the Spanish [Venezuelans] it was done with the assistance of the Spanish Caribs. We were brought to Carapo and we were tied with our thumbs together until we became submissive to them. (BGB-BC VII, 229)

Yet even here there is an echo of the days of Carib hegemony, since, at the very last, they were needed to hunt down their own. As the Prefect of the Capuchins correctly divined,

> . . . this is a unique nation, which is permanently indomitable, and for whose conversion it will be necessary to apply, both spiritually and temporally, the *maximum force.* (AGI-SD 592, 23/12/1755)

CONCLUSION

Various themes emerge in the analysis of Carib warfare over the years 1500–1820 which have a general significance for any attempt to reach an anthropological understanding of warfare. Among the more important of these is a strong contrast between the basic historical trajectories of Amerindian and European warfare with consequent differences in what might be termed their "war-cultures." Paradoxically it has been the Hobbesian notion of war where ". . . every man is the enemy to every man" (1651 I:xiii) that has often been thought to correctly characterize "primitive" conflict. In the case of the Caribs, however, such an intensity of conflict seems to have been more closely associated with the involvement of the Europeans. The limited aims of Amerindian raiding and relative underdevelopment of their military technology was as apparent to the Europeans in the sixteenth century as it is to us today. Subsequently, the social consensus which underlay such traditional conflicts as that of the Karinya and Saliva or Achagua, the Kalinago and the Lokono, or the Tupi and Tapuya (Lévi-Strauss 1943, Balée 1984), was disrupted by the sudden and unpredictable effects of European involvement in these struggles. New military strategies and weaponry, new types of economic and political influence and the ever present

167

possibility of deadly epidemics all combined to challenge the stability and autonomy of the Amerindian polity. Under such conditions Hobbesian "warre" easily flourished as the long succession of European adventurers and freebooters came to seek their fortunes in the New World.

The response of most Carib communities to this challenge proved highly successful, since it combined a justly famous exploitation of the new trading opportunities with a minimal loss of political independence to the Europeam merchants. However, it was precisely the ambiguity of this relationship that also permitted the growth and continuation of the image of the Carib as intractably savage. In point of fact, as we have seen from the evidence presented above, the role of cannibalism in the ideology of the Carib warrior was not principally, as in the case of the Cauca Valley chiefdoms (see Carneiro this volume), to stimulate aggression or satisfy a desire for revenge. Rather the eating of human flesh represented a "rite de passage" – animistic and liminal in the terminology of Van Gennep's schema (1960) – from the domain of the Tiger-Spirit and the world of war and killing, to the human domain and the world of the village and kin. Our own cultural revulsion towards acts of physical cannibalism thus should not distract us from the possibility that it was precisely an equivalent disgust that Carib rituals were designed to elicit, thus placing a clear boundary between the civil and military aspects of their society.

More generally it will be apparent that no single factor, out of the many which have been advanced to explain the phenomenon of war, will, by itself, be adequate to explain the historical development of Carib warfare. Ecological determinants, variations in social structure and ideology, and the costs/benefits for powerful individuals are all components of such an explanation. However important these factors appear in their particular ethnographic contexts, no single element emerges as continuously determinant when seen in historical perspective. In such a situation the challenge becomes one of constructing a truly anthropological, rather than just ethnographic, explanation in which the variability of ecological, sociological and biological factors is analysed in real time. Thus, as Hobbes perceived:

The cause of war is that men know not the causes of war nor peace, there being but few in the world that have learned the rules of civil life sufficiently. (1839: I,8)

Carib warfare, ca. 1500–1820

Archival and Documentary Sources

Abbreviations used are as follows:

Archive	Name of document collection
AGI – Archivo General de Indias	C – Audiencia de Caracas
	SD — Audiencia de Santo Domingo
AZ – Archief Staten van Zeeland (Middelburg)	H – Handschriftenverzameling
BL – British Library	VP – Venezuela Papers (Additional MSS. 36314–55)
	BGB – British Guiana Boundary (Printed extracts from above collection published London, 1898)
PRO – Public Record Office	CO – Colonial Office (Dutch Association Papers)

Notes

1. The designation "tiger" is used since this was the term employed in Spanish territories and in the Guianas. The word "Jaguar" is quite inappropriate since it is of Tupi/Brazilian derivation and currently used zoologically to refer exclusively to the one species of large cat *Panthera onca*.
2. "Poyto" is a Carib term, given various orthographic renderings in the literature, which has had a number of applications in their history. As Riviere points out: " It has variously been translated as 'slave,' 'client,' 'brother-in-law,' 'son-inlaw,' and 'sister's son' . . . but always connote[s] affinal relations . . . which offer the best idiom for expression of relationships that involved domination and subordination" (1977: 40–1). That the Spanish came to use this term to refer to Amerindian captives traded to the Dutch gives us an important indication as to how Carib society was adapted to meet novel conditions of European colonization. It should thus, also, make us wary of any simplistic identifications of the conditions and character of black slavery with that of Amerindian servitude.
3. Harcourt says the name of the spirit that the *piaii* conversed with was *Wattipa*, who was feared rather than loved since he ". . . often times bear them blacke and blew" (1613: 26), while a Dutch report of the 1590's noted that:

When a captain of the [Carib] Indians, taken prisoner by the Spaniards, was going to be hanged, he said that he had spoken with the Spirit Wattipa, and that he had prophesied deliverance through the Dutch and English. (Jonge 1862: 153–60)

However, the wider role of prophetic and divinatory practices, a recurrent theme in Carib history, is not yet clear.

4. Gumilla (1745:I:317) noted that, among the Otomaco and Saliva, ceremonies of peace were concluded by individuals inter-changing as many blows with a club (though not the war club!) as amounted to complete satisfaction for both parties. This practice, and its context, is very reminiscent of the chest-pounding and club duels of the Yanomamö, as reported by Chagnon (1968b).

5. Lévi-Strauss (1943: 143) and, more recently, Balée (1984: 258) similarly note that war and trade between the Tapuya and Tupinamba ". . . performed as logical counterparts of one social system." Indeed, the natural inter-dependency of traditional enemies was recognized as an important social principle in the world of the Ancient Greeks. Thus Lycurgus, Law-Giver of the Spartans, forbade that war should always be waged against the same enemies for fear that they might grow more experienced in military affairs (see Plutarch's "Lives" – many editions).

6. The Dutch were not so successful in Brazil, however, where the Potiguar Chief, Camarao, led fierce Amerindian resistance against the Dutch between 1632 and 1648, nor in Surinam where a "peace" was only established after the Dutch had militarily supported Arawak groups against the Caribs (AZ: 20035-no. 182, 1626).

8
Warfare and the evolution of tribal polities in the prehistoric Southwest

JONATHAN HAAS

This paper examines the role of warfare in the process of tribalization in a prehistoric and precolonial social environment. It differs from the others in the volume by looking at warfare in an archaeological context rather than ethnographically or ethnohistorically; by taking a diachronic rather than a synchronic view of the development and impact of prestate warfare; and – like Carneiro's paper – by looking more at the effects of warfare on society than at its causes.

There are both advantages and disadvantages to an archaeological analysis of warfare. On the negative side, archaeology lacks the rich descriptive detail of individual behavior and specific events provided by ethnographers and early observers. We are largely unable to look at intention, individual motivations, emic explanations of events and patterns of behavior, kin relationships, and most other aspects of the ideological superstructure of the long-dead societies.

On the positive side, archaeology is able to look back to times and cultures before the imperial expansion of European states. As the papers by Whitehead, Gibson, and Robarchek clearly show, contact with colonial states severely impacts native societies and their conduct of war. To factor out the impact of colonial contact and look at social organization, politics, and warfare under "pristine," precontact conditions (Fried 1967), it is necessary to study prehistoric societies archaeologically. Another big advantage of an archaeological analysis is the ability to examine patterns of cultural change over *long* periods of time. While ethnographers such as Chagnon (this volume) can observe societies over several decades, archaeologists have access to records of cultural systems spread over centuries or more (see Haas 1982).

TRIBES AND TRIBALIZATION

Before turning to the possible role of warfare in the process of tribalization it is necessary to briefly address the notion of "tribe" itself. Although there are different models of tribal organization (Service 1971; Adams 1975; Sahlins 1968, 1972), and some dispute over the utility of the concept (Fried 1975, 1983), "tribe" remains a useful term for analyzing a general evolutionary stage of prestate development (Creamer and Haas 1985). The tribe generally lies between the "band" with a loosely knit network of related families, and the "chiefdom" with a formal social hierarchy and centralized political and economic system (Service 1971; Steward 1955). In simplest terms, a tribe is a bounded network of communities united by social and political ties and generally sharing the same language, ideology, and material culture. The communities in a tribe are economically autonomous and there is no centralized political hierarchy.

Two different models of tribal evolution have been offered: a "traditional" model offered by cultural anthropologists such as Service, Sahlins, and Adams, and an alternative model offered by archaeologists such as Braun and Plog (Braun and Plog 1980, 1982; Braun 1984; Plog and Braun 1983; see also Bender 1985). The traditional explanation assigns a primary causal role to warfare in the evolution of the tribe. It is argued that in the face of population growth related to the beginnings of plant domestication, groups found themselves in competition over land and other resources. In response to these conditions, groups that joined forces with one another would be better able to complete, and fight, for scarce resources. Out of this competitive milieu, there emerged a new form of polity, a decentralized network of villages allied together in the face of external competition – the tribe.

There is nothing in this demographic situation [population growth] alone which would necessarily lead to a tribal form of organization; probably the earliest growing societies simply divided and spread. With competition, however, the larger and better consolidated would prevail, other things being equal. Here again external offense-defense requirements may well have been the selective factors, signifying as they do the importance of alliance and solidarity. (Service 1971: 101; see also Harner 1970: 70)

This model of tribalization involves consolidation and coordination of different units, but the process also occurs within the context of competition and conflict or warfare. Again, to quote Service:

The external policy of tribes is usually military only. Usually, too, the military posture is consistently held; that is, a state of war or near-war between neighboring tribes is nearly perpetual. Tribal warfare by its nature is incon-clusive. Ambush and hit-and-run raids are the tactics rather than all-out campaigns, which cannot of course be economically sustained by a tribal economy and its weak organization. True conquest, furthermore, would be self-defeating, for the productivity of a defeated tribe would not be great enough to sustain the conquerors. Objectives seem to be booty . . . or to drive the enemy out of a favored zone or present him from expanding. (1971: 104; see also Adams 1975: 228; Carneiro 1970, 1978; Sahlins 1968: 17)

Thus, while warfare is seen as central to the process of tribalization, its role is one of inducing consolidation through cooperation rather than conquest. The unified tribe then emerges as a discrete political entity separated from its neighbors by hostile (or potentially hostile) relations.

The second model of tribalization, while also emphasizing coopera-tion, argues that the process of tribal consolidation occurs in response to any number of social and/or environmental "risks" (Braun and Plog 1980, 1982: 506–508; Bender 1985). Warfare may be one of those "risks," but it is not seen as the primary causal force behind the process of tribalization. Basically, Braun and Plog take issue with the notion that resource shortages and other environmental problems will necessarily lead to competition and conflict. They argue instead, that in the face of such problems, there is more likely to be an intensification of coopera-tive interaction and alliance between local communities.

For example, other things being equal, an increase in population density or a reduction in the scale of residential movement would leave coresidential units with increasingly smaller areas for direct exploitation. Under many environmental conditions, such a construction of the area available for direct exploitation would increase the spatial and temporal variance in productive yields among neighboring coresidential units. Such increased local unpredict-ability in yields would present a potential increase in risk to each local community. If this increasing local unpredictability occurs within an already existing social network, we would expect to see an increase in the social connectedness within that network. That is, where lines of cooperation and communication already exist, increased local environmental unpredictability should lead to increased demand on these lines of integration. Except under the most extreme circumstances (e.g. see discussions in Dirks [1980] and in Winterhalder [1980]), sustained increases in such demands should lead to increased formalization of the existing lines of integration, as a consequence of the processes of selection discussed earlier. (Braun and Plog 1982: 508)

Thus, the process of tribalization is seen as one of increased cooperation, integration and communication between communities.

The latter view of tribalization differs from the traditional model in a number of ways. First, in downplaying the role of warfare, the interaction between tribal groups is seen to be significantly different from the competition and conflict in the more traditional model. In Braun and Plog's model, the expectation of intertribal conflict is lacking, and there may well be an increase in certain kinds of positive interaction between tribal units (e.g. ritual exchange), as one tribal group establishes alliance relationships with other groups (Braun and Plot 1980: 36–48).

Further, in the traditional model, tribalization involves not only increased integration (pantribal sodalities in Service's model) and coordination (structural hierarchy in Sahlins' model), but also formation of social boundaries around the "tribe." This boundary formation is a logical outgrowth of the emphasis on the importance of warfare in tribal formation. In a cooperative model, however, the process of boundary formation is quite distinct from the intensification of integration and coordination (Braun and Plog 1982: 505; Bender 1985: 55). Accordingly, the process of tribalization can take place in the absence of the formation of concrete bounded tribes. In a sense then, it might be possible to have a tribal *form* of organization, without having a discrete social unit readily identifiable as a bounded *tribe*.

THE ARCHAEOLOGY OF TRIBES

In the remainder of this paper, I will examine the process of tribalization and the possible role of warfare in that process in the context of prehistoric polities in the southwestern United States. Specifically, I will look at the evolutionary development of the prehistoric Anasazi Indians of northeast Arizona prior to A.D. 1300. (The entire northern Southwest including the study area was abandoned at approximately 1300, and remained largely unoccupied until after the time of

174

European contact.) Before turning to the data base, however, it is necessary to operationalize the concepts of tribe and tribalization such that they can be recognized in the archaeological record (Creamer and Haas 1985). From the different models of tribalization, several key elements must be operationalized to study the evolution of tribal organization in prehistoric societies: interaction, environmental stress and warfare.

Interaction

In tribalization there will be an increase in interaction and "connectedness" between the members of an emerging tribal unit. A number of scholars have recently attempted to measure interaction by looking at patterns of exchange between communities (Braun and Plog 1982; Hodder 1982; Plog 1980, 1983; Wobst 1977) and at shared patterns of material culture (ceramic design styles, arrowhead types, etc.) (Bender 1985; Graves 1981; Voss 1980; Washburn 1978). Another means of examining changing patterns of interaction in the process of tribalization is through an analysis of evidence for cooperative activities. The increased connectedness predicted for tribes should be characterized by greater degrees of cooperation between the member units of the tribal unit. Thus, there should be more joint activities carried out at all levels of the tribe, including households, kin units, communities, subtribal units and the tribe itself. Such activities should be manifested in small scale communal labor projects or centrally located work areas or ceremonial structures.

Internal cooperation within a tribe may also be manifested in the economic and social interdependence of the various tribal units. With the high level of integration predicted for tribal forms of organization, social and economic responsibilities may be consolidated and assigned or assumed by different parts of the tribal unit. Social consolidation for ceremonial or political activities is to be expected as a means of explicitly uniting and integrating the member units of a tribe. Such social consolidation is exhibited by communal or shared ceremonial architecture and possibly other kinds of communal activity areas not directly related to the mode of production; for example, formal plazas or non-religious communal buildings ("town halls").

Consolidation or economic responsibilities can be expected as an adaptive response in emergent tribes, given that tribes are argued to arise in response to increased stress, and competition and conflict with neighboring groups. Under such conditions limited pooling of resources and labor as well as small-scale specialization would enhance the economic viability and competitive position of the tribe as a whole. Pooling of resources and labor may be manifested archaeologically in communal storage facilities, small-scale communal labor projects, such as field preparations, water control devices, or defensive walls and fortifications.

The economic specialization in tribes can be expected to be limited to the production of craft items such as ceramics and lithics. Specialization in construction activities, warfare or the production of food would not be expected in these decentralized, nonhierarchical societies. Surplus production serves to ensure long-term survival rather than the support of discrete social strata of craftsmen, warriors, laborers and economic elite. This level of specialization in tribes stands in contrast to the large-scale labor specialization and class formation characterizing more complex, politically centralized societies (Haas 1982). Economic specialization in the prehistoric tribe would be marked by the concentration of specific productive tools in the burials or residences of a small minority of the population. The large majority of the residences and burials on the other hand should not be marked by major economic differences or artifactual indications of specialization.

Another form of interaction is to be found in the interaction between different components of the tribal polity. Sahlins (1968, 1972) has argued that a tribe can be seen as a "pyramid of social groups" (1968: 15), in which the parts are not necessarily subordinate to one another, but play different roles in the social system. For example, at the basic level of the household, certain kinds of activities are carried out, while at the clan or lineage level there is another set of activities, and so on, up to the "tribal" level at the apex of the pyramid. Each level then has responsibility for the accomplishment of different kinds of tasks.

An analysis of artifacts and architecture, therefore, should reveal specific activities that are carried out jointly by the member units of each hierarchical level. Consequently, there should be certain activities, such as sewing, eating, or cooking, which are carried on predominantly at the household level; others, such as food storage, farming, or food processing, carried on at the suprafamilial kin group level; others, such as construction or architectural maintenance, carried on at the community level; others, such as water control or ceremonial behavior, carried on at the multicommunity or subtribal level; and finally activities, such as defense and offense, carried on at the tribal level. The precise nature of such a functional hierarchy should change from one tribe to another, as may the activities carried out at each level. However, if the basic model is an accurate one, there should be evidence of distinct organizational levels and of distinct activities carried out at each.

Environmental stress

Environmental stress on human populations may result from variability in climate, changes in hydrologic or erosional factors, overexploitation of natural resources including land, or population densities beyond the carrying capacity of the surrounding area. Looking at possible environmental stress in the archaeological record involves analysis of ecofact – botanical, pedological, pollen and dendrochronological samples. It is expected from Braun and Plog's model that the actual process of tribalization would be preceded or accompanied by environmental changes which introduced new sources of risk or stress into the local ecosystem.

Indirectly, environmental stress may also be exhibited in the diet of the population. Food shortages resulting from drought or other environmental causes will be reflected in a variety of skeletal markers of malnutrition and related diseases.

Warfare

In relation to "advanced" forms of warfare found in chiefdoms, states and other complex societies, tribal warfare is relatively simple. It will usually consist primarily of small-scale sporadic raiding occurring with limited physical contact. The objectives of such raids would be wife-stealing, limited acquisition, and general destruction of an enemy's resources (Service 1971). Clearly, raiding of this sort will not leave a dramatic mark on the archaeological record. Nevertheless, there should be signs that a prehistoric tribal group was either engaged in conflict with foreign groups or was at least concerned about potential conflict. The latter may be objectified in the construction of defensive features, such as walls or moats, or the deliberate selection of defensible site locations. "Deliberate" selection of such locations may be inferred when ready access to resources, water or arable land is sacrificed in exchange for elevation, difficult access, unrestricted or strategic vistas, or physical protection from attack.

Direct manifestations of warfare can be seen in human skeletal remains exhibiting signs of violence consistent with warfare. One manifestation of this would be a higher frequency of fractured skulls and forearms, and another would be evidence of violent death (e.g. an arrowhead lodged in the body). The frequency of deaths of young adult males, between the ages of roughly 18 and 35 might be significantly higher in the presence of tribal warfare, as those are the individuals most likely to be engaged in the fighting. At the same time, there might be significantly lower frequencies of young adult males in the burial population if warriors are accorded special burial removing them from the archaeologically recoverable record (e.g. placed in trees or left in the open). Arson or the deliberate burning of structures would be another indication of raiding and conflict. In addition to the deliberate burning of structures, tribal warfare should result in differential burning of storage facilities, since one of the goals of raiding may be destruction of the enemy's resource base (see Zier 1976).

THE STUDY AREA

Turning from the archaeological manifestations of tribal organization and formation to the prehistory of northeast Arizona, I will concentrate on the period between A.D. 1100 and 1300. This period has been selected for two reasons: first, this is a time for which there is a good body of survey, excavation and paleoenvironmental data; second, during this period there are the clearest indications of the formation of discrete tribal units throughout the northern Southwest (Haas 1986). However, it should be pointed out that the first stages in the evolution of tribal systems in this region clearly appear to have taken place centuries earlier.

Following A.D. 500, as the population became increasingly sedentary and population grew, there was an intensification of localized interaction. It was at about this time that the residents of northeast Arizona developed a local cultural assemblage quite different from neighboring Anasazi groups elsewhere in the northern Southwest. Their artifacts are distinctive, as are ceramic design styles, domestic and religious architecture, burial practices and the like. These differences, easily recognizable in the archaeological record, have led researchers to identify the residents of northeast Arizona as a separate "branch" of the Anasazi – the Kayenta Anasazi. It is the relative cultural homogeneity that gives the first indication that the residents of the area were evolving from simple bands to the more complex and systematic interaction networks characteristic of tribal organization. The close similarities in material culture, particularly in the ceramic design styles are an indication of some degree of group identity and what Bender refers to as "societal closure" (Bender 1985: 55). At the same time, aside from sharing a wide range of cultural traits, there are no overt manifestations of systematic interaction of coordination between communities. There are also no signs of clear cut boundaries either around the Kayenta as a whole or around component parts within the Kayenta region. Thus in the centuries immediately following A.D. 500, the Kayenta appear to be in the initial stages of the process of tribalization, but without a concrete tribal organization uniting the individual villages.

The next stages in Kayenta tribalization take place centuries later, and exhibit some localized variability in different parts of northeast Arizona. I will concentrate on one area roughly in the center of the Kayenta region, Long House Valley and the surrounding areas of Klethla Valley, Kayenta Valley, and Tsegi Canyon. This area of roughly 1000 sq km was the focus of my own research for five years and the subject of extensive research by others over the past century. Long House Valley itself was completely surveyed in the late 1960s and early 1970s (Dean, et al. 1978), and two sites within the valley have been excavated and several others have been intensively mapped and recorded. In the 1930s, the Rainbow Bridge–Monument Valley Expedition conducted an intensive survey of the Tsegi Canyon system (Beals, et al. 1945), and excavated one large site in the Kayenta Valley and several smaller sites in the general vicinity (Crotty 1983; Christensen 1983). More recently extensive sample surveys have been conducted in Klethla Valley to the south and west and Kayenta Valley to the east and in the Tsegi Canyon system to the north (Haas and Creamer 1987). Complementing the survey and excavation data is a detailed reconstruction of the prehistoric environment. Based on data from tree rings, pollen and paleo-hydrology, it has been possible to reconstruct accurate patterns of past rainfall, ground water, and soil erosion and aggradation. The arch-aeological and paleoenvironmental data together provide a foundation for examining the process of tribal formation in the Kayenta region

179

during the twelfth and thirteenth centuries.

At A.D. 1100, the residents of Long House Valley were living in numerous small villages of two to ten rooms for one to four families. Some had kivas (ceremonial structures) while others did not. Sites are distributed fairly evenly along the edges and across the floor of the valley. Although exact population estimates are not available, the relative population density in the valley was higher at the beginning of the twelfth century than previously, though not at a maximum which comes in the thirteenth century (Dean, et al. 1978; Effland 1979). The environment at A.D. 1100 across northern Arizona is quite favorable for subsistence horticulture, with relatively high water table, high annual precipitation and near the top of a cycle of soil aggradation (Dean, et al. 1985).

Regarding social relationships, the Long House residents continue to share the same material cultural assemblage as people residing in other parts of the Kayenta region. There are also indications that ceramics and the raw materials for making stone tools are being exchanged between valleys at this time (Green 1983, 1986; Garrett 1986), but there is no sign of systematic interaction or coordination either within the valley or between neighboring valleys. Warfare and conflict are not manifested in any way in the settlement pattern or the burial population. Overall, the available data base from the Kayenta heartland at the beginning of the twelfth century does not point to a supra-village tribal organization.

STRESS AND INTERACTION

Beginning at approximately A.D. 1150, the environment in northern Arizona began to change and the local population changed with it. There was a drop in the alluvial ground water levels, and major short-term drought, and the start of a period of soil degradation caused by erosion (Dean, et al. 1985). In response to these environmental shifts, portions of the Kayenta region were abandoned completely. Black Mesa, immediately to the south and east of Long House Valley, was always fairly marginal for horticulture, and with the drop in precipitation and the water table, the residents of this area left completely by 1150 (Powell 1983).

In Long House Valley between A.D. 1150 and 1250 there was a substantial shift of the population toward the northern half of the valley. This would have increased the population density locally, though the total population in the valley as a whole did not go up substantially. The villages remained small, and there are no material indications of increased interaction or the emergence of a tribal organization uniting the communities within the valley or bringing together the Long House residents with residents of neighboring valleys. At the same time, it can be inferred from the increased densities and clustering of villages in the northern half of the valley, there would have been increased coordination and/or cooperation in the distribution and utilization of limited field systems. There are still no signs of either competition or conflict at either the valley or regional level. However, the shift of the population out of the southern half of the valley resulted in the beginning of a de facto physical boundary between Long House residents and the people living in Klethla Valley to the south and east. The fact that Black Mesa to the south and west was also completely abandoned at this time further extended the physical boundary around the Long House population.

   The latter half of the thirteenth century saw a continued degradation of the environment. Arable land continued to erode and the water table dropped even further, probably drying up many stable sources of drinking water. While annual precipitation was variable, another major drought occurred in the 1260s (Dean 1969). These environmental trends were accompanied by dramatic cultural changes among the Kayenta Anasazi. In Long House Valley, population increased to its maximum, probably through immigration. The southern half of the valley was completely abandoned. In the northern half, the population came to reside in five discrete clusters of villages (Effland 1979; Dean, et al. 1978), in which there appeared for the first time a clear differentiation between two kinds of villages.

   Archaeologically, each of the five clusters consists of a single "focal" site of 75 to 400 rooms around which lie 2 to 13 "satellite" sites of 2 to 25 rooms each. In addition to being large, each of the focal sites is distinguished by the presence of open plaza areas and a "spinal" roomblock – a large, open room, 20 to 50 m long, constructed with cored, double-faced masonry and positioned along the back edge of the site (Dean, et al. 1978: 33). Reservoirs for collecting and storing water have been located at four of the five focal communities. All of the focal sites are situated in defensible positions – hilltops, knolls or isolated small mesas, overlooking the land around the satellite sites in the cluster. Significantly, the focal sites are located so that there is a clear line of sight with each of the others and overlooking all the primary

181

access routes leading into the valley.

Based on the placement and distribution of sites within the valley, the Long House data fits the expected pattern for a population undergoing a transformation to a more concrete tribal form of organization. Clearly there is an "increase in social connectedness" (Braun and Plog 1982: 508) during this period, as the villages move closer together into discrete settlement clusters with central focal sites and dispersed satellites. The functional hierarchy of Sahlins' tribal model would appear to be reflected in the organization and distribution of the different sites, with households, villages, clusters of villages and the interlocking network of clusters representing distinct interacting levels within the hierarchy.

Looking beyond settlement, additional data confirm the appearance of greatly increased social interaction in the Valley in the latter half of the thirteenth century. At the level of the individual villages, excavations have shown the construction of multi-household dwellings, and common rooms for grinding corn shared by multiple households in neighboring villages (see also Dean 1969). At the cluster level, cooperation and interaction are manifested in the construction of the large, centrally located "spinal" roomblocks in the focal sites as well as the communal water reservoirs in four clusters.

Also at the cluster level, it is interesting to note that a detailed map of the largest focal site (Long House Pueblo) reveals 400 rooms, but only a single small kiva. In contrast, within the same cluster, kivas are common at almost all of the satellites. In fact, there are as many as three kivas at a single satellite with only 10 habitation rooms. Either the residents of the larger villages were not participating in the ceremonial activities associated with the kivas, or, more likely, the residents of the focal sites shared in the activities carried out in the kivas at the satellite sites.

Above the cluster, at valley level, the strategic position of the focal sites points to some degree of valley-wide cooperation and coordination. In their defensive locations, the focal sites are all carefully positioned so as to collectively oversee all access routes into the Valley and at the same time maintain visual contact and communication between communities. Indeed, the importance of establishing visual contact between focal sites is reinforced by the discovery that a deep notch was excavated prehistorically in the side of a hillslope that otherwise would have interfered with the line of sight from one site to the other. The notch then allowed visual contact and communication between the two focal communities. As I will discuss below, the visual network of defensive sites is not confined to the limits of Long House Valley, but continues out to the east; nevertheless, it does indicate that at A.D. 1250 there was a pan-valley, supra-village interaction network in the Valley corresponding to the expected pattern for a tribal form of organization.

WARFARE VERSUS ENVIRONMENTAL STRESS

There remains a central question with regard to this emergent polity in Long House Valley: what was the role of warfare and/or environmental stress in stimulating the formation of the new polity. In 1984 and 1985, research was designed and implemented to address this question.

Environmental stress

Turning to the reasons why a tribal type of organization emerged in northeastern Arizona in the thirteenth century, there is evidence that both environmental stress and warfare contributed to the evolutionary process. The stress comes from continuing long-term environmental degradation coupled with high relative population densities. As outlined above, beginning in A.D. 1150, there was a steady loss of arable land due to both erosion and a lowering of the water table. These climatic conditions were aggravated by periodic drought and the highest local population densities witnessed prehistorically. (It is important to note that the environmental degradation had a significant impact on the local adaptive strategies only in the face of high population densities. Earlier, similar environmental conditions had had little effect on the evolutionary trajectory of the local population when there were fewer people around [Dean, et al. 1985].) The loss of land would have restricted the population to even smaller farming plots with an inevitable long-term decrease in yield as the options for leaving fields fallow were washed away with soil. On top of the precarious general conditions, the periodic short-term droughts introduced yet another element of stress and uncertainty into the lives of the prehistoric residents.

Direct evidence of the effects of the environmental stress can be seen in the fact that through the period from A.D. 1150 to 1300, the Kayenta population was suffering from increasing nutritional problems (Ryan 1977). There was increased mortality of infants and children, and a

183

progressive increase in the severity of anemia, causing porotic hyperostosis. Both of these patterns reached their peak in the latter half of the thirteenth century (Ryan 1977: 200).

The combination of environmental degradation with the pattern of increased social interaction and social connectedness corresponds well with the theoretical model of tribalization outlined by Braun and Plog. In the face of high population densities, loss of land, and periods of drought, the archaeological record indicates that the residents of Long House Valley and surrounding areas began to come together physically in the beginning of the twelfth century. There are also indirect signs that they began to cooperate in the exploitation of the limited and decreasing local resource base. As the environmental problems continued in the thirteenth century, the pattern of interaction and cooperation intensified at least on the local level. The members of the separate clusters worked together in building communal structures, shared water reservoirs, and participated in joint ceremonial activities. However, all was not peace and light in the lives of the Kayenta Anasazi.

Warfare

In all three of the adjoining valleys as well as in the Tsegi Canyon system to the north, the thirteenth century witnessed an overwhelming movement of large sites into inaccessible and defensible locations. In Long House Valley, all five of the focal sites are situated on defensible positions, and together they hold commanding views of all access routes into the valley. At least two of them have clearly defensive features. At the first, Long House Pueblo, the site is positioned on a sandstone outcrop with a vertical drop along the entire north half. On the south half, the slope is gradual and the natural access is relatively easy. The residents of the pueblo, however, constructed a continuous wall across the entire south side of the community, and artificially restricted access to two narrow corridors going up along the east and west sides. Access was further restricted by the construction of additional walls across these access corridors. Thus, in order to get into the pueblo, a person had to go up one of the two access corridors and pass through a "check-point" along the way.

The second overtly defensive pueblo, Organ Rock Ruin, is at the mouth of Tsegi Canyon perched on top of an isolated sandstone cliff. The site (and all of its satellites) is naturally protected by 70 m high cliffs on all sides. The only access route on to the top of the cliff is by climbing up a near vertical hand-and-toe trail through a narrow crack in the cliff edge. Anyone attempting to climb through this crack is immediately vulnerable to easy attack from above. There is no water on top of the cliff (though they did build at least one reservoir to catch runoff from the bedrock) and no arable land.

Patterns similar to those found in Long House Valley were found in the neighboring Klethla and Kayenta valleys, with some focal sites on isolated cliff tops, and others either surrounded by defensive walls or accessible only by long, tortuous routes. As in Long House, visual links between the focal sites in Klethla and Kayenta would have allowed for direct communication between the villages in the event of attack, and thus would have enhanced the collective defensive posture of the resident populations. Significantly, the first defensive sites to appear in both Klethla and Kayenta date to the fifty-year period just prior to A.D. 1250. These few earlier defensive sites are all small, and preceded by decades the emergence of the focal/satellite site clusters and the general pattern of increased integration.

In the Tsegi Canyon system a similar pattern appears. In the canyons, the majority of the thirteenth-century communities are "cliff dwellings," and are located in large protected rockshelters, in contrast to the open sites in the valleys. In each case, these cliff dwellings are defensively positioned. Some are located in shelters 200-300 m up from the canyon floor, and can be reached only by climbing long, steep talus slopes. Others have a combination of walls and natural rock faces which create an unbroken wall 5-10 m high across the entire front of the site. Still others can be entered only by way of near-vertical climbs up narrow cracks or chimneys.

Although it has been argued that the people moved into caves and rockshelters to take advantage of the natural protection and access to water supplies, the large majority of the most inaccessible shelters were occupied for the first time between A.D. 1250 and 1300 (Dean 1969). Furthermore, many of the most accessible shelters with long occupations in earlier centuries were abandoned in the thirteenth century. Overall, thirteenth-century sites in Tsegi Canyon were consistently difficult to get into, while shelters with easy access from the canyon floor went unoccupied during the same time period. The pattern again suggests that the people were concerned about attack and took major steps to defend themselves and their stored resources. While the shelters in the canyons were occupied at different times for different purposes, and in the late 1200s, the inaccessible and defensible locations were selected for their defensive attributes in a time of war.

The inaccessibility of sites both in the canyons and open valleys is not indisputable "proof" of warfare in this area in the thirteenth century. However, warfare does offer the most parsimonious explanation of this highly consistent site location pattern. Alternative explanations include the possibility that sites were located in inaccessible places for religious reasons, or because the cliff tops and rock shelters offered some advantage in terms of warmth or protection. Neither of these explanations is complete. Citing religious reasons for selecting particular village locations only pushes the explanation back one step. It then becomes necessary to explain why there was a major change in their religion at A.D. 1250 that demanded relocation of the villages to inaccessible locations. Similarly, if the Kayenta people retreated to the cliff tops and remote rock shelters for the advantages of warmth or protection, then the question arises of why they never lived in these locations in earlier times. The onset of warfare in the mid-thirteenth century explains not only why the people selected the remote, inaccessible places for their villages, it also explains why they moved to those places at that point in time. Warfare started in the Kayenta area in the thirteenth century, and in response the people moved their houses, their goods, and their families up onto mesa tops, hills, and high shelters. In the face of attack or threatened attack, they were protected by a deliberate combination of natural and cultural defensive features.

Some additional evidence relating to possible warfare can be found in the available burial population. Of four burials excavated in Long House Valley, two were females with no unusual features. The other two were male and had features that might indicate some kind of physical conflict. One had his head removed and placed beside him on the bedrock, while the second was missing his head altogether. In neither case, however, was it possible to determine the direct cause of death of either of these two individuals.

In the neighboring Kayenta Valley, the Rainbow Bridge–Monument Valley expedition excavated a large burial population from one of the defensive focal sites. Of the 42 whole or partial skeletons, 7 were subadults of indeterminate sex, 10 were young adult females, 13 were older adult females, 5 were adult females of indeterminate age, and only five (possibly 6) were older adult males (over 30 years of age) (Berry 1983:

68–69). Only five males out of 42! The low frequency of males and the absence of younger adult males fits an expected pattern for warfare. Warriors often are accorded special burial away or distinct from the rest of the population, and the regular burial ground of a community at war may be expected to have lower frequencies of adult males of fighting age. (It should be pointed out that of all the burials from this area, there are no signs of violence on any of the individuals in this group of burials [e.g. arrows stuck into bodies].)

Elsewhere in the northern Southwest, where there are somewhat better excavation data, there are clear signs of warfare and violence appearing in the second half of the thirteenth century. In southwest Colorado, for example, (approximately 150 km northeast of Long House Valley) excavations at Sand Canyon Pueblo (Bradley 1987) have revealed a completely walled village which was almost entirely burned at the time of abandonment. There are dead bodies lying on the floors of a number of the rooms, and artifacts in the rooms have been deliberately smashed.

Taken as a whole, the survey and burial data from Long House Valley and vicinity point to the initiation of a pattern of warfare in the middle of the thirteenth century. Although the exact causes of the warfare cannot be specified at this time, it can be directly related to the pattern of high relative population density, environmental degradation and periodic severe drought. The negative impact of these variables can be seen in the nutritional problems mentioned above, and warfare is a predictable response under such conditions of ecological stress and uncertainty (see Vayda 1976; Ember 1982; Ember and Ember n.d.; Ferguson 1984a; Harris 1984a).

CONCLUSIONS

Returning to the alternate models of tribalization, the data from northeast Arizona reveal that localized tribal formation is associated both with severe environmental stress or risk and with some degree of conflict and warfare. Looking at the long-term diachronic evolution of the system in Long House Valley, it is apparent that the initial stages of social consolidation and increased integration begin at approximately A.D. 1150 and develop in response to environmental variables. There is simply no evidence for any kind of conflict, competition or warfare at this time period. At 1250, however, an organizational transformation of the local political system with much greater consolidation of communities within the valleys is directly associated with the appearance of warfare.

Is then the evolution of a tribal organization in Long House and neighboring valleys a result of the warfare as argued in the traditional model of tribalization, or a result of the environmental stress as argued in a more recent cooperative model of tribalization? The most reasonable answer is that discrete tribal units in the Kayenta area evolved in response to a combination of warfare, high population density and a deteriorating environment.

On one level, the ecological conditions appear to have brought about localized consolidation beginning at A.D. 1150. When faced with too little water and land for a large and growing population, the people in Long House Valley began to move together and coordinate their efforts in cultivating their diminishing fields. As the situation worsened into the thirteenth century, there was greater consolidation and cooperation as tight residential clusters emerged which were centered around large focal sites. These focal sites were centers of communal activities and water storage efforts, while their surrounding satellites were the loci of ceremonial activities associated with kivas. These changes fit well with Braun and Plog's argument that there is an "increase in social connectedness" in response to increased environmental stress and risk.

On a second level, there is evidence that the declining environmental conditions also stimulated conflict and raiding between groups on a broader, regional scale. With insufficient food and increasing mortality among children and babies, raiding would have been an alternative, though expensive, means of procuring additional resources for the residents of northeast Arizona. In the central Kayenta area, the first signs of conflict actually appear slightly before A.D. 1250 in the valleys neighboring Long House. At this time, at least some of the people in these areas found it expedient to move into inaccessible, defensible locations. The level of conflict or threat of conflict then appears to have increased markedly at A.D. 1250, when the residents of the adjoining valleys positioned their key focal sites in positions that were not only highly defensible but which also allowed visual contact and communication with other focal sites and their associated satellite clusters. These interlinked focal sites thus effectively brought together the residents of a large, multivalley area in a coordinated defensive network. At this point in the research, it is uncertain whether the people in neighboring valleys were raiding each other, as might be indicated by the wide "no-man's-land" between Long House and Klethla, or if the Kayenta were being subject to attack from outside groups such as the Mesa Verde in southern Colorado or the Cibola further to the south in Arizona. Nevertheless, as argued by the traditional theorists, the available evidence does indicate that warfare played a causal role in uniting communities beyond the local level.

Viewed from the perspective of the archaeological record, it becomes evident that tribalization is not a one time historical event that suddenly transforms a band society into a tribe. Rather, it is clearly a process that takes place in stages and can be stretched out over centuries or even millenia. In northeast Arizona, survey and excavation data reveal the beginnings of tribalization at around A.D. 500 with the emergence of the Kayenta "branch" of the Anasazi, and the final stages of tribal development occurring at A.D. 1250 with the appearance of con- solidated regional defensive networks. It is not possible to observe subsequent changes after the transformation in the thirteenth century, since the entire region was completely abandoned at A.D. 1300. In other parts of the southwest, however, tribal polities continued to evolve with the appearance of much larger pueblo aggregations and regional alliances (see Upham 1982, for example). Although the material and dusty data base of archaeology limits the picture that can be drawn of early tribal polities, the diachronic perspective of archaeology provides a different and valuable dimension to the study of tribalization and the possible role of warfare, stress and demography in the evolution of human political systems.

9
Chiefdom-level warfare as exemplified in Fiji and the Cauca Valley

ROBERT L. CARNEIRO

The emergence of chiefdoms marked the first great step in political evolution. With this step, local autonomy was at last transcended and villages were fused into multi-village political units. But it was a step not easily taken. Local autonomy had been stubbornly clung to during more than three million years of human history, and only through the application of force was this autonomy overthrown. Like the even larger states that followed them, chiefdoms were, from their inception, creatures of war (Carneiro 1970; 1981).

This view of the centrality of war in political evolution has come to be accepted only slowly. Indeed, it is still resisted by many anthropologists.[1] Thus, several theorists who have concerned themselves with chiefdoms, such as Service (1962), Sahlins (1968), Fried (1967), Flannery (1972), and Renfrew (1984), if not flatly denying the role of war in creating chiefdoms, certainly tend to minimize it.

This resistance to using war as an explanatory mechanism in political development has a long history. Scholars in many fields have often treated war as an abnormal or aberrant condition. Thus, for example, James Collier (1903: 139), once Herbert Spencer's research assistant,

190

wrote that "War in all its phases is a pathological phenomenon . . . it is the action of society in a state of disease." But, as Edmund Leach (1968: 24) has observed, "Why should we suppose that peace is normal and war an aberration when the whole weight of European history has been just the other way around?"

It seems to me that an objective examination of the evidence leads irresistibly to the conclusion that war has been the principal agent by which human societies, starting as small and simple autonomous communities, have surmounted petty sovereignties and transformed themselves, step by step, into vast and complex states (cf. Robarchek and Gibson, this volume).

THE CHANGING PHASES OF WAR

War, of course, is a very old phenomenon, going back deep into the Paleolithic (compare Haas, this volume), but it did not assume great significance until the coming of agriculture. Then, as the growth of population led to a shortage of arable land, war became redirected from the avenging of personal offenses, its traditional cause, to the taking of territory. With this change in objectives, war became at once more frequent, more intense, and more important. But it was not only the causes and nature of war that changed. It was also its consequence, which now became much more far reaching.

During the earlier stages of Neolithic warfare, its net effect was *dispersion*. The prevailing process of "fight and flight" meant that villages that engaged in war remained not only at arms' length spatially but autonomous politically.

However, as population grew and warfare intensified, something totally new occurred. Rather than pushing villages apart, warfare began leading to the subjugation of the losers by the winners, and to the seizure and incorporation of their territory as well. Now, for the first time in history, the *coalescing* and consolidation of formerly independent villages into larger political units became the order of the day. And the polities thus formed were *chiefdoms*.

Given the universal disinclination of human groups to relinquish their sovereignty, the surmounting of village autonomy could not have occurred peacefully or voluntarily. It could – and did – occur only by force of arms. Thus, it is important to examine war as a mechanism of political evolution.

191

CIRCUMSCRIPTION AND WAR

The factor that did most to intensify warfare and to redirect it toward conquest was, as I have said, the pressure of human numbers on the land. Acting most acutely in areas of circumscribed agricultural land, population pressure led, step by step and almost irresistibly, to the rise of the state (Carneiro 1970). The chiefdom was, of course, a necessary stepping stone toward the state (Carneiro 1981). Thus, to understand state formation we must first understand the formation of chiefdoms. And this leads us to a study of chiefdom-level war.

Chiefdom-level warfare has been the subject of very little study. Thus it is not well understood. Certain questions arise about it which must be answered if we are to fully understand the rise of the state. For one thing, if chiefdom-level warfare were conquest warfare, pure and simple, then chiefdoms, as a general level, should have been of brief duration. Through successive conquests of one by another, chiefdoms would have quickly been transcended, giving way to states.

But in many parts of the world chiefdoms were not readily transcended at all. They lasted centuries, if not millennia. Reasons other than outright conquest, then, must have prompted warfare among chiefdoms. What were they? And what were their results? The only way to answer these questions, and others like them, is to look carefully at actual instances of warfare among chiefdoms in all of their dimensions. This is precisely what I propose to do in this paper.

In attempting to do so here, I have chosen two areas of the world where chiefdom-level culture flourished – Fiji in the Southwest Pacific and the Cauca Valley of Colombia. Though widely separated geographically, both had the common characteristic that they were areas of circumscribed agricultural land.

In these two regions political development by contact times had reached the level of "typical" or "maximal" chiefdoms (see Carneiro 1981: 47). The warring units in each area were thus no longer small, autonomous villages, but multi-village polities of considerable size. Moreover, warfare on Fiji and in the Cauca Valley was observed and recorded in considerable detail while it was still being waged under essentially aboriginal conditions.

WARFARE IN FIJI AND THE CAUCA VALLEY

Frequency and Intensity

Warfare at the chiefdom level may well be more frequent than at the state level, if for no other reason than that the contending units, being smaller in size, are greater in number, and thus the total incidence of war is higher. At any rate, warfare among chiefdoms is certainly widespread and recurring. "Fiji is rarely free from war . . . The chiefs have ever been warring among themselves," wrote Thomas Williams (1870: 34, 14), a close observer of events on that island during the early decades of contact. The same was true of the Cauca Valley, where warfare was universal, acute, and unending. It was "total war," observed Hermann Trimborn (1949: 284–285, 195), a careful scholar who compiled the early Spanish sources relating to the valley. Elaborating further on this point, Trimborn (p. 284) wrote:

We can only comprehend the true character of war in the Cauca Valley if we realize the total nature of these struggles and conflicts. These were not episodes carried out in the manner of tournaments or within recognized rules among the warriors of opposing groups, leaving the "civilian" population unaffected. On the contrary, it was a case of the war of all against all, carried out through every coercive means, military and non-military.[2]

The causes of war

The sorts of grievances that provoked warfare between autonomous villages continued to provoke it at the chiefdom level. But in addition, such things as offenses against the dignity of persons of rank, especially the paramount chief, began to play a role. Thus, Williams (p. 34) cites "pride and jealousy of the chiefs" as a common cause of war among the Fijians. And of course, the very existence of multi-village chiefdoms is *prima facie* evidence that the seizure of land and the subjection of peoples had already been acting as causes – or at least consequences – of war. Thus for Fiji, Williams (p. 34) noted that "the fact of there being so many independent governments, each of which seeks aggrandizement at the expense of the rest," was a common motive for hostilities.

In the Cauca Valley, a chief's desire to expand his domain and gain control of natural resources such as gold mines and salt deposits are cited by Trimborn (p. 283) as leading causes of war. Territorial conquest was a particular incentive for Guaca and Popayán, two chiefdoms of the

193

valley which, when the Spaniards arrived in the early 1500s, were actively expanding their territory and apparently well on their way to becoming states (pp. 280, 335).

However, the primary motive for going to war among most Cauca Valley chiefdoms seems to have been the taking of prisoners. Most war captives were killed and eaten outright, although some were first sacrificed to the god of war before being devoured. A smaller number of captives was kept alive to use as slaves in tilling the fields or as personal retainers of the chiefs and nobles. Even these could expect to be killed and eaten at some later date (Trimborn, p. 369).

The fact that Fiji and the Cauca Valley were permanently on a war footing was reflected in many aspects of everyday life. "When on his feet," Williams (p. 34) noted, "the Fijian is always armed; when working in his garden or lying on his mat, his arms are always at hand . . . The club or spear is the companion of all his walks." A similar readiness for war marked the Cauca Valley. Of the Indians of this region Trimborn wrote (p. 281), "When they are planting or working the fields, in one hand they hold a club to slash the fallow and in the other a lance to fight."

Preparations for war

A Fijian chief sought to put as many warriors as possible in the field. "Orders are sent by the chief to all under his rule to be in readiness . . . A flat refusal to comply with the summons of the chief, by any place in which he has a claim, would, sooner or later, be visited by the destruction of the offenders" (Williams, p. 35). Moreover, whatever military alliances might exist with other chiefdoms were now activated: ". . . application is made to friendly powers for help" (p. 35). Military alliances were also concluded among the chiefdoms of the Cauca Valley as each sought to gain an advantage over its enemies (Trimborn, pp. 331–334; but cf. pp. 66, 277, 281).

On Fiji, "efforts are made [by opposing chiefs] to neutralize each other's influence. A sends a whale's tooth to B, entreating his aid against C, who, hearing of this, sends a larger tooth to B, to *bika* – "press down" – the present from A; and thus B joins neither party" (Williams, p. 35).

When, as among the Yanomamö or the Dugum Dani, wars are waged between autonomous villages, only those persons fight who want to. The chief of such a village usually lacks the power to force anyone to

194

go to war.[3] Among the chiefdom-level Fijians, though, while there was no formal military draft, and certainly nothing like a standing army, every able-bodied man was expected to fight when called upon. Failure to do so would subject him to dire consequences. A Fijian army was thus essentially coextensive with the entire able-bodied adult male population of the society. "The military of Fiji," wrote Williams (p. 36), "do not form a distinct class, but are selected from every rank, irrespective of age or size: any who can raise a club or hurl a spear are eligible. At the close of a war, all who survive return to their ordinary pursuits." In the Cauca Valley the fighting forces were apparently marshaled and discharged in much the same way.

Rallies preceding combat

Before going into battle, the forces that had been gathered under the banner of a Fijian chief assembled at a designated spot. Here a kind of military review called a *taqa* took place. An important part of this review consisted of making great threats, by word and gesture, of what each warrior would do to the enemy. A man might run up to his chief and shout, "Sir, do you know me? Your enemies soon will." Another might strike the ground violently with his club and boast, "I cause the earth to tremble: it is I who meet the enemy tomorrow!" (Williams, p. 37).

With warfare now serious business, and the risk of dying in battle greatly increased, courage-instilling rituals become more elaborate. Fijian chiefs helped stiffen the nerve of their men by promising them rich rewards for valor. "Incentives to bravery are not withheld," says Williams (p. 38). "Young women, and women of rank, are promised to such as shall, by their prowess, render themselves deserving."

Size of armies

While autonomous villages can seldom muster more than a few dozen men for war, at the chiefdom level this number increases by one or two orders of magnitude. In Fiji, the warriors brought together under one banner generally numbered in the hundreds, and on occasion, as many as a thousand men might be assembled. There were even times – though apparently rare – when an army of 4,000 or 5,000 men might be marshaled (Williams, p. 38).

In the Cauca Valley, which was more densely populated than Fiji, somewhat larger armies were mobilized. Again, the average size was probably in the neighborhood of 200–400 (Trimborn, pp. 335–337), but according to early Spanish chroniclers, the Carrapa could mount 4,000 warriors, the Pozo 4,000 to 6,000, and the Guaca 12,000 (Trimborn, pp. 335–337).

The commencement of hostilities

Warfare between chiefdoms no longer consists of a pre-dawn sneak attack followed by a quick withdrawal. If nothing else, the large size of the attacking force precludes this. Instead, the onset of hostilities is now often attended by a certain amount of protocol and ceremony. Williams (p. 35) tells us that on Fiji: "When war is decided upon between two powers, a formal message to that effect is interchanged . . . [as are] informal messages in abundance, warning each other to strengthen their fences and carry them up to the sky."

War leadership

At the chiefdom level, it is the paramount chief who typically leads his warriors into battle. After all, it was through his war exploits that he attained his position in the first place,[4] and it was by continued demonstrations of military prowess that he confirmed it. Williams does not devote a separate section to the chief's role in war, but from passages scattered throughout his treatment of politics and warfare (e.g., pp. 15, 20, 31, 36, 39–40, 48), it is quite clear that the chief not only led his men into battle, but often showed himself the bravest and most redoubtable warrior among them. He tells, for example (p. 48), of a chief named Tui Wainunu, who along with a younger man stormed into a defended position, and with war clubs flailing, killed 27 of the enemy.

Not only was the paramount chief in the Cauca Valley the one who initiated war, he also led his army into battle (Trimborn, p. 241). "Fundamentally it can be said that military command – as long as not prevented by illness or age – generally belonged to the chief . . ." (Trimborn, p. 337). The only exceptions were the polities of Guaca and Popayán, among whom the chief's younger brother was the war leader (pp. 256, 337). Councils of war involving "captains" and lesser chiefs took place prior to battle during which matters of strategy and tactics were discussed (p. 244).

Weapons

Peoples at the autonomous village level usually carry out warfare at medium-to-long range, with the bow-and-arrow as the favorite weapon. At the chiefdom level, though, since it is now a matter of personal honor and prowess, warfare is much more likely to be fought hand-to-hand. This is reflected in the choice of weapons. "The club is the favorite weapon of the Fijians," says Williams (p. 47), and those of a distinguished warrior have such menacing names as "Damaging beyond hope" (p. 48). In addition to clubs, the Fijians used the spear, the bow, and the sling. Spears were 10–15 feet long, of hard wood, and their points were wickedly barbed. One type of spear was suggestively called, "The priest is too late" (Williams, p. 47).

In the Cauca Valley, warriors also preferred hand-to-hand weapons, their favorite being the hard, sharp-edged, palm-wood sword club referred to by the Spaniards as a *macana*. And, as on Fiji, secondary use was made of lances and slings (Trimborn, pp. 297–306).

Fortifications

Battles on an open field where opposing armies met and clashed in close order were not the rule, either on Fiji or in the Cauca Valley. Usually the attackers had to seek out the enemy in a defended position. With warfare as prevalent as it was, fortified places were common in both areas. In the Cauca Valley, villages themselves were usually defended with palisades made from stout bamboo. But in the face of an impending attack, villages were often abandoned in favor of less accessible and therefore more defensible positions (Trimborn, pp. 290–292, 344).

On Fiji, places difficult of access, often at some distance from the village, were strengthened by fortifications, often of stone. Literally thousands of them have been found in the course of archeological surveys (Frost 1979: 70). But even when not located in a natural fastness, a Fijian village might be defended against attackers, in which case it was strongly fortified (Williams, p. 38).

The battle

Taunts and challenges preceded an assault. Williams (p. 40) cites a Fijian commander who, just before attacking a strong position, cried out loudly enough so both sides could hear: "The *men* of that fort have been dead a long while: those who occupy it now are a set of old women." Besides taunts, unearthly yells meant to intimidate the enemy were also part of an attack. In addition to uttering fierce cries, Cauca Valley tribes blew trumpets made from the long bones of slain enemies and beat drums whose heads were made from skin flayed from these same victims. For good measure, during an assault, warriors in the Cauca Valley also threatened to devour their enemies after they killed them (Trimborn, pp. 359–362), and similar cannibalistic threats were hurled by Fijian attackers. Shouting out the name of an enemy chief, a bold Fijian warrior might declare his intention to "cut out his tongue, eat his brains, and make a cup of his skull" (Williams, p. 40).

Of the Fijians, Williams (p. 39) writes: "An attack being decided upon, a command to that effect is issued by the Vu-ni-valu [General], who names the order in which the several companies are to advance, and specifies which is to have the honor of the first assault." The Cauca Valley groups also went into battle in formations and organized into sub-units. The Spaniards, who fought against them many times, were much impressed with the military discipline and bravery of these people (Trimborn, pp. 339, 378–381).

It is unnecessary for our purposes to go into every detail of an assault. It is enough to say that they were violent and ferocious, and are fully described by the early sources. Let us proceed, then, to other aspects of warfare.

Casualties of war

It is often said of prestate war that, once blood has been drawn, both sides break off the engagement and retire. This view, I think, tends to minimize the actual facts of the matter. It is true, though, that warfare at the autonomous village level seldom leads to great loss of life. However, when chiefdoms fight, the picture changes drastically. It is true that at one point Williams (p. 42) says of Fijian war that "In a pitched battle comparatively little mischief is done," but he adds that in most battles the number of persons killed ranges from 20 to 200, a not inconsiderable figure. The largest number of deaths he personally knew of in a war was about 400, most of them women and children. And even though he believed the report to be exaggerated, Williams notes: "Old natives speak of as many as a thousand being killed in some battles when they were young . . ." (p. 41). As late as the 1860s, when European influence had already begun to lessen the amount of fighting, the loss of life in war on Fiji was still reckoned as high as 1,500 to 2,000 a year (p. 42).

I have found no casualty figures in Trimborn, but since Cauca Valley armies were larger than those of Fiji and their battles even fiercer, a greater loss of life seems indicated. The only mitigating factor was that Cauca Valley peoples were more likely to take prisoners than the Fijians.

Warfare among the Fijians was all-out and bloody, with no respect shown for sex or age. Women and children were killed ruthlessly and indiscriminately. The Cauca Valley tribes also killed women, no matter how young or attractive they might be, and slaughtered children as well (Trimborn, pp. 284–285).

War prisoners

The stage of culture at which economic exploitation of war captives becomes uppermost in the minds of their captors so that prisoners are enslaved rather than executed, had not been reached either in Fiji or the Cauca Valley. The usual fate of vanquished enemies was the same in both societies: to be devoured. In fact, cannibalism was so important an element of warfare in the two regions that it will be described in some detail in a separate section later in this paper.

We should note here, though, that Fijian cannibalism seems to have been primarily of men slain in warfare. Those who managed to survive the battle seem usually to have been spared this fate, although they too were accorded harsh treatment. According to Williams (p. 43): "The terms dictated to the conquered are severe, including, generally . . . the abject servitude of its inhabitants."

Cauca Valley tribes took more prisoners than did Fijians, since, as we have said, this was a major reason for going to war. The fate that awaited these captives, however, varied considerably. Some were brought back to the village to be killed and eaten outright, their skulls and other body parts being kept as trophies (Trimborn, p. 201). Most captives, though, were probably kept alive – at least temporarily. Of these, some might

199

later be killed for cannibalistic feasts which were sometimes preceded by human sacrifices to the gods (pp. 203, 369). A certain number of captives were nonetheless allowed to survive these hazards in order to be made permanent slaves (p. 200). These slaves were used mostly to till the soil, permitting their masters to farm more land and thus improve their economic status (pp. 204, 410).

Destruction of property

The destruction of the enemy's physical possessions was a frequent outcome of war (Williams, pp. 48, 176). On Fiji, the peace terms imposed on a vanquished foe generally included "the destruction of their town and its defences . . .", especially if the enemy had put up a particularly stiff resistance (pp. 43, 40).

Cauca Valley peoples were even more systematic and unrelenting in their decimation of a defeated enemy. Warfare, wrote Trimborn (p. 295), was often "a fight for annihilation, carried out by every available means . . .", and burning an enemy's village and destroying his gardens was one of them (pp. 290–292). Indeed, among some groups, like the Pozo, the aim of war was nothing less than the total extermination of their adversaries (pp. 280–281, 184).

Warriors' rise in status

Warfare being of such great importance in both Fiji and the Cauca Valley, successful warriors were conspicuously rewarded. Among the Fijians, a man who had clubbed an enemy to death was given the honorary name of *Koroi* (Williams, p. 43). And if a man of rank had distinguished himself in battle, he received a grandiloquent title such as "divider of such-and-such a district," "waster of such-and-such a coast," "depopulator of such-and-such an island," etc. (Williams, pp. 43–44). He might also be "consecrated" in a special anointing ceremony held before the paramount chief and other leading men (pp. 44–47).

Of the six social classes or ranks recognized by the Fijians, commoners who fought bravely could expect to rise to the rank just below that of town chiefs and priests (Williams, p. 25). However, heredity counted for a great deal on Fiji, and there was a limit to how high a man's war exploits could carry him. "Common men," Williams (p. 27) noted, "though esteemed for superior prowess and rewarded with an honorable name, do not rise in rank [beyond that already mentioned], their original grade being always remembered."

In the Cauca Valley, the taking of war prisoners was the principal way for a man to raise his status. The braver the warrior and the more captives he took, the higher his rank would become (Trimborn, p. 202). Killing enemy warriors in battle also brought prestige, and by this means a man could achieve the position of war captain.

Warfare and the status of the chief

Fijian chiefs, who were men of high rank to begin with, rose even higher in power and status by expanding their domain, adding to the number of their subjects, and increasing the amount of tribute paid to them. And of course, all three were achieved by force of arms. The net effect of a successful military campaign, then, was a considerable augmentation of a chief's power. And for higher Fijian chiefs, this power was virtually unlimited. According to Williams (p. 17): "The will of the king is, in most cases, law . . ."

In the Cauca Valley, the paramount chief got most of the credit for success in warfare, since it was he who initiated war and led his men to victory. And the political rewards of his military prowess were great. Trimborn (e.g., pp. 237, 283, 338) repeatedly affirms that the roots of strong chiefly power lay in war. Enemy skulls and other war trophies, which were commonly exhibited in and around a chief's house, were tangible evidence of his military triumphs (p. 234). Indeed, Trimborn (p. 241) goes so far as to state that "as a result of the continuous state of war, the power of the chief increased until it became unlimited."

Growth in size of political units

In both Fiji and the Cauca Valley, warfare often led to the conquest of territory. This was marked ceremonially in Fiji: ". . . a basket of earth . . . is presented by the weaker party, indicating the yielding up of their land to the conqueror" (Williams, p. 25).

Conquest warfare had resulted, as I have said, in the surmounting of village autonomy and the aggregation of villages into chiefdoms. But the process of political expansion did not stop there. In both regions some chiefdoms had themselves been conquered and incorporated by other, stronger ones, leading to the formation of still larger political units.

Whether these larger polities deserve to be called states depends on one's definition. If to be a state a society merely has to have three levels of political organization – the village, the district, and the supra-district level – then states had emerged in Fiji, and their rulers warranted the title of "kings," which Williams (pp. 14, 17, 18, 19, etc.) freely bestows on them. However, if we require of states such functional attributes as the decreeing and enforcing of laws and a monopoly on the internal use of force, then the largest Fijian polities were probably not states but only "maximal" chiefdoms (see Carneiro 1981: 46–48). This would be so since, as Williams (p. 23) noted with regard to the punishment of criminal offenses: "Injured persons often take the law into their own hands; an arrangement in which the authorized powers gladly concur."

In the Cauca Valley, both Guaca and Popayán were clearly pushing beyond the bounds of chiefdoms. Popayán in particular, which had more than a dozen formerly independent chiefdoms under its suzerainty, was well on its way to becoming a state, if it had not reached that level already (Trimborn, pp. 211, 248–249).

Cannibalism

Let us now turn back to a practice which in both Fiji and the Cauca Valley was perhaps the most striking accompaniment of warfare: cannibalism. From warfare, cannibalism had extended its influence to many other aspects of life. In fact, Williams (p. 175) was led to observe of the Fijians that "Cannibalism among this people is one of their institutions; it is interwoven in the elements of society; it forms one of their pursuits, and is regarded by the mass as a refinement."

When Europeans first arrived on the scene, cannibalism in both Fiji and the Cauca Valley was already deeply rooted. Thus the original cause of this practice cannot be stated with assurance. However, since the victims of cannibalism were, first and foremost, hated enemies, it is reasonable to suppose that the practice began as a way of wreaking vengeance on them. Williams (p. 187), in fact, says this outright: "Revenge is undoubtedly the main cause of cannibalism in Fiji . . ." And no doubt the intimidation of the living that accompanied the ingestion of the dead was part of the aim as well.[5] Certainly one could hardly show greater hatred and disdain towards an enemy than by eating him. Let us turn, then, to an examination of cannibalism as it was practiced by these two societies.

When men marched off to war in the Cauca Valley, they took with them special ropes with which to bind their captives (Trimborn, p. 389). Being trussed up, though, was no guarantee that a prisoner would arrive back in his captor's village alive. Along with ropes, warriors carried flint knives with which to decapitate their prisoners (p. 389), who sometimes were cooked and eaten right on the field of battle (p. 398).

Fijians, on the other hand, almost always brought their war captives home before eating them. Returning war parties carrying a *bakolo* – a dead body destined to be eaten – beat on drums as they approached the village, giving advance notice of their success. At the sound, those who had remained behind – mostly the women – did a wild dance of anticipation and delight (Williams, p. 177).

A prisoner brought back to his captor's village in the Cauca Valley was usually made to kneel and bow his head before he was knocked senseless with a club and then decapitated. He was then quartered in preparation for cooking (Trimborn, p. 390). In Fiji, the butchering was done by a man skilled in wielding a bamboo knife with which he "cut off the several members, joint by joint" (Williams, p. 177).

To add to the grisliness of the occasion, prisoners in both regions were sometimes dismembered while still alive, and their limbs eaten in front of them (Williams, p. 178; Trimborn, p. 393). Williams (p. 181), who evidently witnessed these practices himself, wrote: "Nothing short of the most fiendish cruelty could dictate some of these forms of torment, the worst of which consists of cutting off parts and even limbs of the victim while still living, and cooking and eating them before his eyes, sometimes finishing the brutality by offering him his own cooked flesh to eat."

In both areas, the blood of the victim was caught and drunk fresh (Williams, p. 178; Trimborn, p. 394). Some Cauca Valley chiefdoms went so far as to render the body of a victim of its fat which was later used as lighting oil for miner's lamps (Trimborn, p. 393).[6]

Baking in a special oven was the most common way for Fijians to cook a *bakolo*, but boiling was practiced too (Williams, p. 178). In the Cauca Valley, bodies were roasted or boiled (Trimborn, pp. 395–396), and in some areas human flesh was also eaten raw (pp. 394–395, 285) – something which evidently never occurred in Fiji (Williams, p. 179). In both areas, dead bodies were cut into pieces before cooking, although Williams (p. 178) mentions the occasional practice of placing a whole corpse in an oven.

In neither area did cannibalism respect sex or age. Captive women and children were eaten just as readily as men (Williams, p. 179; Trimborn, pp. 401–402). Cauca Valley women often took part in cannibalistic feasts along with their menfolk (Trimborn, pp. 298–300), but among the Fijians, Williams (p. 180) remarks that "Women seldom eat *bakolo* . . ."

Most of the body was eaten. In the Cauca Valley, the limbs were favored, but the internal organs, including the heart, liver and intestines were also consumed (Trimborn, pp. 394, 397). The torso, though, was sometimes discarded. To the Fijians, "The heart, the thighs, and the arm above the elbow are considered the greatest dainties" (Williams, p. 180). In eating human flesh, the Fijians made use of the famous "cannibal forks" (p. 180).

On rare occasions, a Fijian chief might have the skull of an enemy made into a soup dish or a drinking cup, and human shin-bones were prized as sail needles. However, on Fiji, body parts were not used extensively as war trophies (Williams, p. 180), as they were in the Cauca Valley, where successful warriors were lavish in their display of parts cut from the bodies of their fallen enemies. Chiefs especially kept skulls or dried heads of enemy warriors impaled on bamboo poles outside their houses. This grim display served the purpose of acquainting visitors with the greatness of their hosts' power, thus inspiring fear and respect (Trimborn, pp. 369, 370, 372, 400).

Among at least one Cauca Valley chiefdom, that of the Lile, the entire corpse of an enemy was smoke-dried in order to preserve it. The paramount chief of this group had a large house built for this purpose, and when first visited by the Spaniards it contained the smoked and stuffed bodies of some 400 enemy warriors, their bodies arranged in various poses, each corpse holding his weapons (Trimborn, pp. 375, 415).

What was the magnitude of cannibalism in these two areas? Evidently, it was very substantial. Of the 1,500 to 2,000 annual Fijian war dead estimated by Williams for the 1860s, most no doubt were consigned to the pot or to the oven. Being more populous than Fiji, the Cauca Valley cannibalistic toll was even higher. Indeed, Cieza de León, one of the most reliable of the early Spanish chroniclers, says that in the large polity of Popayán during the famine year of 1538, "the living buried the dead in their stomachs" (quoted in Trimborn, p. 404), and that altogether during the course of that year, 50,000 persons were killed

204

and eaten. Trimborn (p. 387) regards this estimate as excessive, and of course it reflected famine conditions rather than normal times. But even so, it points to a rather wholesale cannibalism.

Among the Arma, another Cauca Valley group, Herrera reported that 8,000 persons were eaten, apparently in one year (Trimborn, pp. 387–388). Trimborn again questions this figure, but even if substantially reduced, it still betokens cannibalism on a large scale.

More specific, and therefore probably more accurate, is Cieza's report that after defeating their traditional enemies, the Pozo, the Carrapa and Picara ate more than 300 of them. Later, when the tables were turned and the Pozo defeated the Carrapa, Picara, and Paucura, a Pozo chief named Perequita and his retinue ate 100 of his enemies in a single day (Trimborn, p. 388).

Although commoners were allowed to partake of human flesh it was the chiefs who were by far the most accomplished cannibals. Many Fijian chiefs were famous for the quantity of human flesh they had consumed. In this regard, a certain chief named Ra Undreundre stood head and shoulders above his fellows. Behind his house this chief kept a tally of his victims by lining up stones, one for each body he had eaten. According to an eyewitness, the line in back of Ra Undreundre's house extended 232 paces and contained 872 stones. Moreover, several stones were missing from the line, and when added to the tally, brought the grand total of bodies consumed to 900 (Williams, p. 181).[7]

Interpretation of cannibalism

As lurid as this description of cannibalism may seem, it is presented here with a higher purpose than merely to shock or to titillate. The implacable cannibalism of Fiji and the Cauca Valley says something important about the warfare out of which it grew. It is also perfectly clear that, while arising out of war, cannibalism had infiltrated into other aspects of the culture. It had become, as Williams noted, an institution.

Regardless of how ritualistic and vengeful cannibalism may have been at the outset, in time it became *gastronomic* as well (Trimborn, p. 412; Williams, p. 179). People *liked* human flesh. No doubt exists, wrote Williams (p. 179) of the Fijians, "that there is . . . a large number who esteem such food a delicacy, giving it a decided preference above all others." The same was true in the Cauca Valley. Indeed one chief, Tateepe of Buritica, was said to eat *only* human flesh (Trimborn, pp.

400–401). In some parts of the valley, chiefs even "grew their own," war captives being kept inside bamboo cages to fatten until the chief deemed them ready to eat (pp. 400, 410).

So pervasive was cannibalism in these two areas that it had become a common, even a necessary, part of social functions unrelated to war. Thus, Williams (p. 175) tells us:

Human bodies are sometimes eaten in connection with the building of a temple or canoe; or on launching a large canoe; or on taking down the mast of one which has brought some chief on a visit; or for feasting of such as take tribute to a principal place. A chief has been known to kill several men for rollers, to facilitate the launching of his canoes, the "rollers" being afterwards cooked and eaten.

Cannibalism had also extended into the realm of religion. War captives and even members of the society itself were sacrificed and eaten when the god of war was being worshipped or a new civic structure was being built (Williams, p. 177). In the Cauca Valley, human sacrifices, followed by cannibalism, were conducted in front of an idol representing a god in order to gain success in war and other enterprises (Trimborn, p. 296).

At the beginning of his discussion of Cauca Valley cannibalism, Trimborn expresses a certain wonderment that societies that had advanced politically to the relatively high level of chiefdoms, and had achieved the technical virtuosity required to produce such outstanding goldwork as that of the Quimbaya, could still be "barbarous" enough to devour each other. It seems to me, though, that the practice of cannibalism was not really out of place or inconsistent in those societies. Cannibalism was part and parcel of the intense and deeply-rooted war complex that existed here. Indeed, it can be said to be a *logical culmination* of that complex.

When warfare is as violent and unrelenting as it was in the Cauca Valley and Fiji, and mutual slaughter on the battlefield leaves the survivors without fathers or brothers or sons, an ever-increasing tide of hatred is engendered toward the enemy. And as the killing continues, this feeling becomes so strong as to know no bounds and to seek the most vehement form of expression. Sooner or later in the escalation of outrages and indignities heaped by one side on the other, the final rung on the ladder is almost bound to be reached. And that rung is cannibalism.

Indeed, so important did cannibalism become on Fiji and in the

Cauca Valley that the taking of prisoners to kill and eat became more and more of a factor in going to war. Thus, it is probably fair to say that what started out as a *consequence* of war eventually became a *cause*.

Final considerations

In our survey of Fiji and the Cauca Valley, we have examined two peoples with a very striking war complex. Yet, these peoples were not particularly unusual or aberrant in this respect. Rather, they were reasonably typical of societies at the chiefdom level of political development. Warfare at this stage often manifests several opposing characteristics. From the point of view of political evolution, the salient feature of chiefdom-level warfare is, of course, that it led to conquest. Defeated enemies and their lands were often incorporated into the political unit of the victors. And even when not fully subjugated, the vanquished often lost their autonomy to the extent of becoming subordinate and tributary to the group that had defeated them.

But chiefdom-level warfare, as we have seen, was not conquest warfare pure and simple. It had not laid aside many of its earlier, prechiefdom characteristics. In fact, it often retained and intensified them.

We have noted that the principal objective of many chiefdom-level wars was revenge, just as it had been among autonomous villages. What had changed, though, was the scale and intensity of this revenge. Now it became greatly heightened. The aim of much of the fighting in Fiji and the Cauca Valley was the destruction, even annihilation, of the enemy, not only his person but his property. Thus, chiefdom-level warfare often exhibits the "regressive" element of destruction and dispersion rather than the "progressive" one of amalgamation and consolidation.

As a result, success in war at the chiefdom level often did more to increase the power and status of the paramount chief than it did to enlarge his domain. Thus, it was not uncommon for the leaders of chiefdoms of even moderate size to hold the power of life and death over their subjects, a power often associated with despotic rulers of larger kingdoms.

A question often asked about societal conflicts is, what motivates an individual warrior to go to war? At the chiefdom level of war, we begin to see the question losing some of its import. For whatever might be in the head of a Fijian or Cauca Valley warrior as he marched off to battle, be it visions of revenge, glory, booty, or whatever, the fact is, he went to war on *orders* from his chief. And this marks a radical departure from the reasons that impel a typical warrior of an autonomous village to go to war.

Viewed in the short run, then, chiefdoms may seem to be in a continual state of tumult and ferment. They may occasionally grow in size by conquest, but often fragment back to a lower level in short order. Over the long run, though, the picture is quite different. Short-term fluctuations are damped down, and chiefdoms – at least the victorious ones – can be seen becoming progressively larger and more con-solidated. However reversible the process may appear in the short run, then, the general trend is upward. And the final result, after chiefdoms have been around for a while, is often the building up and welding together of larger political units whose size, complexity, and leadership warrant their being called states.

CHIEFDOMS AS THEOCRACIES

There is another aspect to chiefdoms that bears indirectly on warfare which I would like to discuss before concluding this paper. This is the question of whether chiefdoms are, in any real sense, "theocracies." In general discussions of chiefdoms, it is often noted that the paramount chief is something more than a political leader. He frequently enjoys supernatural standing in the society and may play a specific religious role. Service (1962: 171), for example, writes that ". . . sometimes the priest and chief are the same person. For this reason many chiefdoms have been called theocracies with considerable appropriateness."

Some theorists even stress the religious role of the paramount chief to the exclusion of his military functions. Thus, Kent Flannery (1972: 403) writes: " 'Chiefs' in rank societies [= chiefdoms] are not of noble birth, but usually divine; they have special relationships with the gods which are denied commoners and which legitimize their right to demand community support and tribute." But he adds nothing about the paramount chief normally being the war leader, nor that his power to issue commands and have them followed derives largely from this basis.

Another theorist, Morton Fried (1967:133), in describing rank societies, writes as follows: ". . . leaders can lead, but followers may not follow. Commands are given, but sometimes they may not be obeyed . . . In rank society . . . there are few if any effective sanctions that can

208

be used to compel compliance." Noting that in rank societies the role of chief and priest are often fused in one person, Fried (1967:141) observes: ". . . the chiefly figures bring little in the way of power to their priestly roles. Instead, it seems more accurate to believe that such small power as they control is likely to stem from their ritual status . . ."

But what we know of Fiji and the Cauca Valley suggests a very different view of the power of the chief and of the respective roles of secular and sacred factors in giving rise to it. Let us look at the matter more closely.

Williams (p. 19) writes of the typical paramount chief in Fiji: "The person of a high-rank king . . . is sacred. In some instances these Fijian monarchs claim a divine origin, and . . . assert the right of deity, and demand from their subjects respect for those claims." And again: "The chiefs profess to derive their arbitrary power from the gods . . . Their influence is also greatly increased by that peculiar institution found so generally among the Polynesian tribes – the *tabu* . . ." (p. 20).

However, the real issue here is not the *validation* of chiefly power but its ultimate *basis*. And it is clear from Fijian ethnohistory that what allowed this power to arise in the first place was not any religious aura but a secular force – the demonstrated prowess of the chief in war.

What about Fijian priests? Was their power in any way equal to that of the chief, and thus a challenge to his authority? Priests certainly existed in Fiji, and indeed a head priest took part in the installation ceremony for a high chief (Williams, p. 19). But it is quite clear that Fijian priests were decidedly subordinate to the paramount chief. Thus, while priests might not hesitate to inform a chief of adverse public opinion about some unpopular act of his: "Generally . . . a good understanding exists between the chief and the priest, and the latter takes care to make the god's utterances agree with the wishes of the former" (p. 191).

That priests were subservient to chiefs may be gleaned from this remonstrance reported by Williams (p. 192): " 'who are you?' angrily asked the chief of the priest who sought to turn his purpose: 'Who is your god? If you make a stir, I will eat you!' "

In the Cauca Valley, the religious standing of paramount chiefs was apparently less than on Fiji. Thus Trimborn (p. 237) writes: "The existence of priestly functions among Cauca Valley chiefs cannot be demonstrated," and he was led to conclude from this and other evidence that "it does not appear that chieftainship arose from a priestly base."

This is not to say, of course, that the chief had nothing to do with the supernatural. While there were no temples as such in the Cauca Valley, cult objects, such as trophy heads, mummified bodies of former chiefs, and idols, were often lined up inside the chief's house (pp. 237–238).

Priests existed in the Cauca Valley but their political influence was very limited. They mediated between members of the society and certain supernatural beings, but they also cured, revealing their shamanistic roots (p. 193). Feeding the corpses of war captives to the gods seems to have been an important religious function, and priests were probably the ones to do so (p. 238).

While they enjoyed a higher status than commoners, Cauca Valley priests did not form a separate caste (p. 194). Summing up their role, Trimborn says: "Although priests exercised a notable influence on public life, they did not involve themselves directly in political matters" (p. 242).

In summary, then, if chiefdoms are to be painted in bold, contrasting colors, they are more accurately portrayed as secular military despotisms than as peaceful theocracies.

Now if an entire island or valley should become politically unified, warfare might come to an end or at least be substantially curtailed. Deprived in this way of his military role, the paramount chief might then begin to arrogate onto himself more and more religious functions as he sought other means to maintain the powers of his office. As a result, his chiefdom might in time take on the appearance of a peaceful theocracy. But merely because the lion had retracted his claws, we should not be deluded into thinking that he never had them. Concealed as the initial basis of chiefly power might have been by the donning of clerical robes, it remained, at its root, the ability to exercise physical coercion over others by successful leadership in war.

Elsewhere in this volume, Ferguson remarks that "In states, compulsion replaces consensus as the ultimate basis of organization." I am convinced that by the time chiefdoms had arisen, this transition was already well under way.

Notes

1. For example, the theorist Henri Claessen, even when surrounded by very substantial evidence to the contrary, still feels impelled to say, "It seems improbable that war should be considered the, or

even a, prime mover behind the evolution of sociopolitical forms" (Claessen and van de Velde, 1985: 253).

2. In this and subsequent quotations from Trimborn, the translation from the Spanish text of his work is mine.

3. "Dani leaders initiate war actions but do not have the power to force warriors to participate" (Heider, 1970: 127).

4. Unless, of course, the principle of hereditary chieftainship had already become established. Even then, it was usual for the heir to the chieftainship to be trained from childhood in the martial arts, since eventually he would become the military as well as the political leader of his people.

5. In the Cauca valley, cannibalism was also a way to incorporate the martial virtues of a dead warrior into oneself (Trimborn, pp. 405, 414), and this may also have been true on Fiji, although I have not found an explicit statement in Williams to this effect.

6. This practice may have given rise to the widespread and still-current Andean Indian belief in *pishtacos*, white men who are said to kill Indians for their fat, which they use as grease or fuel for airplanes, cars, trucks, or machinery.

7. It should not go unmentioned that Ra Undreundre had eaten all these corpses by himself, never deigning to share so much as a single morsel with anyone else (Williams, p. 181).

REFERENCES

Adams, Richard N. 1975. *Energy and Structure: A Theory of Social Power*. Austin: University of Texas Press.

Alexander, Richard 1979. *Darwinism and Human Affairs*. Seattle: University of Washington Press.

1985. A Biological Interpretation of Moral Systems. *Zygon* 20:3–20.

1987. *The Biology of Moral Systems*. New York: Aldine De Gruyter.

Alexander, Richard, and Gerald Borgia 1978. Group Selection, Altriusm, and the Levels of Organization of Life. *Annual Review of Ecological Systems* 9: 449–474.

Alland, Alexander 1972. *The Human Imperative*. New York: Columbia University Press.

Andreski, Stanislav 1968. *Military Organization and Society*. Berkeley: University of California.

Axelrod, R. 1984. *The Evolution of Cooperation*. New York: Basic Books.

Balee, William 1984. The Ecology of Ancient Tupi Warfare. In *Warfare, Culture, and Environment*. B. Ferguson, ed. pp. 241-265. Orlando: Academic Press.

1985. Ka'apor Ritual Hunting. *Human Ecology* 13: 485–510.

1988. The Ka'apor Indian Wars of Lower Amazonia, ca. 1825–1928. In *Dialectics and Gender: Anthropological Approaches*. Richard Randolph, David Schneider, and May Diaz, eds. pp. 155–169. Boulder: Westview Press.

Ballard, Charles. 1981. Trade, Tribute and Migrant Labor: Zulu and Colonial Exploitation of the Delagoa Bay Hinterland 1818–1979. In *Before and*

After Shaka: Papers in Nguni History. J. Peires, ed. pp. 100–124. Institute of Social and Economic Research, Rhodes University, Grahamstown, South Africa.

Barash, D. 1977. *Sociobiology and Behavior.* New York: Elsevier, North-Holland.

Barnett, S. A. 1983. Humanity and Natural Selection. *Ethnology and Sociobiology* 4: 35–51.

Barrere, P. 1743. *Nouvelle Relation de la France Equinoxiale.* Paris.

Basso, E. B. 1973. *The Kalapalo Indians of Central Brazil.* New York: Holt, Rinehart and Winston.

Baxter, P. T. W. 1979. Boran Age-Sets and Warfare. In *Warfare Among East African Herders.* K. Fukui and D. Turton, eds. pp. 69–95. Osaka: National Museum of Ethnology.

Beals, Ralph L., George W. Brainerd, and Watson Smith 1945. *Archaeological Studies in Northeast Arizona.* University of California Publications in American Archaeology and Ethnology, Vol. 4, No. 1, Berkeley and Los Angeles: University of California Press.

Beemer, Hilda 1937. The Development of the Military Organization in Swaziland. *Africa* 10: 55–74, 176–205.

Bell, F. L. S. 1935. Warfare Among the Tanga. *Oceania* 5: 253–279.

Bender, Barbara 1985. Emergent Tribal Formations in the American Midcontinent. *American Antiquity* 50: 52–62.

Benedict, Ruth 1934. *Patterns of Culture.* New York: Houghton Mifflin.

1974. *The Chrysanthemum and the Sword: Patterns of Japanese Culture.* New York: New American Library.

Bennett Ross, Jane 1971. Aggression as Adaptation: The Yanomamo Case. Unpublished manuscript on file at Department of Anthropology, Columbia University, New York.

1980. Ecology and the Problem of Tribe: A Critique of the Hobbesian Model of Preindustrial Warfare. In *Beyond the Myths of Culture: Essays in Cultural Materialism.* E. Ross, ed. pp. 33–60. New York: Academic Press.

1984. Effects of Contact on Revenge Hostilities Among the Achuara Jivaro. In *Warfare, Culture, and Environment.* B. Ferguson, ed. pp. 83–109. Orlando: Academic Press.

Berkowitz, L. 1982. Adversive Conditions as Stimuli to Aggression. In *Advances in Experimental Social Psychology.* New York: Academic Press.

Berndt, Ronald 1962. *Excess and Restraint.* Chicago: University of Chicago.

Berndt, Ronald, and Peter Lawrence, editors 1973. *Politics in New Guinea: Traditional and in the Context of Change, Some Anthropological Perspectives.* Seattle: University of Washington.

Berry, David R. 1983. Skeletal Remains from RB568. Appendix I, in *Honoring the Dead: Anasazi Ceramics from the Rainbow Bridge–Monument Valley Expedition*, by Helen Crotty. Museum of Cultural History Monograph Series 22, pp. 64–69. University of California, Los Angeles.

Betzig, L. L. 1986. *Despotism and Differential Reproduction: A Darwinian View of History*. Chicago: Aldine.

Biet, A. 1664. *Voyage de la France Equinoxiale en l'isle de Cayenne, entrepris par les Français en l'année MDCLII*. Paris.

Bigalke, T. 1983. Dynamics of the Torajan Slave Trade in South Sulawesì. In *Slavery, Bondage and Dependency in Southeast Asia*, (ed.) A. Reid, St. Lucia, Queensland: U. of Queensland Press.

Biocca, Ettore 1971. *Yanoama: The Narrative of a White Girl Kidnapped by Amazonian Indians*. New York: E. P. Dutton.

Biolsi, Thomas 1984. Ecological and Cultural Factors in Plains Indian Warfare. In *Warfare, Culture, and Environment*. B. Ferguson, ed. pp. 141–168. Orlando: Academic Press.

Bishop, Charles 1970. The Emergence of Hunting Territories Among the Northern Ojibwa. *Ethnology* 9: 1–15.

Boehm, Christopher 1983. *Montenegrin Social Organization and Values: Political Ethnography of a Refuge Area Tribal Adaptation*. New York: AMS.

1984. *Blood Revenge: The Anthropology of Feuding in Montenegro and Other Tribal Societies*. Lawrence: University Press of Kansas.

Bonner, P. L. 1981. The Dynamics of Late Eighteenth-Century, Early Nineteenth-Century Northern Nguni Society – Some Hypotheses. In *Before and After Shaka: Papers in Nguni History*. J. Peires, ed. pp. 74–81. Institute of Social and Economic Research, Rhodes University, Grahamstown, South Africa.

Boone, James 1983. Noble Family Structure and Expansionist Warfare in the Late Middle Ages: A Socioecological Approach. In *Rethinking Human Adaptation: Biological and Cultural Models*. R. Dyson-Hudson and M. Little, eds. pp. 79–96. Boulder: Westview.

Borch, T. and J. Galtung 1966. Belligerence among the Primitives. *Journal of Peace Research* 3: 33–45.

Borgerhoff Mulder, Monique 1987. On Cultural and Reproductive Success: Kipsigis Evidence. *American Anthropologist* 89: 617–634.

Boulding, Kenneth 1963. *Conflict and Defense: A General Theory*. New York: Harper Torchbooks.

Braun, David P. 1984. Midwestern Hopewellian Exchange and Supralocal Interaction. In *Peer Polity Interaction and Sociopolitical Change*, edited by C. Renfrew and J. Cherry. Cambridge University Press.

Braun David P. and Stephen Plog 1980. Evolution of "Tribal" Social Networks: Theory and Prehistoric North American Evidence. Paper presented at the 79th annual meeting of the American Anthropological Association, Washington, D.C.

1982. Evolution of "Tribal" Social Networks: Theory and Prehistoric North American Evidence. *American Antiquity* 47: 504–25.

Brett, W. H. 1868. *The Indian Tribes of Guiana*. London: Bell & Daldy.

Broch, Tom, and Johan Galtung 1966. Belligerence Among the Primitives: A Re-Analysis of Quincy Wright's Data. *Journal of Peace Research* 3: 33–45.

Brown, Paula 1964. Enemies and Affines. *Ethnology* 3: 335–356.
Brown, R. 1985. *Social Psychology: The Second Edition.* New York: Free Press.
Burch, Ernest 1974. Eskimo Warfare in Northwest Alaska. *Anthropological Papers of the University of Alaska* 16: 1–14.
Burch, Ernest, and Thomas Correll 1971. Alliance and Conflict: Inter-Regional Relations in North Alaska. In *Alliance in Eskimo Society.* L. Guemple, ed. pp. 17–38. Seattle: American Ethnological Society and University of Washington Press.
Buss, A. H. 1961. *The Psychology of Aggression.* New York: Wiley.
    1971. Aggression Pays. In *The Control of Aggression and Violence,* by J. Singer. New York: Academic Press.
Carneiro, Robert L. 1961. Slash and Burn Cultivation Among the Kuikuru and Its Implications for Cultural Development in the Amazon Basin. In *The Evolution of Horticultural Systems in Native South America: Causes and Consequences.* J. Wilbert, ed. pp. 47–67. Anthropologica, Supplement No. 2. Caracas: Sociedad de Ciencias Naturales la Salle.
    1970. A Theory of the Origin of the State. *Science* 169: 733–38.
    1978. Political Expansion as an Expression of the Principle of Competitive Exclusion. In *Origins of the State: The Anthropology of Political Evolution,* Ronald Cohen and Elman R. Service, eds., pp. 205–24. Philadelphia: Institute for the Study of Human Issues.
    1981. The Chiefdom: Precursor of the State. In *The Transition to Statehood in the New World,* G. D. Jones and R. R. Kautz, eds. pp. 37–79. New York: Cambridge University Press.
Chagnon, N. A. 1966. Yanomamö warfare, Social Organization and Marriage Alliances. Unpublished Ph.D. dissertation, Department of Anthropology, University of Michigan, Ann Arbor: University Microfilms.
    1968a. Yanomamö Social Organization and Warfare. In *War: The Anthropology of Social Conflict and Aggression.* M. Fried, M. Harris, and R. Murphy, eds. pp. 109–159. New York: Doubleday.
    1968b. *Yanomamö: The Fierce People.* New York: Holt, Rinehart and Winston.
    1973. The Culture-Ecology of Shifting (Pioneering) Cultivation Among the Yanomamö Indians. In *Peoples and Cultures of Native South America.* D. Gross, ed. pp. 126–142. Garden City: Natural History.
    1974. *Studying the Yanomamö.* New York: Holt, Rinehart and Winston.
    1977. *Yanomamö: The Fierce People,* 2nd edition. New York: Holt, Rinehart and Winston.
    1979a. Mate Competition, Favoring Close Kin, and Village Fissioning Among the Yanomamö Indians. In *Evolutionary Biology and Human Social Behavior.* N. Chagnon and W. Irons, eds. pp. 86–132. Duxbury: North Scituate, MA.
    1979b. Is Reproductive Success Equal in Egalitarian Societies? In *Evolutionary Biology and Human Social Behavior: An Anthropolitical Perspec-*

tive, N. A. Chagnon and W. Irons, eds. pp. 374–401. North Scituate, MA: Duxbury Press.

1980. Kin Selection Theory, Kinship, Marriage and Fitness Among the Yanomamö Indians. In *Sociobiology: Beyond Nature/Nurture?* G. Barlow and J. Silverberg, eds. pp. 545–571. Boulder: Westview Press.

1981. Terminological Kinship, Genealogical Relatedness and Village Fissioning Among the Yanomamö Indians. In *Natural Selection and Social Behavior: Recent Research and New Theory*, R. Alexander and D. Tinkle, eds., pp. 490–508. New York: Chiron Press.

1982. Sociodemographic Attributes of Nepotism in Tribal Populations: Man the Rule Breaker. In *Current Problems in Sociobiology*, King's College Sociobiology Group, eds., pp. 291–318. Cambridge, England: Cambridge University Press.

1983. *Yanomamö: The Fierce People*, 3rd edition. New York: Holt, Rinehart and Winston.

1988a. Life Histories, Blood Revenge and Warfare in a Tribal Population. *Science* 239: 985–992.

1988b. Male Yanomamö Manipulations of Kinship Classifications of Female Kin for Reproductive Advantage. In *Human Reproductive Behavior*, L. Betzig, M. Borgerhoff Mulder and P. Turke, eds. pp. 23–48. Cambridge, England: Cambridge University Press.

Chagnon, Napoleon, and Paul Bugos 1979. Kin Selection and Conflict: An Analysis of a Yanomamö Ax Fight. In *Evolutionary Biology and Human Social Behavior: An Anthropological Perspective*, N. A. Chagnon and W. Irons, eds., pp. 213–228. North Scituate, MA: Duxbury Press.

Chagnon, Napoleon, and Raymond Hames 1983. The Social Effects of Mortality and Divorce on the Yanomamö Nuclear Family. National Science Foundation Research Proposal, BNS-8319644, Washington, D.C.

Chagnon, Napoleon, and William Irons, eds. 1979. *Evolutionary Biology and Human Social Behavior: An Anthropological Perspective*. North Scituate, MA: Duxbury Press.

Christenson, Andrew L. 1983. The Archaeological Investigation of the Rainbow Bridge–Monument Valley Expedition, 1933–1938. In *Honoring the Dead: Anasazi Ceramics from the Rainbow Bridge–Monument Valley Expedition*, by Helen Crotty, Museum of Cultural History Monograph Series 22, pp. 9–23. University of California, Los Angeles.

Claessen, Henri 1979. The Balance of Power in Primitive States. In *Political Anthropology: The State of the Art*. S. Lee Seaton and H. Claessen, eds. pp. 183–195. New York: Mouton.

Claessen, Henri, and Pieter van de Velde 1985. Sociopolitical Evolution as Complex Interaction. In *Development and Decline: The Evolution of Sociopolitical Organization*, H. Claessen, P. van de Velde, and M. E. Smith, eds. pp. 246–263. South Hadley, Mass.: Bergin and Garvey Publishers, Inc.

Codere, Helen 1950. *Fighting with Property: A Study of Kwakuitl Potlatching and Warfare*, 1792–1930. American Ethnological Society Monograph No. 18.

Cohen, Ronald 1984. Warfare and State Formation: Wars Make States and States Make War. In *Warfare, Culture, and Environment*. B. Ferguson, ed. pp. 329–358. Orlando: Academic Press.

Collier, James 1903. The Struggle for Existence in Sociology. I. *Knowledge* 26: 138–140.

Collins, June 1950. Growth of Class Distinctions and Political Authority Among the Skagit Indians During the Contact Period. *American Anthropologist* 52: 331–342.

Colson, E. 1953. Social Control and Vengeance Among the Plateau Tonga. *Africa* 23: 199–211.

Cook, S. F. and Borah, W. H. 1963. The Aboriginal Population of Central Mexico on the Eve of Spanish Conquest. *Ibero-Americana* 45.

Cook, Sherburne 1973. Interracial Warfare and Population Decline Among the New England Indians. *Ethnohistory* 20: 1–24.

Coser, Lewis 1956. *The Functions of Social Conflict*. New York: Free Press.

Creamer, Winifred and Jonathan Haas 1985. Tribe versus Chiefdom in Lower Central America. *American Antiquity* 50: 738–754.

Crotty, Helen 1983. *Honoring the Dead: Anasazi Ceramics from the Rainbow Bridge–Monument Valley Expedition*. Museum of Culture History Monograph Series 22, University of California, Los Angeles.

Crummey, Donald, editor 1986. *Banditry, Rebellion and Social Protest in Africa*. Heinemann: Portsmouth.

Daly, Martin and Margo Wilson 1983. *Sex, Evolution and Behavior*. 2nd edition. Boston: Willard Grand Press.

1988. *Homicide*. New York: Aldine de Gruyter.

Dawkins, Richard 1976. *The Selfish Gene*. Oxford: Oxford University Press.

Dean, Jeffrey S. 1969. Chronological Analysis of Tsegi Phase Sites in Northeastern Arizona. *Papers of the Laboratory of Tree-Ring Research*, No. 3. Tucson: University of Arizona Press.

Dean, Jeffrey, S., Robert C. Euler, George J. Gumerman, Fred Plog, Richard H. Hevly, and Thor N. V. Karlstrom 1985. Human Behavior, Demography, and Paleoenvironment on the Colorado Plateaus. *American Antiquity* 50(3): 537–554.

Dean, Jeffrey, S., Alexander J. Lindsay, Jr., and William Robinson 1978. Prehistoric Settlement in Long House Valley, Northeastern Arizona. In *Investigations of the Southwestern Anthropological Research Group: An Experiment in Archaeological Cooperation: The Proceedings of the 1976 Conference*, Robert C. Euler and George Gumerman, eds., pp. 25–44. Flagstaff: Museum of Northern Arizona.

Dentan, Robert K. 1968. *The Semai: A Non-Violent People of Malaya*. New York: Holt, Rinehart and Winston.

1978. Notes on Childhood in a Nonviolent Context: The Semai Case (Malaysia). In *Learning Non-Aggression*. A. Montagu ed. New York: Oxford University Press.

217

Depons, F. 1806. *Travels in Parts of South America, During the Years 1801–1804.* London.

Dibble, Vernon 1967. The Garrison Society. *New University Thought* 5: 106–115.

Dickemann, Mildred 1981. Paternal Confidence and Dowry Competition: A Biocultural Analysis of Purdah. In *Natural Selection and Social Behavior: Recent Research and New Theory,* R. Alexander and D. Tinkle, eds., pp. 417–438. New York: Chiron Press.

Dirks, Robert 1980. Social Responses During Severe Food Shortages and Famine. *Current Anthropology* 21: 21–44.

Divale, William 1971. An Explanation for Primitive Warfare: Population Control and the Significance of Primitive Sex Ratios. *New Scholar* 2: 173–192.

    1985. Matrilocal Residence in Pre-Literate Society. In *Studies in Cultural Anthropology,* UMI Research Press.

Divale, William, F. Chameris and D. Gangloff 1976. War, Peace, and Marital Residence in Pre-Industrial Societies. *Journal of Conflict Resolution* 20: 57–78.

Divale, William, and Marvin Harris 1976. Population, Warfare, and the Male Supremacist Complex. *American Anthropologist* 78: 521–538.

Dole, G. E. 1956–58. Ownership and Exchange Among the Kuikuru Indians of Mato Grosso. *Revista do Museu Paulista,* n.s. X: 125–33.

    1966. Anarchy Without Chaos: Alternatives to Political Authority Among the Kuikuru. In *Political Anthropology.* Marc Swarz et al., eds. Chicago: University of Chicago Press.

Dollard, J., et al. 1939. *Frustration and Aggression.* New Haven: Yale University Press.

Drago, Harry 1970. *The Great Range Wars: Violence on the Grasslands.* Lincoln: University of Nebraska Press.

Drucker, Philip 1951. The Northern and Central Nootkan Tribes. *Bureau of American Ethnology Bulletin* 144. Washington: Smithsonian Institution.

Durham, W. H. 1976. Resource Competition and Human Aggression, Part I: A Review of Primitive Warfare. *Quarterly Review of Biology* 51: 385–415.

Dyson-Hudson, Rada, and Eric Smith 1978. Human Territoriality: An Ecological Reassessment. *American Anthropologist* 80: 21–41.

Eckhardt, William 1975. Primitive Militarism. *Journal of Peace Research* 12: 55–62.

Effland, Richard W. 1979. A Study of Prehistoric Spatial Behavior: Long House Valley, Northeastern Arizona. Unpublished Ph.D. dissertation, Arizona State University. Ann Arbor: University Microfilms.

Ekvall, Robert 1961. The Nomadic Pattern of Living Among the Tibetans as Preparation for War. *American Anthropologist* 63: 1250–63.

    1964. Peace and War Among the Tibetan Nomads. *American Anthropologist* 66: 1119–1148.

Ellis, Florence Hawley. 1951. Patterns of Aggression and War Cult in the

Southwestern Pueblos. *Southwestern Journal of Anthropology* 7: 177–201.

Ember, Carol, Melvin Ember, and Burt Pasternak 1974. On the Development of Unilineal Descent. *Journal of Anthropological Research* 30: 69–94.

Ember, Melvin 1982. Statistical Evidence for an Ecological Explanation of Warfare. *American Anthropologist* 84(3): 645–649.

Ember, Melvin, and Carol Ember 1971. The Conditions Favoring Matrilocal Versus Patrilocal Residence. *American Anthropologist* 73: 571–594.

n.d. The Predictors of Warfare. Unpublished manuscript.

Engels, Frederick 1939. *Herr Eugen Duhring's Revolution in Science*. New York: International.

Epstein, A. L. 1975. Military Organization and the Pre-Colonial Polity of the Bemba of Zambia. *Man* 10: 199–217.

Evans-Pritchard, E. E. 1940. *The Nuer*. Oxford: University Press.

Fabbro, D. 1978. Peaceful Societies: An Introduction. *Journal of Peace Research* 12: 67–84.

Fadiman, Jeffrey 1976. Mountain Warriors: Traditional Warfare Among the Meru of Mt. Kenya. Ohio University Africa Series.

1982. *An Oral History of Tribal Warfare: The Meru of Mt. Kenya*. Athens: Ohio University.

Fathauer, George 1954. The Structure and Causation of Mohave Warfare. *Southwestern Journal of Anthropology* 10: 97–118.

Ferguson, R. Brian 1983. Warfare and Redistributive Exchange on the Northwest Coast. In *The Development of Political Organization in Native North America: 1979 Proceedings of the American Ethnological Society*. E. Tooker, ed. pp. 133–147. Washington: American Ethnological Society.

1984a. Introduction: Studying War. In *Warfare, Culture, and Environment*. B. Ferguson, ed. pp. 1–81. Orlando: Academic Press.

1984b. A Reexamination of the Causes of Northwest Coast Warfare. In *Warfare, Culture, and Environment*. B. Ferguson, ed. pp. 267–328. Orlando: Academic Press.

1988a. *The Anthropology of War: A Bibliography*. New York: The Harry Frank Guggenheim Foundation.

1988b. War and the Sexes in Amazonia. In *Dialectics and Gender*, Richard Randolph, May Diaz, and David Schneider, eds. pp. 136–154. Boulder: Westview Press.

1989a. Anthropology and War: Theory, Politics, Ethics. In *The Anthropology of War and Peace*. David Pitt and Paul Turner, eds. pp. 141–159. South Hadley, MA: Bergin and Garvey.

1989b. Game Wars? Ecology and Conflict in Amazonia. *Journal of Anthropological Research* 45: 179–206.

1989c. Ecological Consequences.

Festinger, L. 1954. A Theory of Social Comparison Processes. *Human Relations* 7: 117–140.

219

Fisher, Raymond 1930. *The Genetical Theory of Natural Selection*. (Revised 2nd edition, 1958.) New York: Dover Press.

Flannery, Kent V. 1972. The Cultural Evolution of Civilization. *Annual Review of Ecology and Systematics* 3: 399–426.

Flinn, Mark 1988. Mate Guarding and Daughter Guarding in a Trinidadian Village. *Ethology and Sociobiology* 9: 1–28.

Flinn, Mark and R. D. Alexander 1982. Culture Theory: The Developing Synthesis from Biology. *Human Ecology* 10: 383–400.

Forbes, Jack 1960. *Apache, Navaho, and Spaniard*. Norman: University of Oklahoma.

Forsyth, D. W. 1983. The Beginnings of Brazilian Anthropology – the Jesuits and Tupinamba Cannibalism. *Journal of Anthropological Research* 39(2): 147–178.

Fortes, Meyer, and E. E. Evans-Pritchard, editors 1940. *African Political Systems*. New York: Oxford.

Fox, Richard G. 1969. Professional Primitives: Hunters and Gatherers of Nuclear South Asia. *Man In India* 49(2): 139–60.

Freeman, D. 1967. Shaman and Incubus. *Psychoanalytic Study of Society* 4: 315–344.

1968. Thunder, Blood and the Nicknaming of God's Creatures. *The Psychoanalytic Quarterly* 37: 353–399.

1970. *Report on the Iban*. London: Athlone Press.

1979. Severed Heads That Germinate. In *Fantasy and Symbol*. R. H. Hook, ed., pp. 233–246. London: Academic Press.

1981. Reflections on the Nature of Iban Society. Occasional Paper of the Department of Anthropology, Research School of Pacific Studies, A.N.U. Canberra.

Fried, Morton H. 1961. Warfare, Military Organization, and the Evolution of Society. *Anthropologica* N.S. 3: 134–147.

1967. *The Evolution of Political Society: An Essay in Political Anthropology*. New York: Random House.

1975. *The Notion of Tribe*. Menlo Park: Cummings.

1983. Tribe to State or State to Tribe in Ancient China? In *The Origins of Chinese Civilization*, David N. Keightley, ed., pp. 467–493. Berkeley: University of California Press.

Fried, Morton H., Marvin Harris and Robert Murphy, eds. 1968. *War: The Anthropology of Social Conflict and Aggression*. New York: Doubleday.

Frost, Everett L. 1979. Fiji. In *The Prehistory of Polynesia*, ed. by J. D. Jennings, pp. 61–81. Cambridge, MA: Harvard University Press.

Fukui, Katsuyoshi, and David Turton, eds. 1979. *Warfare Among East African Herders*. Osaka: National Museum of Ethnology.

Galtung, J. 1968. Peace. *International Encyclopedia of the Social Sciences*.

Galvao, E. 1953. Cultura e sistems de Parentesco das tribos do Alto Rio Xingu. *Boletim do Museu Nacional* 10: 1–56.

Gamst, Frederick 1986. Conflict in the Horn of Africa. In *Peace and War:*

Cross-cultural Perspectives. M. Foster and R. Rubinstein, eds., pp. 133–151. New Brunswick: Transaction Press.

Gardner, P. M. 1972. The Paliyans. In *Hunters and Gatherers Today,* Marco Bicchieri ed. New York: Holt, Rinehart and Winston.

Garrett, Elizabeth M. 1986. A Petrographic Analysis of Black Mesa Ceramics. In *Spatial Organization and Exchange: Archaeological Survey on Northern Black Mesa,* edited by Stephen Plog, pp. 114–142. Southern Illinois University Press, Carbondale.

Gibson, T. 1985. The Sharing of Substance Versus the Sharing of Activity Among the Buid. *Man* 20(3): 391–411.

1986. *Sacrifice and Sharing in the Philippine Highlands: Religion and Society Among the Buid of Mindoro.* London: Athlone Press.

Giddens, Anthony 1985. *The Nation-State and Violence:* Volume Two of *A Contemporary Critique of Historical Materialism.* Berkeley: University of California.

Givens, R. D., and M. A. Nettleship 1976. *Discussions on War and Human Aggression.* The Hague: Mouton.

Glasse, Robert 1959. Revenge and Redress Among the Huli: A Preliminary Account. *Mankind* 5: 273–289.

Gluckman, Max 1940. The Kingdom and the Zulu. In *African Political Systems.* M. Fortes and E. E. Evans-Pritchard, eds. pp. 25–55. New York: Oxford.

1955. *Custom and Conflict in Africa.* Glencoe, IL: Free Press.

1965. *Politics, Law, and Ritual in Tribal Society.* Chicago: Aldine.

1969. *Custom and Conflict in Africa.* New York: Harper and Row.

Goldberg, Neil, and Frank Findlow 1984. A Quantitative Analysis of Roman Military Aggression in Britain, circa A.D. 43–238. In *Warfare, Culture, and Environment.* B. Ferguson, ed. pp. 359–385. Orlando: Academic Press.

Golden, Peter 1986. Aspects of the Nomadic Factor in the Economic Development of Kievan Rus'. Manuscript.

Golob, Ann 1982. The Upper Amazon in Historical Perspective. Doctoral Disseration, Dept. of Anthropology, The City University of New York.

Goody, Jack 1980. *Technology, Tradition and the State in Africa.* New York: Cambridge University Press.

Gordon, Robert 1983. The Decline of the Kiapdom and the resurgence of "Tribal Fighting" in Enga. *Oceania* 53: 205–223.

Gould, S. J. 1986. Cardboard Darwinism. *New York Review of Books,* 25 Sep.: 47–54.

Graham, Edward 1974. Yuman Warfare: An Analysis of Ecological Factors from Ethnohistorical Sources. In *War, Its Causes and Correlates.* M. Nettleship, R. D. Givens, and A. Nettleship, eds. pp. 451–462. The Hague: Mouton.

Graves, Michael W. 1981. Ethnoarchaeology of Kalinga Ceramic Design.

Unpublished Ph.D. Dissertation, Department of Anthropology, University of Arizona. Ann Arbor: University Microfilms.

Green, Margerie 1983. The Relationship of Source Distance to Conservation of Chipped Stone Raw Materials. In *Papers on the Archaeology of Black Mesa*, Arizona, Volume II, edited by Stephen Plog and Shirley Powell, pp. 173–188. Southern Illinois University Press, Carbondale.

1986. The Distribution of Chipped Stone Raw Materials at Functionally Nonequivalent Sites. In *Spatial Organization and Exchange: Archaeological Survey on Northern Black Mesa*, edited by Stephen Plog, pp. 143–168. Southern Illinois University Press, Carbondale.

Gregor, Thomas 1977. *Mehinaku: The Drama of Daily Life in a Brazilian Indian Village*. Chicago: The University of Chicago Press.

1985. *Anxious Pleasures: The Sexual Lives of an Amazonian People*. Chicago: The University of Chicago Press.

Gross, Daniel 1975. Protein Capture and Cultural Development in the Amazon Basin. *American Anthropologist* 77(3): 526–549.

Gumilla, J. 1745. *El Orinoco Illustrado Y Defendido*. Madrid.

Haas, Jonathan 1982. *The Evolution of the Prehistoric State*. New York: Columbia University Press.

Haas, Jonathan and Winifred Creamer 1987. Warfare and Tribalization in the Prehistoric Southwest. Report submitted to the Harry Frank Guggenheim Foundation. New York.

Hall, Kenneth R. 1985. *Maritime Trade and State Development in Early Southeast Asia*. Honolulu: University of Hawaii Press.

Halloway, R. L. 1968. Human Aggression: The Need for a Species Specific Framework, In *War: The Anthropology of Armed Conflict and Aggression*, by M. Fried, M. Harris, and R. Murphy, pp. 29–48. New York: Doubleday.

Hallpike, C. R. 1977. *Bloodshed and Vengeance in the Papuan Mountains: The Generation of Conflict in Tauade Society*. London: Oxford University Press.

Hames, Raymond 1983. A Settlement Pattern of a Yanomamö Population Bloc: A Behavioral Ecological Interpretation. In *Adaptive Responses of Native Amazonians*. R. Hames and W. Vickers, eds. pp. 393–427. New York: Academic Press.

Hamilton, J. 1820. Journal of a Trek from St. Tome de Angostura in Spanish Guayana to the Capuchin Missions of the Caroni. *Quarterly Journal of Science, Literature and The Arts* 8: 260–87, 9: 1–32.

Hamilton, William 1964. The Genetical Evolution of Social Behavior, I and II. *Journal of Theoretical Biology* 7: 1–52.

Harcourt, R. 1613. *A Relation of a Voyage to Guiana*. London.

Harner, Michael J. 1970. Population Pressure and the Social Evolution of Agriculturalists. *Southwestern Journal of Anthropology* 26: 67–86.

1973. *The Jivaro: People of the Sacred Waterfalls*. Garden City: Anchor.

Harris, Marvin 1964. *The Nature of Cultural Things*. New York: Random House.

1968. *The Rise of Anthropological Theory: A History of Theories of Culture.* New York: Thomas Crowell.

1971. *Culture, Man and Nature: An Introduction to General Anthropology.* New York: Thomas Crowell.

1972. Warfare, Old and New. *Natural History* 81(3): 18–20.

1974. *Cows, Pigs, Wars and Witches: The Riddles of Culture.* New York: Vantage Press.

1977. *Cannibals and Kings.* New York: Random House.

1979a. *Cultural Materialism: The Struggle for a Science of Culture.* New York: Random House.

1979b. The Yanomamö and the Causes of War in Band and Village Societies. In *Brazil: Anthropological Perspectives: Essays in Honor of Charles Wagley*, M. Margolies and W. Carter, eds., pp. 121–132. New York: Columbia University Press.

1984a. A Cultural Materialism Theory of Band and Village Warfare: The Yanomamö Test. In *Warfare, Culture, and Environment.* B. Ferguson, ed. pp. 111–140. Orlando: Academic Press.

1984b. Animal Capture and Yanomamö Warfare: Retrospect and New Evidence. *Journal of Anthropological Research* 40: 183–201.

1985. *Culture, People, Nature: An Introduction to General Anthropology,* 3rd edition. New York: Harper and Row.

Harris, Marvin and Eric Ross 1987. *Death, Sex and Fertility: Population Regulation in Preindustrial and Developing Societies.* New York: Columbia University Press.

Hayano, David 1974. Marriage, Alliance, and Warfare: A View from the New Guinea Highlands. *American Ethnologist* 1: 281–293.

Heider, Karl 1970. *The Dugum Dani: A Papuan Culture in the Highlands of West New Guinea.* New York: Wenner-Gren Foundation for Anthropological Research, 49.

Hickerson, Harold 1965. The Virginia Deer and Intertribal Buffer Zones in the Upper Mississippi Valley. In *Man, Culture, and Animals: The Role of Animals in Human Ecological Adjustments.* A. Leeds and A. Vayda, eds. pp. 43–65. Washington: American Association for the Advancement of Science.

Hilhouse, W. 1825. *Indian Notices.* Demerara.

Hobbes, Thomas 1651. *Leviathan.* London. (Fontana Edition, 1972)

1839. *The English Works of Thomas Hobbes.* 11 volumes, edited by Sir William Molesworth. London.

Hobhouse, L. T., G. C. Wheeler, and M. Ginsberg 1965. *The Material Culture and Social Institutions of the Simpler Peoples: An Essay in Correlation.* New York: The Humanities Press.

Hodder, Ian 1982. Toward a contextual approach to prehistoric exchange. In *Contexts for Prehistoric Exchange*, Jonathan E. Ericson and Timothy K. Earle, eds., pp. 213–235. New York: Academic Press.

Hoebel, E. Adamson 1978. *The Cheyennes: Indians of the Great Plains,* 2nd edition. New York: Holt, Rinehart and Winston.

Hoff, B. 1968. *The Carib Language*. KITLV-Verhandelingen Series No. 55. The Hague: M. Nijhoff.

Humboldt, A. von 1852. *Personal Narrative of Travels to the Equinoctial Regions of America*. London.

Hunt, George 1940. *The Wars of the Iroquois: A Study in Intertribal Trade Relations*. Madison: University of Wisconsin.

Im Thurn, E. F. 1883. *Among the Indians of Guiana*. London.

Irons, William 1979. Cultural and Biological Success. In *Evolutionary Biology and Human Social Behavior*. N. A. Chagnon and W. Irons, eds. Duxbury: North Scituate, MA. pp. 257–272.

Jablow, Jacob 1950. *The Cheyenne in Plains Indian Trade Relations*. American Ethnological Society Monograph No. 19. Seattle: University of Washington.

Johnson, Allen and Timothy Earle 1987. *The Evolution of Human Societies: From Foraging Group to Agrarian State*. Stanford: Stanford University Press.

Jonge, J. K. L. de 1862. *De Opkonst van det Nederlandisch Gezag in Oost-Indie*. 's-Gravenhage.

Kaberry, Phyllis 1973. Political Organization Among the Northern Abelam. In *Politics in New Guinea: Traditional and in the Context of Change, Some Anthropological Perspectives*, R. Berndt and P. Lawrence, eds. pp. 35–73. Seattle: University of Washington.

Kang, Gay Elizabeth 1979. Exogamy and Peace Relations of Social Units: A Cross-Cultural Test. *Ethnology* 18: 85–99.

Kelly, Raymond 1985. *The Nuer Conquest: The Structure and Development of an Expansionist System*. Ann Arbor: University of Michigan.

Kennedy, John 1971. Ritual and Intergroup Murder: Comments on War, Primitive and Modern. In *War and the Human Race*, M. Walsh, ed. pp. 40–61. New York: Elsevier.

Kiefer, Thomas 1968. Institutionalized Friendship and Warfare Among the Tausug of Jolo. *Ethnology* 7: 225–244.

1970. Modes of Social Action in Armed Combat: Affect, Tradition and Reason in Tausug Private Warfare. *Man* 5: 586–596.

1972. *The Tausug: Violence and Law in a Philippine Moslem Society*. New York: Holt, Rinehart and Winston.

Knivet, A. 1625. The Admirable Adventures and Strange Fortunes of Master Antonie Knivet, Anno 1591. In *Purchas his Pilgrimes*, by S. Purchas. London.

Kobben, André 1973. Cause and Intention. In *A Handbook of Method in Cultural Anthropology*, Raoul Naroll and Ronald Cohen, eds., pp. 89–98. New York: Columbia University Press.

Koch, Klaus-Friedrich 1974a. *War and Peace in Jalemo: The Management of Conflict in Highland New Guinea*. Cambridge: Harvard University Press.

1974b. The Anthropology of Warfare. *Addison-Wesley Modules in Anthropology* No. 52. Reading: Addison-Wesley.

1979. Epilogue. Pacification: Perspectives from Conflict Theory. In *The*

Pacification of Melanesia. M. Rodman and M. Cooper, eds., pp. 199–207. Ann Arbor: University of Michigan.

Kopytoff, Igor 1982. Slavery. *Annual Review of Anthropology* 11: 207–230.

Kopytoff, Igor, and Suzanne Miers 1977. African "Slavery" as an Institution of Marginality. In *Slavery in Africa: Historical and Anthropological Perspectives*. S. Miers and I. Kopytoff, eds. pp. 3–81. Madison: University of Wisconsin.

Krader, Lawrence 1968. *Formation of the State*. Englewood Cliffs: Prentice Hall.

Krebs, D. L., and D. T. Miller 1985. Altruism and Aggression. In *The Handbook of Social Psychology*, Vol. II, by G. Lindzey and E. Aronson. New York: Random House.

Lance, C. D. 1876. *Recollection of Four Years in Venezuela*. London.

Langness, L. L. 1964. Some Problems in the Conceptualization of Highlands Social Structures. *American Anthropologist* 66: 162–182.

1968. Sexual Antagonism in the New Guinea Highlands: A Bena Bena Example. *Oceania* 3: 161–177.

1973. Bena Bena Political Organization. In *Politics in New Guinea: Traditional and in the Context of Change, Some Anthropological Perspectives*. R. Berndt and P. Lawrence, eds. pp. 298–316. Seattle: University of Washington.

Larson, Lewis 1972. Functional Considerations of Warfare in the Southeast During the Mississippi Period. *American Antiquity* 37: 383–392.

Leach, Edmund 1968. Ignoble Savages. *The New York Review of Books* 11(6): 24–29.

Leacock, Eleanor 1978. Women's Status in Egalitarian Society: Implication for Social Evolution. *Current Anthropology* 19: 247–275.

Leacock, Eleanor, and Richard Lee, editors 1982. *Politics and History in Band Societies*. Cambridge: Cambridge University Press.

Lee, Richard 1982. Politics, Sexual and Non-Sexual in an Egalitarian Society. In *Politics and History in Band Societies*. E. Leacock and R. Lee, eds. pp. 37–59. Cambridge: Cambridge University Press.

Leeds, A. 1968. General Discussion. In *War: The Anthropology of Armed Conflict and Aggression*, by M. Fried, M. Harris, and R. Murphy, pp. 100–102. New York: Doubleday.

Lepervanche, Marie de 1968. Descent, Residence and Leadership in the New Guinea Highlands. *Oceania* 3: 163–189.

Lerius, J. 1625. Extracts Out of the Historie of John Lerius A Frenchman, Who Lived in Brasil With Monsieur Villagagnon, Anno 1557 and 1558. In *Purchas his Pilgrimes*, by S. Purchas. London.

Lesser, A. 1968. War and the State. In *War: The Anthropology of Armed Conflict and Aggression*, by M. Fried, M. Harris, and R. Murphy, eds. pp. 92–96. New York: Doubleday.

Lévi-Strauss, Claude 1943. Guerre et Commerce chez les Indiens de l'Amérique de Sud. *Renaissance* 1: 122–139.

Lewis, Oscar 1970. The Effects of White Contact upon Blackfoot Culture. In

Anthropological Essays. O. Lewis, ed. pp. 137–212. New York: Random House.

Li Puma, Edward 1985. Social and Cultural Factors Which Influence Aggression, Part I. In *Aggression: Functions and Causes*. J. Ramirez and P. Brain, eds. pp. 49–66. Publicacion de la Universidad de Sevilla.

Livingstone, F. B. 1968. The Effects of Warfare on the Biology of the Human Species. In *War: The Anthropology of Armed Conflict and Aggression* M. Fried, M. Harris, and R. Murphy, eds. pp. 3–15. New York: Doubleday.

Lizot, Jacques 1985. *Tales of the Yanomami*. Cambridge, England: Cambridge University Press.

1989. Sobre la Guerra: Una Repuesta a N.A. Chagnon (*Science* 1988). *La Iglesia en Amazonas* 44: 23–34.

Lovejoy, Paul 1983. *Transformations in Slavery: A History of Slavery in Africa*. Cambridge: Cambridge University Press.

Lowie, Robert 1963. *Indians of the Plains*. Garden City: American Museum of Science Book.

Maine, Henry 1861. *Ancient Law*. London: J. Murray.

Mair, Lucy 1977. *Primitive Government: A Study of Traditional Political Systems in Eastern Africa*. Bloomington: Indiana University.

Malinowski, Bronislaw 1964. An Anthropological Analysis of War. In *War: Studies from Psychology, Sociology, Anthropology*. L. Bramson and G. Goethals, eds. pp. 245–268. New York: Basic Books.

1966. War – Past, Present, and Future. In *War as a Social Institution: The Historians' Perspective*. J. Clarkson and T. Cochran, eds. pp. 21–31. New York: AMS Press.

Mann, Michael 1986. *The Sources of Social Power, Volume 1: A History of Power from the Beginning to A.D. 1760*. New York: Cambridge University Press.

Marshall, E. T. 1959. *The Harmless People*. New York: Knopf.

Marshall, S. L. A. 1947. *Men Against Fire*. New York: William Morrow.

Mason, Otis 1966. *The Origins of Invention*. Cambridge: MIT Press.

Mauss, Marcel 1967. *The Gift: Forms and Functions of Exchange in Archaic Societies*. New York: W. W. Norton.

Maybury-Lewis, David 1974. *Akwe-Shavante Society*. New York: Oxford.

Maynard Smith, J. 1964. Group Selection and Kin Selection. *Nature* 20: 1145–1147.

McDonald, George 1979. *Kitwanga Fort National Historic Site, Skeena River, British Columbia: Historical Research and Analysis of Structural Remains*. Ottawa: National Museum of Man.

McNeil, William 1982. *The Pursuit of Power*. Chicago: University of Chicago Press.

Mead, M. 1968. Alternatives to War. In *War: The Anthropology of Armed Conflict and Aggression*. M. Fried, M. Harris, and R. Murphy eds. pp. 215–228. New York: Doubleday.

Meillassoux, Claude, editor 1971. *The Development of Indigenous Trade and Markets in West Africa*. London: Oxford.

Meggitt, Mervyn 1972. System and Subsystem: The Te Exchange Cycle Among the Mae Enga. *Human Ecology* 1: 111–112.

1977. *Blood is Their Argument: Warfare Among Mae Enga Tribesmen of the New Guinea Highlands.* Palo Alto: Mayfield.

Melman, Seymour 1974. *The Permanent War Economy.* New York: Simon and Schuster.

1984. The End of War. In *Warfare, Culture, and Environment.* B. Ferguson, ed. pp. 387–396. Orlando: Academic Press.

Miers, Suzanne, and Igor Kopytoff, editors 1977. *Slavery in Africa: Historical and Anthropological Perspectives.* Madison: University of Wisconsin.

Mishkin, Bernard 1940. *Rank and Warfare Among the Plains Indians.* Seattle: University of Washington.

Mitchell, Donald 1984. Predatory Warfare, Social Status, and the North Pacific Slave Trade. *Ethnology* 23: 39–48.

Mocquet, J. 1696. *The Travels and Voyages of John Mocquet into the West Indies. Anno 1604.* London.

Morren, George 1984. Warfare in the Highland Fringe of New Guinea: The Case of the Mountain Ok. In *Warfare, Culture, and Environment.* B. Ferguson, ed. pp. 169–207. Orlando: Academic Press.

Morris, B. 1977. Tappers, Trappers and the Hill Pandaram (South India). *Anthropos* 71: 225–41.

Murphy, Robert 1956. Matrilocality and Patrilineality in Mundurucu Society. *American Anthropologist* 58: 414–434.

1957. Intergroup Hostility and Social Cohesion. *American Anthropologist* 59: 1018–1035.

1960. *Headhunter's Heritage: Social and Economic Change Among The Mundurucu Indians.* Berkeley: University of California.

Murphy, Robert, and Yolanda Murphy 1974. *Women of the Forest.* New York: Columbia University Press.

Nadel, S. F. 1953. *The Foundations of Social Anthropology.* London: Cohen and West.

Naroll, Raoul 1966. Does Military Deterrence Deter? *Trans-Action* 3(2): 14–20.

Netting, Robert 1973. Fighting, Forest and the Fly. *Journal of Anthropological Research* 29: 164–179.

1974a. Functions of War. *Man* 9: 485–487.

1974b. Kofyar Armed Conflict: Social Causes and Consequences. *Journal of Anthropological Research* 30: 139–163.

1977. *Cultural Ecology.* Menlo Park, CA: Cummings.

Newcomb, W. W. 1960. Toward an Understanding of War. In *Essays in The Science of Culture in Honor of Leslie A. White.* G. Dole and R. Carneiro, eds. pp. 317–336. New York: Thomas Crowell.

Numelin, Ragnar 1950. *The Beginnings of Diplomacy: A Sociological Study of Intertribal and International Relations.* London: Oxford.

1963. Intertribal relations in Central and South Africa. *Commentationes Humanarum Litterarum, Societas Scientiarum Fennica* 32(3).

Ogot, Bethwell, editor 1972. *War and Society in Africa: Ten Studies.* London: Frank Cass.

Oliver, Douglas 1967. *A Solomon Island Society: Kinship and Leadership Among the Siuai of Boudainville.* Boston: Beacon.

Otterbein, Keith 1968. Internal War: A Cross-Cultural Study. *American Anthropologist* 70: 277–289.

1970. *The Evolution of War: A Cross-Cultural Study.* New Haven: HRAF Press.

1977. Warfare: A Hitherto Unrecognized Critical Variable. *American Behavioral Scientist* 20: 693–710.

1980. The Evolution of Zulu Warfare. In *Law and Warfare: Studies in the Anthropology of Conflict.* P. Bohannan, ed. pp. 351–357. Austin: University of Texas.

1985. *The Evolution of War: A Cross-Cultural Study*, 2nd edition. New Haven: HRAF Press.

Peires, J. B. 1981a. *Before and After Shaka: Papers in Nguni History.* (ed.) Institute of Social and Economic Research, Rhodes University, Grahamstown, South Africa.

1981b. Introduction. In *Before and After Shaka: Papers in Nguni History.* Institute of Social and Economic Research, Rhodes University, Grahamstown, South Africa.

1981c. Chiefs and Commoners in Precolonia Xhosa Society. In *Before and After Shaka: Papers in Nguni History.* Institute of Social and Economic Research, Rhodes University, Grahamstown, South Africa.

Pelleprat, P. 1965. *Relato de las Misiones de los Padres de la Compania de Jesus en las Islas y en Tierra Firme de America Meridional.* Biblioteca de la Academia Nacional de la Historia, Vol. 77. Caracas.

Penard, A. P. and Penard, F. P. 1907. *De Menschetende Aanbidders der Zonnesslang.* Paramaribo.

Pershits, Abraham 1979. Tribute Relations. In *Political Anthropology: The State of the Art.* S. Lee Seaton and H. Claessen, eds. pp. 149–156. New York: Mouton.

Peters, E. L. 1967. Some Structural Aspects of the Feud Among the Camel-Herding Bedouin of Cyrenaica. *Africa* 37: 261–282.

Phillips, H. B. 1965. *Thai Peasant Personality.* Berkeley: University of California Press.

Pitt-Rivers, A. L. 1906. *The Evolution of Culture and Other Essays.* J. L. Myers, ed. Oxford: Clarendon Press.

Plog, Stephen 1980. *Stylistic Variation in Prehistoric Ceramics.* Cambridge: Cambridge University Press.

1983. Analysis of Style in Artifacts. In *Annual Review of Anthropology* 12, Bernard J. Siegel, Alan R. Beals, and Stephen A. Tyler, eds., pp. 125–142. Palo Alto: Annual Reviews.

Plog, Stephen and David Braun 1983. Some Issues in the Archaeology of "Tribal" Social Systems. *American Antiquity* 48: 619–625.

Podolefsky, Aaron 1984. Contemporary Warfare in the New Guinea Highlands. *Ethnology* 23: 73–87.

Powell, Shirley 1983. *Mobility and Adaptation: The Anasazi of Black Mesa, Arizona.* Carbondale: Southern Illinois University Press.

Price, Barbara 1982. Cultural Materialism: A Theoretical Review. *American Antiquity* 47: 709–741.

1984. Competition, Productive Intensification, and Ranked Society: Speculations from Evolutionary Theory. In *Warfare, Culture, and Environment.* B. Ferguson, ed. pp. 209–240. Orlando: Academic Press.

Price, David 1981. Nambiquara Leadership. *American Ethnologist* 8: 686–708.

Pringle, Robert 1970. *Rajahs and Rebels: The Ibans of Sarawak under Brooke Rule, 1841–1941.* Ithaca, NY: Cornell University Press.

Ralegh, W. 1596. *The Discoverie of the Large, Rich and Bewtiful Empire of Guiana.* London.

Rappaport, Roy 1967. Ritual Regulation of Environmental Relations Among a New Guinea People. *Ethnology* 6: 17–30.

1968. *Pigs for the Ancestors: Ritual in the Ecology of a New Guinea People.* New Haven: Yale University.

Reay, Marie 1973. Structural Co-Variants of Land Shortage Among Patrilineal Peoples. In *Politics in New Guinea: Traditional and in the Context of Change, Some Anthropological Perspectives.* R. Berndt and P. Lawrence, eds. pp. 175–190. Seattle: University of Washington.

Reid, Anthony 1980. The Structure of Cities in Southeast Asia, 15th–17th Century. *Journal of Southeast Asian Studies* 11(2): 235–50.

1983. Introduction: Slavery and Bondage in Southeast Asian History and Closed and Open Slave Systems in Pre-Colonial Southeast Asia. In *Slavery and Bondage in Southeast Asia.* (ed.) A. Reid. St. Lucia, Queensland: U. of Queensland Press.

1984. The Pre-Colonial Economy of Indonesia. *Bull. Indonesian Economics Studies* (ANU) 20(2): 151–167.

Renfrew, Colin 1984. *Approaches to Social Archaeology.* Cambridge, MA: Harvard University Press.

Ritter, E. A. 1957. *Shaka Zulu: The Rise of the Zulu Empire.* New York: Putnam.

Riviere, P. 1977. Some Problems in the Comparative Study of Carib Societies. In *Carib-Speaking Indians: Culture, Society and Language.* E. B. Basso, ed. Tucson: University of Arizona Press.

Robarchek, Carole J. 1981. Cash Economy and the Evolution of Ambilineal Ramages among the Semai Senoi. Paper presented at the annual meeting of the Southwestern Anthropological Association, Los Angeles.

Robarchek, Clayton A. 1977a. Semai Nonviolence: A Systems Approach to Understanding. Unpublished Ph.D. dissertation, Department of Anthropology, University of California, Riverside, CA.

1977b. Frustration, Aggression and the Nonviolent Semai. *American Ethnologist* 4(4): 762–779.

1979a. Learning to Fear. *American Ethnology* 6(3): 555–617.

1979b. Conflict, Emotion and Abreaction: Resolution of Conflict Among the Semai Senoi. *Ethos* 7(2): 104–123.

1981. The Image of Nonviolence: World View of the Semai Senoi. *Journal of the Federated States Museums* 24. Kuala Lumpur.

1985. Danger, Dependence and Nonviolence: The Motivational Context of Semai Social Relations. Paper presented at the 84th annual meeting of the American Anthropological Association, Washington, D.C.

Robarchek, Clayton and Robert Dentan 1987. The Unmaking of Another Anthropological Myth: Blood Drunkenness and the Myth of the Blood-thirsty Semai. *American Anthropologist* 89(2): 356–365.

Robbins, Sterling 1982. *Auyana: Those Who Held Onto Home*. Seattle: University of Washington.

Rochefort, C. de 1665. *Histoire Naturelle et Morale des Iles Antilles de l'Amérique*. 2nd Edition Rotterdam. (1st edition, Poincy, L. de Rotterdam, 1658).

Rodman, Margaret, and Matthew Cooper, editors 1979. *The Pacification of Melanesia*. Ann Arbor: University of Michigan.

Rosaldo, Michelle Z. 1980. *Knowledge and Passion*. Cambridge: Cambridge University Press.

Rosaldo, Renato 1980. *Ilongot Headhunting, 1883–1974: A Study in Society and History*. Stanford: Stanford University.

1981. The Social Relations of Ilongot Subsistence. In *Adaptive Strategies and Change*. H. Olofson, ed. Laguna: Forest Research Institute.

Rosenfeld, Henry 1965. The Social Composition of the Military in the Process of State Formation in the Arabian Desert. *Journal of the Royal Anthropological Institute of Great Britain and Ireland* 95: 75–86.

Ross, Eric 1978. Food Taboos, Diet and Hunting Strategy: The Adaptation to Animals in Amazonian Cultural Ecology. *Current Anthropology* 19(1): 1–36.

1980a. Introduction. In *Beyond the Myths of Culture*, Eric Ross, ed., pp. xix–xxix. New York: Academic Press.

ed. 1980b. *Beyond the Myths of Culture*. New York: Academic Press.

Ross, Jane Bennett 1984. Effects of Contact on Revenge Hostilities among Achuara Jivaro. In *Warfare, Culture, and Environment*. R. Brian Ferguson, ed. Orlando: Academic Press.

Rousseau, J. 1980. Iban Inequality. *Bijdragen tot de Taal-, Land- en Volkenkunde* 136: 52–63.

Roy, Sarat Chandra 1925. *The Birhors*. Ranchi, India: G. E. L. Mission Press.

Russell, E. W. 1972. Factors of Human Aggression. *Behavior Science Notes* 7: 275–312.

Ryan, Dennis J. 1977. The Paleopathology and Paleoepidemiology of the Kayenta Anasazi Indians in Northeastern Arizona. Unpublished Ph.D. Dissertation, Department of Anthropology, Arizona State University.

Sabloff, Jeremy, and C. C. Lambert-Karlovsky, editors 1975. *Ancient*

Civilization and Trade. Albuquerque: School of American Research, University of New Mexico.

Sahlins, Marshall 1958. *Social Stratification in Polynesia.* Seattle: University of Washington.

1965. On the Sociology of Primitive Exchange. In *The Relevance of Models for Social Anthropology.* M. Banton, ed. pp. 139–227. London: Tavistock.

1967. The Segmentary Lineage: An Organization of Predatory Expansion. In *Comparative Political Systems: Studies in the Politics of Pre-Industrial Societies.* R. Cohen and J. Middleton, eds. pp. 89–119. Garden City: Natural History.

1968. *Tribesmen.* Engelwood Cliffs: Prentice-Hall.

1972. *Stone Age Economics.* Chicago: Aldine.

1976. *Culture and Practical Reason.* Chicago: University of Chicago Press.

Schweder, R. A., and J. G. Miller 1985. The Social Construction of the Person: How Is It Possible? In *The Social Construction of the Person,* by K. J. Georgen and K. E. Davis. New York: Springer-Verlag.

Scott, J. P. 1976. Individual Aggression as a Cause of War. In *Discussions on War and Human Aggression,* by R. D. Givens and M. R. Nettleship. The Hague: Mouton.

Scott, W. H. 1979. Class Structure in the Unhispanicized Philippines. *Philippine Studies* 17(2): 137–59.

1982. Boatbuilding and Seamanship in Classic Philippine Society. In *Cracks in the Parchment Curtain,* pp. 60–95. Quezon City: New Day Publishers.

Service, Elman R. 1962. *Primitive Social Organization: An Evolutionary Perspective.* New York: Random House.

1968. War and Our Contemporary Ancestors. In *War: An Anthropology of Armed Conflict and Aggression.* M. Fried, M. Harris, and R. Murphy eds. pp. 160–167. New York: Doubleday.

1971. *Primitive Social Organization: An Evolutionary Perspective,* 2nd edition. New York: Random House.

1971. *Cultural Evolutionism: Theory in Practice.* New York: Holt, Rinehart and Winston.

1975. *Origins of the State and Civilization: The Process of Cultural Evolution.* New York: W. W. Norton.

Sillitoe, Paul 1978. Big Men and War in New Guinea. *Man* 13: 252–271.

Sipes, R. G. 1973. War, Sports and Aggression: An Empirical Test of Two Rival Theories. *American Anthropologist* 75: 64–86.

Siskind, Janet 1973. Tropical Forest Hunters and the Economy of Sex. In *Peoples and Cultures of Native South America.* D. Gross, ed. pp. 226–240. Garden City: Natural History.

1978. Kinship and Mode of Production. *American Anthropologist* 80: 860–872.

Skinner, B. F. 1981. Selection by Consequences. *Science* 213: 501–504.

Smith, Marian 1951. American Indian Warfare. *Transactions of the New York Academy of Sciences* 13: 348–365.

Sparrey, F. 1625. The Description of the Ile of Trinidad, the Rich Countrey of Guiana, and the Mightie River of Orinoco. Anno 1595. In *Purchas his Pilgrimes*, by S. Purchas. London.

Spencer, Robert, and Jesse Jennings 1965. *The Native Americans*. New York: Harper and Row.

Spiro, Melford 1967. *Burmese Supernaturalism*. Englewood Cliffs, NJ: Prentice Hall.

Staden, H. 1557. *Warhaftige Historia und Beschreibung Eyner Landtschaff der Wilden*. Marburg.

Staehelin, F. 1912. *Die Mission der Brudergemeinde in Suriname und Berbice im Achtzehnten Jahrhundert*. Herrnhut.

Stedman, J. G. 1796. *Narrative of a Five Years Expedition Against the Revolted Negroes of Surinam*. London.

Steward, Julian H. 1955. *Theory of Cultural Change: The Methodology of Multilinear Evolution*. Urbana: University of Illinois Press.

Stewart, Kenneth 1947. Mohave Warfare. *Southwestern Journal of Anthropology* 3: 257–277.

Stouffer, S. A., et al. 1949. *The American Soldier*. Princeton: Princeton University Press.

Suls, J. M., and R. L. Miller 1977. *Social Comparison Processes: Theoretical and Empirical Perspectives*. New York: Wiley.

Sumner, William 1911. *War and Other Essays*. New Haven: Yale University Press.

Suttles, Wayne 1961. Subhuman and Human Fighting. *Anthropologica* 3: 148–163.

Sweet, Louise 1970. Camel Raiding of North Arabian Bedouin: A Mechanism of Ecological Adaptation. In *Peoples and Cultures of the Middle East*, Vol. 1: *Depth and Diversity*. L. Sweet, ed. pp. 265–289. Garden City: Natural History.

Symons, Donald 1979. *The Evolution of Human Sexuality*. Oxford: Oxford University Press.

Tambiah, S. J. 1976. *World Conqueror and World Renouncer: A Study of Buddhism and Polity in Thailand Against a Historical Background*. Cambridge, England: Cambridge University Press.

Taylor, D. M. 1954a. A Note on the Arawakan Affiliation of Taino. *IJAL* 20: 153–154.

1954b. Diachronic Note on the Carib Contribution to Island Carib. *IJAL* 20: 28–33.

Teft, S. 1975. Warfare Regulations: A Cross-Cultural Test of Hypotheses. In *War, Its Causes and Correlates*. M. A. Nettleship, R. Dalegivens, and A. Nettleship, eds. pp. 693–712. The Hague: Mouton.

Thoden van Velzen, H. U. E., and W. van Wetering 1960. Residence, Power Groups, and Inter-Societal Aggression. *International Archives of Ethnography* 49: 169–200.

Thomas, D. J. 1982. *Order Without Government — The Society of the Pemon Indians of Venezuela*. Illinois Studies in Anthropology, No. 13, University of Illinois Press.

Tiger, L. 1969. *Men In Groups*. New York: Random House.

Tournay, Serge 1979. Armed Conflict in the Lower Omo Valley, 1970–1976: An Analysis from within Nyangatom Society. In *Warfare Among East African Herders*. K. Fukui and D. Turton, eds. pp. 97–117. Osaka: National Museum of Ethnology.

Trigger, Bruce 1976. *The Children of Aataentsic: A History of the Huron People to 1660*, two volumes. Montreal: McGill-Queen's University.

Trimborn, Hermann 1949. *Senorió y Barbarie en el Valle del Cauca*. Translated from the German by José Mariá Gimeno Capella. Madrid: Consejo Superior de Investigaciones Científicas, Instituto Gonzalo Fernandez de Oviedo.

Trivers, Robert 1971. The Evolution of Reciprocal Altruism. *Quarterly Review of Biology*. 46: 35–57.

Turney-High, Harry 1971. *Primitive War: Its Practice and Concepts*. Columbia: University of South Carolina.

—— 1981. *The Military: The Theory of Land Warfare as Behavioral Science*. West Hanover: Christopher.

Upham, Steadman 1982. *Polities and Power: An Economic and Political History of the Western Pueblo*. New York: Academic Press.

Van Berkel, A. 1695. *Amerikaansche Voyagien*. Amsterdam.

Van den Berghe, Pierre 1979. *Human Family Systems: An Evolutionary View*. New York: Elsevier.

Van der Kraan, A. 1983. Bali: Slavery and the Slave Trade. In *Slavery, Bondage and Dependency in Southeast Asia*, (ed.) A. Reid. St. Lucia, Queensland: U. of Queensland Press.

Van Gennep, A. 1960. *The Rites of Passage*. London: Routledge and Kegan Paul.

Vansina, Jan 1971. A Traditional Legal System: The Kuba. In *Man in Adaptation: The Institutional Framework*. Y. Cohen, ed. pp. 135–148. Chicago: Aldine Press.

Vayda, Andrew 1960. *Maori Warfare*. Polynesian Society Maori Monographs No. 2. Wellington, New Zealand.

—— 1961. Expansion and Warfare Among Swidden Agriculturalists. *American Anthropologist* 63: 346–358.

—— 1969a. Expansion and Warfare Among Swidden Agriculturalists. In *Environment and Cultural Behavior: Ecological Studies in Cultural Anthropology*. A. Vayda, ed. pp. 202–220. Garden City: Natural History.

—— 1969b. The Study of the Cause of War, with Special Reference to Head-Hunting Raids in Borneo. *Ethnohistory* 16: 211–224.

—— 1976. *War in Ecological Perspective: Persistence, Change, and Adaptive Processes in Three Oceanian Societies*. New York: Plenum Press.

—— 1979. War and Coping. *Reviews in Anthropology*: 191–198.

Voget, Fred 1964. Warfare and the Integration of Crow Indian Culture. In *Explorations in Cultural Anthropology*. W. Goodenough, ed. pp. 483–509. New York: McGraw-Hill.

Von Clausewitz, Carl 1968. *On War*. New York: Penguin.

Voss, Jerome A. 1980. Tribal Emergence During the Neolithic of Northwestern Europe. Unpublished Ph.D. Dissertation, Department of Anthropology, University of Michigan. Ann Arbor: University Microfilms.

Wagner, Gunther 1940. The Political Organization of the Bantu of Kavirondo. In *African Political Systems*. M. Fortes and E. E. Evans-Pritchard, eds. pp. 196–236. New York: Oxford University Press.

Wallace, Anthony F. C. 1968. Psychological Preparation for War. In *War: An Anthropology of Armed Conflict and Aggression*. M. Fried, M. Harris, and R. Murphy, eds. pp. 173–182. New York: Doubleday.

1972. *The Death and Rebirth of the Seneca*. New York: Vintage Press.

Warren, James Francis 1981. *The Sulu Zone, 1768–1898*. Singapore: University Press.

1982. Slavery and the Impact of External Trade: The Sulu Sultanate in the 19th Century. In *Philippine Social History: Global Trade and Local Transformations*. A. W. McCoy and C. de Jesus, eds. pp. 415–444. Quezon City: Ateneo de Manila University and Asian Studies Association of Australia.

Washburn, D. K. 1978. A Symmetry Classification of Pueblo Ceramic Design. *Papers of the Peabody Museum of Archaeology and Ethnology* 68. Cambridge: Peabody Museum Press.

Watson, James, editor 1980. *Asian and African Systems of Slavery*. New York: Oxford University Press.

Webb, Malcom 1975. The Flag Follows Trade: An Essay on the Necessary Interaction of Military and Commercial Factors in State Formation. In *Ancient Civilizations and Trade*. J. Sabloff and C. Lamberg-Karlovsky, eds. Albuquerque: School of American Research, University of New Mexico.

Weber, Max 1964. *The Theory of Social and Economic Organization*. Talcot Parsons, ed. New York: The Free Press.

Webster, David 1977. Warfare and the Evolution of Maya Civilization. In *The Origins of Maya Civilization*. R. Adams, ed. pp. 335–372. Albuquerque: University of New Mexico.

Werner, Dennis 1983. Fertility and Pacification Among the Mekranoti of Central Brazil. *Human Ecology* 11: 227–245.

Westing, A. 1982. War as a Human Endeavor: The High Fatality Wars of the Twentieth Century. *Journal of Peace Research* 3: 261–4.

White, Leslie 1949. *The Science of Culture*. New York: Farrar, Strauss and Giroux.

Whitehead, N. L. 1984. Carib Cannibalism — The Historical Evidence. *Journal de la Société des Américanistes* 70: 69–88.

234

1986. A Note on John Gabriel Stedman's Collection of Amerindian Arti-
facts. *Nieuwe West-Indische Gids* 60: 203–208.
1988. *The Caribs, 1498–1820: A History of the Karinya in Colonial
Venezuela and Guyana*. KITLV-Caribbean Studies Series, No. 10
Providence: Foris Publications.
Wiberg, H. 1981. What Have We Learned About Peace? *Journal of Peace
Research* 15: 110–149.
Willems, Emilio 1975. *Latin American Culture: An Anthropological Syn-
thesis*. New York: Harper and Row.
Williams, George 1966. *Adaptation and Natural Selection: A Critique of
Some Current Evolutionary Thought*. Princeton: University Press.
ed. 1971. *Group Selection*. New York: Aldine-Atheron.
Williams, Thomas 1870. *Fiji and the Fijians*, 3rd edition. London: Hodder
and Stoughton.
Wilson, Edward 1975. *Sociobiology: The New Synthesis*. Cambridge, MA:
Harvard University Press.
Winterhalder, Bruce 1980. Environmental Analysis in Human Evolution
and Adaptational Research. *Human Ecology* 8: 135–70.
Wobst, H. Martin 1977. Stylistic Behavior and Information Exchange. In
For the Director: Research Essays in Honor of James B. Griffin, Charles
Cleland, ed., pp. 317–342. University of Michigan Museum of
Anthropology, Anthropological Papers 61.
Wolf, Eric 1973. *Peasant Wars of the Twentieth Century*. New York: Harper.
Wolf, Eric and Edward Hansen 1972. *The Human Condition in Latin
America*. New York: Oxford University Press.
Woodburn, James 1982. Egalitarian Societies. *Man* 17(3): 431–451.
Wright, Q. 1965. *A Study of War*. Chicago: University of Chicago Press.
Zegwaard, Gerard 1959. Headhunting Practices of the Asmat of Netherlands
New Guinea. *American Anthropologist* 61: 1020–1041.
Zier, Christian 1976. Excavations Near Zuni, New Mexico: 1973. Museum
of Northern Arizona Research Paper 2.

Index

237

Index

187, 188; see also climatic change; land; population
equality, relations of, 133, 135–6, 137, 139; see also egalitarian societies; inequity, perception of
Eskimo, 107
Essequibo, 149, 150, 153, 157, 158, 162, 164, 165
ethnocentrism, 17, 22–3, 24, 116–17
Evans-Pritchard, E. E., 122
evolution, socio-cultural, and war, xiii, 47–51, 171, 172–4, 187–9, 190–1
evolutionary biology, 77, 78, 81–4, 102; see also biological selection exchange, 29, 39, 122, 123, 136, 175, 180; see also trade

fangablang (Buid evil spirit), 133
Fiji, chiefdom-level warfare in, 192–209
Flannery, Kent V., 190, 208
food sharing, 132, 137, 141; see also meat distribution
food shortages, 177
fortifications, 197; see also defensive features
French Guiana, 148
French in South America, 162
Freud, Sigmund, 17
Fried, Morton, 90, 190, 208–9
frustration, 17, 64–5
functional hierarchy, 176–7, 182

Galibi, 147, 148
Garriaga, Fr. Benito de la, 150
geographical factors, 107, 141, 143
Groenewegen, Aert von, 162
group: boundaries, 2, 174; extinctions, 29, 35; fissioning, 32, 80, 96, 97, 102, 104; hostility towards outgroup, 14, 21–2, 23, 24, 66–7, 116–17, 118; ingroup cohesion and preference, 21–3, 65–6; interaction, 39, 42, 111–13, 173–4, 175, 182–3, 184; selection, 28–9; vis-à-vis individual 23, 65, 78–9
Gauca Indians, 193–4, 196, 202
Guaypuinavis, 162
Gumilla, José, 148
gun trade, South American, 164
Guyana, 147, 148, 149, 158, 159, 160–7

Hanunoo, 131
Harcourt, Robert, 151
headhunting, 18, 44–5, 133, 138–9, 140, 142
headmen, 94, 95, 142; see also chiefs
hierarchical society, 10, 11, 12, 18, 41–2, 208–9
historical model of causation, xii, 6–10, 107–8, 125

Hobbes, Thomas, 160, 167, 168
human sacrifice, 200, 206
hunter-gatherer societies, 33, 34, 57, 107, 127, 132, 141, 143
hunting, 135

Iban, the, 128, 137–40, 142
ideological manipulation, 51, 54
Illanun, 138
Ilongot, the, 133–7, 140, 142
"inclusive fitness", 3, 4, 5, 7, 83, 84, 103, 144
individual, 5, 6, 9; autonomy, 131–6, 140–1, 142; life effort and conflicts of interest, 79–104; vis-à-vis group, 23, 65, 78–9
inequity, perception of, 22, 23–4
infrastructural explanations, 28, 30–5, 48
insults, verbal, 98
Iyawei-teri (Yanomamö village), 100

James I, King, 151
Java, 128
Jesuits, 164
Jivaro, the, 45, 146
Journal of Peace Research, 121

Kalapalo tribe, 114
Kalingo, the, 147, 156, 161, 167
Kanaima (vengeance cult), 166
Karinya, the, 147, 148, 167
Kayan, the, 128
Kayapo, the, 117
Kayenta region, Arizona, 179–80, 185, 186, 188
killer instinct, hypothesis of, 2
kinship, 5, 8, 30, 35–40, 50, 53, 75, 90–4, 137; kin reclassification, 96–7, 103–4
kivas (Anasazi ceremonical structures), 180, 82
Klethla Valley, Arizona, 179, 181, 185, 189
Kung Bushmen, 107, 123n.

labor: credits and debits, 137, 139; division of, 48–9, 134, 135, 140
land: scarcity, 33, 38, 63, 172, 183–4, 191, 192; seizure of, 193, 201, 207
leaders, leadership, 40, 42–3, 50, 54, 153–4, 156–7, 160, 196–7; difference between interests of followers and, 11–12; prestige of, 97–9; reproductive rewards, 101
Lévi-Strauss, Claude, 170n.
life effort model, 84–6
Lile chiefdom, Colombia, 204
Lokono, the, 147, 151, 157, 161, 167
Long House Pueblo, 182, 184
Long House Valley, Arizona, 11, 179, 180–9
Luzon, 128, 137

239

Index

241